# ELEMENTS OF TIBETAN BUDDHISM

# ELEMENTS OF TIBETAN BUDDHISM

RICHARD E. FARKAS

CHÖMAY BOOKS

FOUNDATION®
BOOKS

Delhi • Bengaluru • Mumbai • Kolkata • Chennai • Hyderabad
Pune • Thiruvananthapuram

Published by
**Cambridge University Press India Pvt. Ltd.**
under the imprint of Foundation Books
Cambridge House, 4381/4 Ansari Road, Daryaganj, **New Delhi** 110 002

**Cambridge University Press India Pvt. Ltd.**
C-22, C-Block, Brigade M.M., K.R. Road, Jayanagar, **Bengaluru** 560 070
Plot No. 80, Service Industries, Shirvane, Sector-1, Nerul, **Navi Mumbai** 400 706
10 Raja Subodh Mullick Square, 2nd Floor, **Kolkata** 700 013
21/1 (New No. 49), 1st Floor, Model School Road, Thousand Lights, **Chennai** 600 006
House No. 3-5-874/6/4 (Near Fernandez Hospital, OP Block), St. No. 5, Hyderguda, **Hyderabad** 500 029
Agarwal Pride, 'A' Wing, 1308 Kasba Peth, Near Surya Hospital, **Pune** 411 011
T.C. 25/2732, Lukes Lane, Ambujavilasam Road, **Thiruvananthapuram** 695 001



This edition has been published by Cambridge University Press India Pvt. Ltd. by arrangement with Chömay Books.
Chömay Books, Lexington, KY
c/o chomay@outlook.com

First South Asia Edition 2014
Reprinted 2014

ISBN 978-93-82993-44-5

Published by Manas Saikia for Cambridge University Press India Pvt. Ltd. and printed at Sanat Printers, Kundli, Haryana

# Contents

This book is dedicated to the people of Tibet
and to
Jetsun Jamphel Ngawang Lobsang Yeshe Tenzin Gyatso,
the 14th Dalai Lama of Tibet

To Julie

*Dedication of Merit*

May any merit generated through this book
be dedicated to the happiness of all sentient beings

THE DALAI LAMA

## FOREWORD

For more than a thousand years Tibetans have preserved and protected the full range of the Buddha's teachings, analysing them, refining them and, most important of all, putting them into practice. Thus, they became the mainstay of Tibetan culture, whose influence, in due course, spread throughout Central Asia and the Himalayan regions.

The impact of the Buddha's teachings on love, kindness and tolerance, the emphasis on compassion and the conduct of non-violence, and especially the theory that all things are relative can be seen in the character of Tibetans and people of the surrounding regions. They are, by and large, mild-mannered, easily contented, satisfied with whatever conditions are available and resilient in the face of hardship. No doubt the rigours of both the climate and the environment contributed to this, but it is the emphasis on compassion that has been the most significant source of their inner peace.

As people from different parts of the world and from quite different cultural backgrounds begin to take an interest in Tibetan Buddhism, it is important that they overcome the misconceptions and mysteries that seem to have been associated with it in the past and reach a clear understanding of what it involves. Readers will find this book by Richard Farkas very helpful in presenting many aspects of Tibetan Buddhism clearly and succinctly in a way that is not only easy to consult, but also easy to understand.

# Preface

**ele-e-ment.** n. 1. a fundamental, essential, or irreducible constituent of a composite entity. 2. the basic assumptions or principles of a subject.

## Why I wrote this book

I first got interested in Buddhism from reading Shirley MacLaine's books in the 1970s. I was especially interested in reincarnation, which led me to Buddhism and then to Tibetan Buddhism.

I took refuge during a retreat held annually by Namgyal Monastery Institute of Buddhist Studies in Ithaca, New York, the North American Seat of the personal monastery of His Holiness the Fourteenth Dalai Lama. I took the retreat because I wanted to receive teachings from a Tibetan Buddhist monk and also to experience the support of a sangha.

After the retreat, I continued to read and research topics on Tibetan Buddhism and found that there are thousands of books available from general concepts to very esoteric topics. The more I learned about Buddhism, the more I wanted to know.

During my search for information, I began to put this book together because I believed others would want the information I had found, too. Each time I found what I wanted to know, it led me to something I didn't know. As the information I collected grew, my goal became to organize it in a way that was easily accessible.

The result—this book—is foremost a compilation of information that may be second nature to one born into the Tibetan Buddhist tradition. But to a newcomer like me, everything was a wondrous mystery of deities, rituals, colors, and traditions. The book is intended for readers who are looking for a guide on the basic concepts, rituals, and elements of Tibetan Buddhism, as it is not a book on Buddhist teachings or a scholarly text.

**Spellings** found here are the ones I determined were most commonly used; alternative spellings may also be shown; other spellings may be as correct (or perhaps even more correct).

**Dates** in this book are ones generally accepted, although other dates might also be correct. The older the date, the more likely there might be dispute about its accuracy, and also the harder it is to verify.

Any errors found in this book should be attributed to me. I have tried to confirm information from multiple sources.

☸

I have had the great fortune to meet His Holiness the Dalai Lama, to whom this book is dedicated. Many people have found his teachings an inspiration and motivation for discovering and practicing Buddhism.

When I think about the many Tibetans who are not able to see him or hear his teachings, I believe that I must have had some good karma ripen at the right times.

It is my hope that the words in this book will illuminate Tibetan Buddhism to those who read them.

# Acknowledgments

Appreciation for their kind help go to: Mr. Tenzin Lekshay of the Department of Information and International Relations at the Central Tibetan Administration (CTA) of the Tibetan government-in-exile; Mrs. Tsering Choezom, Astrologer, Astrology Department of the Men-Tsee-Khang, the Tibetan Medical & Astrological Institute of H.H. the Dalai Lama; Thupten Tsering, Deputy Secretary, Department of Religion & Culture, CTA; and Dr. Kunchok Tsundue, Chief Planning Officer, and Namgyal Chonzom, Planning Commission, CTA, for their assistance in obtaining information.

I acknowledge the following for their guidance on where I am on my path at this point in this lifetime (in no particular order): Ven. Jamyang Lama, Ven. Tenzin Gephel, Ven. Tenzin Deshek, Ven. Tenzin Thutop, Geshe Lobsang Gonpo, Geshe Thupten Jinpa, Namgyal Khen Rinpoche Geshe Dawa-la, Geshe Sangay Gyatso, Geshe Kelsang Rapgyal, Norbu Samphel of TIPA, Tsering Namdol, Mrs. Tashi Lungrig of the TIbetan Children's Village (TCV), Tenzin Deckyi at TCV, Ven. Lobsang Choegyal, Lobsang Chozin and Pema Karpoche, Sidney Piburn, Jeff and Christie Cox, Gail and Art Birnbaum, Palden Oshoe, Wylie Schwartz, the students with whom I took the *Get Acquainted with Namgyal Retreat: An Introduction to Tibetan Buddhism* (four times), Arjia Rinpoche and Mary Pattison at TMBCC, Sam and Renee Farkas, Joan Ann Cohen, Robert and Bettina Barnes, Pradyumna Prasad Karan, Quincy Shimi, my wife, Julie Barnes Farkas, and His Holiness Tenzin Gyatso, the Fourteenth Dalai Lama of Tibet.

# 1 It Started with Buddha

**Bud-dhism.** n. 1. the doctrine, attributed to Shakyamuni Buddha, that suffering is inseparable from existence but that inward extinction of the self and of the senses culminates in a state of illumination beyond both suffering and existence. 2. the religion of eastern and central Asia represented by the many differing sects that profess Buddhism and venerate Shakyamuni Buddha.

Buddhism is the religion/philosophy/ideology/practice/path of Shakyamuni Buddha (c. 563-483 BCE). He was born Siddhartha Gautama, a prince of the Shakya clan that reigned in Kapilavastu in what is now southern Nepal and was born in what is now called Lumbini, near the border of India. Born to a family rich and highly placed in society, Siddhartha grew up in the midst of luxury, insulated from discomfort. His father, the king, kept him in the royal compound, to shield him from seeing what life was really like. Eventually, however, he came to know suffering through the *four sights*—a sick person, an old person, a corpse, and a world-renouncer (ascetic). As a result of this knowledge, he left his father's palace and went out into the world to find a way to overcome suffering.

On his journeys, he first studied with two masters, one of whom specialized in a mental training for the attainment of the "sphere of nothingness" and the other who taught a path of meditation leading to a state of "neither knowing nor not-knowing." After mastering both techniques, Siddhartha concluded that there was more to the truth he was seeking.

The next phase of his search was as an ascetic, one who believed that the body and its desires were obstacles to spiritual realization. For the next six years, Siddhartha kept company with five ascetics; together they starved themselves and gave up all comforts in an effort to bring body and mind under complete control. He eventually realized that this approach was also not the way to the truth he was seeking.

After renouncing the wealth of his father, the teachings of two great masters, and the extremity of asceticism, Siddhartha came to realize what he called the Middle Way. He meditated under the Bodhi Tree in Uruvela in what is now Bodh Gaya, India, for forty-nine days. Vowing to remain there until he attained enlightenment, after defeating the efforts of the demonic figure of Mara (who is associated with death and hindrances to enlightenment), Siddhartha Guatama emerged as the Buddha—one who is enlightened, or awake. From his enlightenment, he emerged with the **Four Noble Truths** (Sans. *Arya-Satya)*:

1. **The truth of suffering** (Sans. *dukkha*)—life is suffering: birth, sickness, inability to fulfill desires, separation from the desired, and, of course, death. If you look deeply enough at anything, the result in the end is always suffering.
2. **The truth of the origin of suffering** (Sans. *trishna*)—suffering is caused by craving and desire: you want something or someone, and even if you get what you desire, it will still ultimately cause suffering, because everything is impermanent—it does not last. You will eventually either lose it or death will take it. Or, if you don't get what you desire, that will also cause you to suffer.
3. **The truth of the cessation of suffering** (Sans. *nirodha*)—the elimination of craving and desire will eliminate suffering.
4. **The truth of the path that leads beyond suffering** (Sans. *magga*)—there is a Path, The Eightfold Path, which is a way of life, a way of thinking, that leads to the abandonment of craving and an end to suffering.

The **Eightfold Path** that leads to the extinction of suffering is composed of:

1. **Right view** (understanding)—knowledge of the Four Noble truths: the truth of suffering; the truth of the origin of suffering (desire and craving); the truth of the cessation of suffering; and the truth of the path to the cessation of suffering.
2. **Right thought** (intention)—to have the mind of renunciation (to be

free from craving); to have good will (to be free from aversion); to have compassion (to be free from heartlessness).

3. **Right speech**—to abstain from false speech (lying), malicious speech (slander), and useless or unnecessary speech (gossip).
4. **Right action**—these include the same as the five novice vows of a monk: to abstain from killing any sentient being; to abstain from stealing (taking what is not given); to abstain from sexual misconduct; to abstain from lying; and to abstain from intoxicants, that dull the mind and prevent progress on the road to enlightenment.
5. **Right livelihood**—one should avoid making a living from those activities that cause harm to oneself or others, such as trading in weapons or poisons, anything to do with killing other sentient beings, or any profession that causes one to deceive, exploit, or cheat others.
6. **Right effort**—to have the energy: to prevent the arising of unwholesome mental states; to eliminate any unwholesome states that already exist within one; to develop wholesome mental states that have not yet arisen; and to maintain and perfect wholesome mental states that already exist within one.
7. **Right mindfulness** (attentiveness)—the practice of being mindful of sensations of the body, feelings, mental states, and concepts that arise from Dharma.
8. **Right concentration**—a state where all mental faculties are directed onto one particular object or point; for the purpose of this Path, it means concentration on wholesome thoughts and actions, such as meditation on any of the previous aspects of the Eightfold Path.

The Buddha also revealed the **Seven Factors of Enlightenment,** some of which correspond to the Eightfold Path:

awareness
investigation of the Dharma
energy
joy
tranquility
concentration
equanimity

At the age of thirty-five, having achieved enlightenment and having been freed from the cycle of rebirth (*samsara*), Siddhartha entered a living nirvana and became a Buddha (literally, "one who is awakened" or "one who is aware"). The Buddha spent his remaining years teaching the Path, and at the age of 80, he passed into parinirvana.

According to the Buddha:

"My teaching is not a philosophy. It is the result of direct experience.
My teaching is a means of practice, not something to hold onto or worship.
My teaching is like a raft used to cross the river.
Only a fool would carry the raft around after he had already reached the other shore of liberation."

Or, as the Buddha is said to have commented to a favorite disciple, Ananda: "If you were to follow the Dharma purely out of love for me or because you respect me, I would not accept you as a disciple. But if you follow the Dharma because you have yourself experienced its truth, because you understand and act accordingly, only under these conditions have you the right to call yourself a disciple of the Exalted One."

The Buddha gave the **Four Reliances**, advice on how to approach teachings:

- Rely on the message, not on the personality of the teacher
- Rely on the meaning, not just the words
- Rely on the real meaning, not just the provisional meaning
- Rely on your wisdom and insight, not just on your ordinary, judgmental mind

Similarly, the Buddha gave what came to be called the **Kalama Discourse**, in which he revealed ten aspects one should consider when listening to any spiritual teachings:

"Do not believe a spiritual teaching because:
- it is repeatedly recited
- it is written in a scripture

- it was handed from guru to disciple
- it is believed by everyone around you
- it has supernatural qualities
- it fits my beliefs anyway
- it sounds rational to me
- it is taught by a respectable person
- it was said to be the truth by the teacher
- one must defend it or fight for it.

However, only when it agrees with your experience and reason, and when it is conducive to the good and gain of oneself and all others, then one should accept the teachings, and live up to them."

## Buddhas of the current kalpa

A *kalpa* (Sans.; Pali, *kappa*) is said to be a period of four hundred and thirty two million years of mortals, measuring the duration of a world, or a "world period;" sometimes called an aeon. It is the period of time between the creation and the recreation of a world or universe. The four kalpas of formation, existence, destruction, and emptiness, a complete period, is called *maha kalpa* or great kalpa.

In the kalpa we are currently in, called Bhaddakappa, there are five buddhas, four of whom have already come to pass, and one who is yet to come. They are:

Kakusandha—lived 40,000 years
Konágamana—lived 30,000 years
Kassapa (Kassapa Dasabala)—lived 20,000 years
Shakyamuni (the Buddha of the present age)—lived 80 years
Maitreya (the Buddha yet to come)

According to www.palikanon.com, the following are true of all Buddhas:

In his mother's womb, he remains cross-legged with his face turned outward
His mother gives birth to him in a standing posture
His birth takes place in a forest grove
Immediately after birth he takes seven steps to the north and roars the "lion's roar"

He makes his renunciation after seeing the four sights and after a son is born to him

He preaches his first sermon in the Deer Park at Isipatana

There can appear only one Buddha in the world at a time

No Buddha can arise until the *sāsana* (doctrines, meditational techniques, rules of conduct, and doctrines) of the previous Buddha has completely disappeared from the world

Earthquakes appear when he is born, when he attains enlightenment, when he preaches his first sermon, when he decides to die, and when he finally does so

The era when a Buddha will appear is when man lives not less than one hundred years and not more than ten thousand years

The Buddha's mother must be wise and virtuous; and her life must be destined to end seven days after the Buddha's birth

The Buddha is born when his mother is in the last third of her middle age

On the night before enlightenment, the Buddha dreams five dreams

After enlightenment, the Buddha does not preach until asked to do so by Mahā Brahmā

The Buddha is omniscient, not in the sense that he knows everything, but in the sense that he could know anything should he so desire

He converts people in one of three ways:

1. by exhibition of miraculous powers
2. by reading their thoughts
3. by teaching them what is beneficial to them according to their character and temperament

Though the Buddha's teaching is never really lost on the listener, he sometimes preaches knowing that it will be of no immediate benefit

Every Buddha founds an order

A Buddha is not completely immune from disease. Every Buddha has the power of living for one whole kalpa, but no Buddha does so; his term of life is shortened by climate and the food he takes

No Buddha dies until the *sāsana* (doctrines, meditational techniques, rules of conduct, and doctrines) is firmly established

After the Buddha's death, his doctrine is gradually forgotten

The Buddha is fond of solitude

# 2 And Then It Came to Tibet

In about 760 CE, more than 1200 years after his passing, the Buddha's teachings came to Tibet. At the request of King Trisong Detsen, second of the Dharma Kings, Indian tantric master Padmasambhava (also known as Guru Rinpoche) came to Tibet. His first task was to pacify the demons that populated Tibet at that time; he did so, and turned many of them into dharma protectors (dharmapalas). Then, along with Indian master Shantarakshita, he began the first diffusion of Buddhism into Tibet.

The two, under the sponsorship of the king, established Samye Monastery between 765 and 780. Among the many significant events that stand out are:

1. The ordination of the first monks in Tibet, called the Seven Examined Men (*misedun*), which took place at Samye c. 779 CE.
2. The Great Debate, taking place at Samye between 792 and 794. The Indian practice of Buddhism and the Chinese practice of Buddhism competed for supremacy in Tibet. After the debate, both claimed victory, but King Trisong Detsen claimed the Indian version was the superior, and it became the state-supported religion.

## THE ROAD TO BUDDHAHOOD

The three vehicles (*yanas*) to Buddhahood are characterized by the practitioner's motive:

- the wish to improve *oneself* (Theraveda/Hinayana)—the First Turning of the Wheel of Dharma by the Buddha, when he taught about the relative reality of the world, about karma and reincarnation, and how to overcome negative actions (at Sarnath)

- the wish to improve *oneself and all sentient beings* (Mahayana)—the Second Turning of the Wheel of Dharma by the Buddha, when he taught about the emptiness of all existence and the self (at Rajgir)

- the wish to improve *oneself and all sentient beings using highly effective techniques* (Vajrayana)—the Third Turning of the Wheel of Dharma by the Buddha, when he clarified all misunderstandings that arose from the previous teachings, and taught that we each already have Buddha nature (at Sravastri)

## FOUR MAJOR SCHOOLS OF TIBETAN BUDDHISM, AND BÖN

Buddhist thought and practice developed in Tibet over the centuries by using the entire scope of the teachings of the Buddha—the Hinayana, the Mahayana, and the Vajrayana vehicles (*yanas*). All four of the Tibetan Buddhist schools are of the Vajrayana vehicle.

"Most people speak of Tibet as having four traditions: Nyingma, Kagyu, Sakya, and Gelug, with Gelug being the reformed continuation of the earlier Kadam tradition. At the nonsectarian conference of tulkus (incarnate lamas) and abbots that His Holiness the Dalai Lama convened in Sarnath, India, in December 1988, however, His Holiness emphasized the importance of adding the pre-Buddhist Tibetan tradition of Bön to the four and always speaking of the five Tibetan traditions. He explained that whether or not we consider Bön a Buddhist tradition is not the important issue. The form of Bön that has developed since the eleventh century of the Common Era shares enough in common with the four Tibetan Buddhist traditions for us to consider all five as a unit." (www.berzinarchives.com/web/en/archives/study/comparison_buddhist_traditions/tibetan_traditions/intro_compar_5_traditions_buddhism_bon.html)

### **Nyingma**—originated with Padmasambhava (9th century)

Oldest of the four schools, the name Nyingma translates as "old school," and because this school relies primarily on older translations traced to the time of King Trisong Detsen (742-797), it is also known as "old translation school" or "the ancient ones." After coming to Tibet in 760, Padmasambhava (also known as Guru Rinpoche) and Shantarakshita, both from India, established Samye Monastery, the first monastery in Tibet (the first monastery which had monks in attendance compared to the many temples that were built earlier). It quickly became a principal center of learning, where most of the Sanskrit texts and literature from India were first translated into Tibetan (a language originally developed to translate the Sanskrit).

Padmasambhava, along with his twenty-five principal disciples, was also said to have hidden hundreds of scripts, ritual articles, and images, collectively known at *terma*. At times in the future, preordained by them, special individuals (called *tertöns*) were destined to find these items and bring their teachings to light.

The head of the Nyingma lineage is His Holiness the Mindrolling Trichen Rinpoche, established at the Mindrolling Monastery in exile in Clementown, Dehradun, India.

**Kagyu**—originated with Tilopa (988-1069), Naropa (1016-1100), and Marpa (1012-1097)

Starting with the Indian yogi Tilopa (whose original source was Buddha Vajradhara), this lineage emphasizes the continuity through oral transmission from master to student. Marpa the Translator brought these teachings to Tibet, where he transmitted them to his disciple Milarepa (1040-1123), one of the most famous yogis and poets of Tibet. It is said that Milarepa, through his teachings and other accomplishments, achieved the ultimate goal of enlightenment in one lifetime.

The head of the Kagyu school is the Karmapa, whose main monastery in Tibet is Tsurphu, west of Lhasa, and in exile is Rumtek Monastery in Sikkim, India.

**Sakya**—originated with Khön Könchog Gyelpo (Kon Chogyal Pho) (1034-1102)

The name "Sakya" in Tibetan means "grey/whitish earth" (considered auspicious), which is what was found on the side of Ponpori (Ponpo Mountain) in southwestern Tibet, where Sakya Monastery was built in 1073 by Könchog Gyelpo.

The origins of Sakya are traced to the Indian mahasiddha Virupa (837-909). Through the transmission of Virupa's teachings, Drogmi Lotsawa (992-1072) introduced to Tibet the LamDre teachings, which have been passed down to the current lineage holders.

The head of Sakya School is called the Sakya Trizin (the holder of the Sakya throne), who is always drawn from the male line of the Khön family. (It is said that one of the first seven monks who took vows in Tibet at Samye Monastery from Padmasambhava was a forebearer of the Khön line.) The head of the Sakya lineage is His Holiness the Sakya Trizin, and resides in exile at Sakya Dolma Phodrang, Rajpur, Dehradun, India.

**Gelug—**originated with Je Tsongkhapa (1357-1419)

The most recent of the four main Tibetan schools, Gelug's founder Tsongkhapa was inspired by the Indian master Atisha and the Kadam school he had founded. What most impressed Tsongkhapa was Kadam's emphasis on the Mahayana principles of universal compassion and altruism as a way of life and not just a spiritual orientation.

Basing his tradition on the works of Shantideva, Nagarjuna, and Candrakirti, Tsongkhapa refined his thoughts into the "Three Principal Aspects of the Path": renunciation, Bodhicitta, and the correct view of emptiness. As a result of this emphasis, the Gelug school is said to represent a most valid union of Sutra and Tantra. Another aspect of this school is the strict adherence to the rules of the Vinaya (the rules of the monastic order).

When he was 52 years old, his disciples asked that Tsongkhapa cut back on his extensive travels. To that end, Ganden Monastery was built, to the east of Lhasa in an area known as Drokri (Drok Mountain). When it was built, Tsongkhapa named it Ganden (Tibetan for the Sanskrit word "Tushita," abode of Maitreya, the Buddha of the future). The followers of Tsongkhapa who gathered at Ganden (also known as Geden [Gaden]) became known as Gelugpa ("those from the Geden school" or "Virtuous Ones").

Tsongkhapa also initiated the Monlam Chenmo (Great Prayer Festival), which is still celebrated in Tibet and Tibetan communities elsewhere with the Tibetan new year celebration (Losar).

The head of the Gelug lineage is the Venerable Ganden Tripa (throne-holder) Rinpoche (abbot of Ganden Monastery) (and not His Holiness the

Dalai Lama, as some might think), who resides in exile at Ganden Monastery in Mungod, Karnataka State, India.

**Bön**—originated with Tönpa Shenrab Miwoche

Bön is the indigenous faith of the Tibetan people that predates the introduction of Buddhism. The acknowledged founder of Bön is Tönpa Shenrab Miwoche, who is said to have lived 16,000-17,000 years ago (or c. 3000 BCE, depending on the source). Some Bönpo (the practitioners of Bön) believe that Tönpa Shenrab was the teacher of Shakyamuni Buddha, who was then sent to India to help eradicate the suffering of the people there. In earlier times, Bön was primarily a shamanistic practice, and animal sacrifices were common to appease the local spirits and demons. Tönpa Shenrab put an end to the animal sacrifices by substituting the forms of animals made from barley flour (a practice very much alive today in Tibetan Buddhism, called *torma*). The teachings in Bön include medicine, astrology, divination, Tantra and Sutra, and Dzogchen, the Great Perfection (brought from India).

The head of Bön worldwide is the Abbot of Menri, residing at a new Menri Monastery built at Dolanji, in Himachal Pradesh, India. In the United States, Geshe Tenzin Wangyal Rinpoche has established the Ligmincha Institute in Charlottesville, Virginia, which has branches in the U.S. and in other countries, to perpetuate the teachings of Bön.

# 3 Tibetan Buddhist Vows and Practices

A main distinction between laypeople and monastics (monks and nuns) in Buddhism is the vows—commitments—made and the willingness to keep those vows.

## Lay Vows

### Refuge

When a practitioner decides to commit to the Buddhist path, he or she may request to take formal Refuge Vows from a qualified teacher, either a monk or a nun. Taking refuge vows from a particular teacher does not necessarily mean a commitment to take this teacher as one's root teacher, or to agree to take the lineage of that teacher as your own. The refuge being taken is in the Buddha, the Dharma, and the Sangha, and not in the teacher.

When you "take refuge" (Tib. *skyabs*), you are committing yourself to the Buddhist path and to the Three Gems.

The Three Gems/Three Jewels/Triple Gems are:

The Buddha (teacher)
The Dharma (teachings of the Buddha)
The Sangha (the community of Buddhist practitioners)

It is not necessary to give up the religion you were raised in in order to take refuge vows. The process of taking refuge is to recite the following lines three times (usually in Tibetan):

I go for refuge to the Buddha
I go for refuge to the Dharma
I go for refuge to the Sangha

An alternative sometimes used in Tibetan Buddhism is:

I take refuge in the Guru
I take refuge in the Buddha
I take refuge in the Dharma
I take refuge in the Sangha

### *Refuge ceremony*

When you take refuge:

1. the first time you repeat the vow is a request for refuge
2. the second time represents your intention to observe your refuge vow
3. the third time is the acceptance of the refuge vow

It is suggested by many that as part of one's daily practice, one should take refuge three times in the morning after waking up, and three times in the evening prior to going to sleep. Although each teacher might conduct the Refuge ceremony differently, in general the elements of the refuge ceremony are:

- Recitating the Refuge Vow three times (see above)
- Taking a small cutting of one's hair, symbolically renouncing worldly activities (as a monk or nun would shave his or her hair off)
- Receiving a Dharma name from the teacher

### *Refuge prayer*

Until I am enlightened
I go for refuge to the Buddha, the Dharma, and the Sangha,
Through the virtue I create by practicing giving and other perfections,
May I become a Buddha to benefit all sentient beings.

### *Five Lay Precepts*

In addition to taking refuge, it is also possible to take lay precepts (Tib. *genyen*). One can make a commitment to take any or all of these precepts.

These are similar to the moral precepts that a novice monk or nun takes. The five moral precepts for Buddhist lay members are:

- do not kill or harm any living being
- do not steal
- do not engage in sexual misconduct
- do not lie or use hurtful speech
- do not use intoxicants that diminish mental capacity

## Bodhisattva vows

Bodhicitta is the mind that is totally dedicated to others and to achieving enlightenment to benefit all sentient beings.

(www.buddhism.kalachakranet.org/bodhisattva_vows.html and www.berzinarchives.com)

1. ***Aspiring Bodhicitta***—"the strong wish to overcome our shortcomings and realize our potentials to benefit everyone"

2. ***Engaged Bodhicitta***—"engaging in the practices that bring about the goal and taking Bodhisattva vows to restrain from actions detrimental to it"

***Root vows*** (18)
Breaking a root vow breaks your bodhicitta ordination, and will require you to take the vows again. It is required that you *abandon*: praising yourself and denigrating others; not giving wealth and Dharma; not forgiving though someone apologizes; abandoning the Mahayana; stealing offerings to the Three Jewels; abandoning the Dharma; disrobing monks or nuns; committing the five heinous crimes; holding wrong views; destroying towns and so on; teaching emptiness to the untrained; reversing others' aspirations for complete enlightenment; causing someone to abandon individual liberation; denigrating the Hinayana; falsely claiming to have realized emptiness; receiving the property of the Three Jewels; the person practicing concentration giving his belongings to others; and giving up on Bodhicitta.

***Secondary (branch) vows*** (46)

Breaking a secondary vow will damage, but not break, your bodhicitta vows. It is required that you *abandon*: neglecting to pay homage to the Three Jewels each day; following the mind of desire; not respecting elders; not replying to questions; not accepting invitations; not accepting gold and so on; not giving the Dharma to those who desire it; forsaking those who have broken their moral discipline; not observing the (Hinayana) trainings in order to generate or sustain faith in others; doing little to benefit other sentient beings; not knowing the full purpose of compassion; deliberately accepting things which are acquired by wrong livelihood; indulging in frivolity with agitation, delusion, and lack of mindfulness (you make fun of others, laugh loudly, make loud noices, and so on); claiming Bodhisattvas should remain in cyclic existence; not avoiding a bad reputation; not employing the methods to overcome others' negativities; not practicing the four noble disciplines (not responding to anger with anger, not responding to physical harm with physical harm, not responding to criticism with criticism; and not responding to verbal argumenting with verbal argumenting); not caring about those who are angry; not accepting others' apologies; not checking the angry mind or acting out thoughts of anger; gathering a circle of followers because of desiring wealth and fame; not eliminating the three types of laziness; engaging in senseless talk through attachment; not seeking the meaning of concentration; not removing obstacles to concentration; viewing the taste of concentration as being its main quality; abandoning the Hinayana; applying great effort to the Hinayana while currently engaged in the Mahayana; applying effort to non-Buddhist teachings while currently engaged in the Buddhadharma; excessive involvement in non-Buddhist subjects; abandoning the Mahayana; praising yourself and denigrating others; making no effort to study Dharma; deriding guru and word rather than relying on the meaning; neglecting to help whoever needs assistance; avoiding taking care of those who are sick; not dispelling suffering of others; not guiding the reckless; not returning kindness; not relieving the grief of others; refusing charity to the needy; not taking care of friends, disciples, servants, etc.; not being considerate of the wishes of others; not praising others' good qualities; not using force when necessary; and not using miracle powers, threatening activities, and so on.

## Tantra

*The 14 Tantric (Vajrayana) Precepts* (www.khandro.net):

1. Show respect for the Guru in body, speech, and mind
2. Have respect for the rules laid down by the Buddha
3. Show respect for one's Vajra companions
4. Show love for all sentient beings
5. Keep Bodhicitta precepts
6. Keep the scriptures of Vajrayana and Mahayana
7. Only transmit tantric teachings with proper empowerment and credentials
8. Do not become attached to the five skandhas
9. Do not harbor skepticism or doubt about the doctrine of Emptiness
10. Do not maintain relationships with those opposed to Buddha and his teachings
11. Do not indulge accomplishments forgetting the purpose of Vajrayana practice
12. Only transmit authentic Dharma
13. Perform tantric ritual practices properly
14. Do not despise or condemn women

## Kalalchakra

*The 14 Kalachakra Tantra Root Downfalls* (www.berzinarchives.com/vows/kalachakra_root_tantric_pledges.html)

1. Disturbing the minds of our Vajra masters
2. Transgressing our teachers' injunctions
3. Because of anger, faulting Vajra brothers or sisters
4. Giving up love for sentient beings
5. Giving up Bodhicitta
6. Holding the view of reality in Sutra to be inferior to that in Tantra
7. Disclosing confidential teachings to those who are unripe
8. Abusing our aggregates
9. Not having faith in the purity of phenomena
10. Having deceitful love
11. Conceptualizing about the blissful awareness that is beyond words

12. Faulting pure beings
13. Rejecting the substances that bond us closely to Tantric practice
14. Deriding women

## Definition of Sangha

There has always been discussion as to what the Sanskrit term *sangha* incorporates. The following is taken from Kalachakranet:

- A currently popular definition is to include all Buddhist practitioners
- Another is that it is composed of those who receive the transmission of Buddha's teachings and practice the instructions
- The most generally applied term includes only the community of ordained monks and nuns
- A more strict definition from the Buddhist scriptures applies to practitioners who have at least realized emptiness

## Practice

Your practice is what you do in order to progress along the path in Buddhism, that which takes you further away from samsara. The primary activity in Buddhism revolves around the transformation of one's mind, and meditation has evolved for many as the main means to accomplish this goal. For many, meditation is the basis of one's practice.

### *What is it that makes up one's practice?*

- Meditation
- Offerings (merit, flowers, fruit, water, light [candles/butter lamps])
- Taking teachings
- Reading books on Buddhist topics
- Supporting a monk, nun, or monastery
- Donating time to your monastery or sangha
- Visiting Buddhist sites, making pilgrimages
- Saying mantras
- Doing circumambulations
- Sharing teachings
- Applying the Buddha's teachings to everyday life

# Monastic Vows

The ten moral precepts for Buddhist monks and nuns are:

1. Do not kill or harm any living being
2. Do not steal
3. Do not engage in sexual activity
4. Do not lie
5. Do not use intoxicants
6. Do not eat after noon
7. Do not participate in entertainment, shows, dancing, singing
8. Do not wear things that adorn the body
9. Do not use a high or luxurious bed
10. Do not use money

## Monastic Vows

**Renunciate** (Tib. *rabjung*)—the first five of the moral precepts: vows not to kill, steal, engage in sexual activity, lie, or use intoxicants. This vow is supposed to be taken when one reaches the age of 7

**Novice** (Tib. *getsul*)— between 10 and 36 vows, depending on the school and lineage. These vows can be taken from the age of 13 or 14. "Both male and female novices take the same 36 precepts, wear the same robes, shave their head in the same manner, and could easily be mistaken for each other. Yet a closer inspection of the social and religious context to which these novices return reveals two very different experiences of detachment. While nuns are detached from the luxurious life, they are [often] forced to participate in the mundane aspects of economic production. Conversely, monks are [usually] removed from the gross material needs and desires of the householder, yet they enjoy wealth, security, and other luxuries. Although nuns and monks participate in a joint rite of passage which moves them into the renunciate life, their paths diverge ever more sharply after that rite." . . . The 36 Novice Vows are (www.gadenrelief.org/chu-novice.html):

1. Avoid killing a human
2. Avoid beating or harming livestock and other living beings

3. Avoid using water containing living creatures
4. Avoid killing animals
5. Avoid stealing
6. Avoid indulging in sexual misconduct
7. Avoid telling lies
8. Avoid accusing [a monk or nun] of a root defeat
9. Avoid slandering [a monk or a nun] by insinuation
10. Avoid creating a schism in the monastic community (sangha)
11. Avoid following such a schism
12. Avoid knowingly tell[ing] a lie
13. Avoid disturbing a householder's faith
14. Avoid making false accusations to favor a friend
15. Avoid slander or derision
16. Avoid accusing [a monk] of teaching Dharma for material gain
17. Avoid accusing [a monk or a nun] of committing a remainder transgression
18. Avoid casting off a teacher's advice
19. Avoid accepting food that is more than one's share
20. Avoid drinking beer
21. Avoid [all] kinds of singing
22. Avoid [all] kinds of dancing
23. Avoid playing musical instruments
24. Avoid wearing [all] kind of ornaments
25. Avoid using aromatic scents
26. Avoid using colorful costumes
27. Avoid wearing garlands, etc.
28. Avoid using high or fancy seats and beds
29. Avoid sleeping or sitting on high and fancy seats and beds
30. Avoid using thrones or beds more than one elbow length high
31. Avoid sleeping or sitting on beds or thrones more than one elbow length high
32. Avoid eating food after noon
33. Avoid accepting gold and silver
34. Avoid maintaining a lay person's lifestyle
35. Avoid abandoning a novice's lifestyle
36. Avoid refusing service to one's abbot or teachers

**Full ordination**—In the Tibetan tradition, there are 253 vows for monks (Tib. *gelong*) and 364 vows for nuns (*gelongma*). These vows are usually taken after reaching the age of 21. (see www.dalailama.com/messages/buddhism/ordination-in-the-tibetan-tradition)

"The nun ordination, the Gelongma, . . . the full ordination for women, does not exist anymore within the Tibetan tradition. If a woman wants to take the full ordination, she has to take it from another tradition, probably from a Theravedan tradition which has maintained this tradition. The cause for this is not the men, but it is due to the fact that in Tibet at some time, it has happened that there were not ten nuns to ordain a new one—because in order to ordain a new Gelong [monk] or a new Gelongma [nun], it is necessary to have the person who ordains plus ten fully ordained witnesses [who have been ordained for at least ten years each]. And the circumstances have made it that, in Tibet, it was at one point no longer possible, thus, the lineage had been broken." (www.dharmaling.org) "Since the early 1980s, [more than] fifty Western women and a handful of Himalayan women who practice in the Tibetan tradition have gone to Taiwan, Hong Kong, Korea, or in more recent years, to the USA, France, or India to receive the bhikshuni [nun's] ordination." (www.thubtenchodron.org) Discussion has been ongoing for some time within the Tibetan government-in-exile to rectify this situation. See below, under Geshe

## Different levels of monk/nun and geshe

### Monk/nun

**Renunciate monk/nun**—one who has taken the first five moral precepts

**Novice monk/nun**—one who has taken the novice vows

**Fully ordained monk/nun**—one who has taken the full *gelong* or *gelongma* vows; in Tibetan Buddhism there are 253 vows for monks and 364 vows for nuns.

### Geshe

This is a degree/title awarded to monks, similar to Doctor of Theology in the west, but taking longer to achieve, sometimes 15 to 20 years. The categories of geshe, assigned to a candidate by the abbot of the monastery according to his ability (starting with highest level) are:

Lharampa ("divine scholar")
Tsorampa ("scholar of the assembly")
Lingtse ("[scholar examined by] mixing of communities")
Dorampa ("scholar [examined on the monastery's] stone [platform]")*

* Definitions from Dreyfus, *The Sound of Two Hands Clapping*

"The 10th Religious Conference (convened on 6-8 March 2009) has advised to submit a proposal for bestowing Geshema degree (Procedures) for the nuns and the same will be finalized in the next conference. Therefore, steps are being taken for issuing geshema degree." (email dated October 9, 2009, from Thupten Tsering, Deputy Secretary, Department of Religion and Culture of the Central Tibetan Administration in Dharamsala.)

In April, 2011, Ven. Kelsang Wangmo, a German Tibetan Buddhist nun, was awarded the degree of Geshe by the Institute for Buddhist Dialectical Studies in Dharamsala, becoming the first nun to have earned this degree.

## Monastic Education

The typical daily schedule of a monk in Sera Je Monastery, located in Bylakuppe, Karnataka State, India (www.fpmt.org/projects/seraje/life.asp):

5:00 AM—Wake up and wash
5:30 AM—Morning prayers. Breakfast will be served during prayer session if there is any sponsor
7:30 to 9:00 AM—Memorizing prayers and scriptures
9:00 to 10:00 AM—Debating class
10:00 to 10:30 AM—Chanting Sutras and reciting prayers as preliminary practices as well as to eliminate obstacles toward one's study and practices
10:30 to 11:30 AM—Debating class
11:30 AM to 12:30 PM—Lunch, with prayers and dedications for sponsors and all sentient beings
12:30 to 1:00 PM—Break time
1:00 to 2:00 PM—Receiving teachings from teachers
2:00 to 4:00 PM—Homework; reading, reflecting, and discussing the subjects covered by the teacher on that day

4:00 to 5:00 PM—Receiving teachings from teachers
5:00 to 5:30 PM—Dinner with prayers
5:30 to 6:00 PM—Break time
6:00 to 7:00 PM—Evening debating class
7:00 to 8:30/9:00 PM—Prayers and meditation; reciting Heart Sutra, 21 Tara praises many times and reciting many other prayers as preliminary practices and to eliminate obstacles toward one's study and practices
9:00 to 10/11:00 PM—Debating class (Some of the monks will continue until midnight or 1 AM)
10/11:00 PM to 12:00 midnight—Reciting the prayers and scriptures which have been memorized so that one does not forget them
12:00 midnight—Bedtime, but many monks will study until 1 or 2 AM

The schedule changes a little during different times of the year. For example, in December, there will be a week of prayers and meditation which start at 2:30 AM and go until 9:30 PM. There will be short debating classes within that period, and many monks will be studying after 9:30 PM. The schedule also changes during the Monlam Chenmo (The Great Prayer Festival), or during the Geshe graduation ceremonies, etc.

## Robes and Hats

### Robes

A Tibetan Buddhist monk's and nun's robes consist of the following:

*Dhonka (Donka)*—vest, usually maroon
*Shemdap (Shamdab, Shamthap)*—lower robe, usually maroon
*Chögu*—cape-like garment, usually yellow, that is wrapped around the upper body and over the left shoulder; usually only worn for teachings and confession ceremonies
*Zen (Zhen)*—similar to the chögu, but maroon, and worn for daily use
*Namjar*—similar to chögu, but larger and yellow; used for special occasions
*Kerag*—yellow belt that cinches the shemdap around the waist
*Dingwa*—a rectangular cloth, usually made of wool, that a monk or nun would use to put on top of a cushion, so as to protect the cushion from damage or getting dirty

According to the Pali tradition, six kinds of cloth are allowed for making the upper and outer robes: plant fibers, cotton, silk, animal hair (e.g. wool), hemp, and a mixture of some or all of them. The Buddha recommended that the robe design should be cut in the pattern of the fields in the Magadha region where he taught. (www.buddhanet) The patchwork design (similar to a planted field) symbolizes simplicity and renunciation. The cloth can be small scraps of cloth sewn together (as was originally done), or it can be one large piece sewn to look like patchwork.

Dyes used to tint the cloth used for robes was generally the cheapest and most readily available, mainly from plants. In the countries near India, the choices were yellow (from saffron and onion) and dark red (from *lac* and madder root). Farther east, grey, black, and brown were the choice for dyes, mostly from tree bark. (www.khandro.net)

The armholes of Tibetan monastic robes and vests are surrounded by blue borders. Three possible explanations have been given for this. One is that blue is a color associated with Padmasambhava. Another is that the blue commemorates Huashang, whose Chinese view of Buddhism was defeated at Samye Monastery in the Great Debate held there in 792. A third is that blue was the color of the vests of the Bönpos, the pre-Buddhist practitioners in Tibet.

**Hats**

*Tsongkhapa hat*

In general, the wearing of hats, except for ritual headdresses, is prohibited. The Gelug tradition is often called the Yellow Hats, because of the color of the hats worn. "Tsongkhapa . . . started a reform that developed into the . . . Gelug Tradition. He told his monk disciples to wear yellow hats. He explained that this would be an auspicious sign for them to be able to bring back pure ethical discipline to the monasteries of Tibet. . . . In this way, the Gelug tradition also became known as the Yellow Hat Tradition." (www.berzinarchives.com) Here are two of the most common types of hats worn during ceremonies:

1. Tsongkhapa hat (Tib. *Naring*)
2. Ceremonial hat (Lama hat or Vinata hat) (Tib. *Tse-sha, Drochama, Tagdroma, Tsogsha*)

*Gelug monks wearing ceremonial hats*

"The red hat worn in the other, earlier Tibetan Buddhist traditions follows the custom of the red hat worn by pandits (learned masters) at the Indian Buddhist Monastery of Nalanda." (www.berzinarchives.com)

The Kagyu sect has been called the Red Hat, and sometimes the Black Hat, depending on which hat and who is wearing it. The Karmapa, head of the Karma Kagyu lineage, has a Black Crown. The Nyingmas are sometimes called the Red Hats. The Sakyas ceremonial hat is often red, but it is not referred to by color as are the other schools.

**Robe colors of monks and nuns**

***Mahayana countries***

Bhutan—burgundy/yellow
China—yellow/brown
Korea—burgundy/white
Japan—black
Mongolia—burgundy/yellow
Nepal—burgundy/yellow
Tibet—burgundy/yellow
Vietnam—yellow/white

***Theravedan countries***

Myanmar (Burma)—burgundy
Sri Lanka—saffron
Thailand—brown

## Monastic Code of Discipline: The Vinaya Pitaka

(translated to mean "basket of discipline")

The monastic code was taken from the Buddha's teachings and codifed following his death. In the language that it was written in, Pali, it was meant for *bhikkhus* (monks) and *bhikkunis* (nuns), and enumerated the rules and the results of breaking the rules.

The Patimokkha (code of monastic discipline) classifies its rules into eight levels:

- *Parajika* (defeat)
- *Sanghadisesa* (entailing communal meetings)
- *Aniyata* (undetermined)
- *Nissaggiya pacittiya* (entailing forfeiture and confession)
- *Pacittiya* (entailing confession)
- *Patidesaniya* (entailing acknowledgement)
- *Sekhiya* (trainings)
- *Adhikarana samatha* (the settlement of issues)

**Examples of each level** (www.accesstoinsight.org/tipitaka/vin/sv/index.html)

***Parajika*** (defeat: expulsion)

Deliberately lying to another person that one has attained a superior human state (right livelihood)

Intentionally bringing about the untimely death of a human being, even if still a fetus (right action)

The theft of anything worth 1/24 ounce troy of gold or more (right action)

***Sanghadisesa*** (communal meeting)

Building a hut with a sponsor, or having it built, destined for one's own use, without having obtained the community's approval (right livelihood)

To persist in one's attempt at a schism, after the third announcement of a formal rebuke in a meeting of the community (community harmony)

***Aniyata*** (undetermined)

If a bhikkhu sits down privately alone with a woman in a place which is secluded and hidden from view and convenient for an immoral purpose and if a trustworthy lay woman (i.e., an Ariya), seeing him, accuses him of any one of the three offenses: (1) a Parajika offense, (2) a Samghadisesa offence, (3) a Pacittiya offense, and the bhikkhu himself admits that he was so sitting, he should be found guilty of one of these three offenses as accused by the trustworthy lay woman.

***Nissaggiya pacittiya*** (forfeiture and confession)

Carrying wool that has not been made into cloth or yarn for more than three leagues (right livelihood)

Asking for a new alms bowl when one's current bowl is not beyond repair (right livelihood)

***Pacittiya*** (confession)

Exhorting a bhikkuni on any topic at all after sunset—except when she requests it (sexual misconduct)

Traveling by arrangement with a bhikkhuni upriver or downriver in the same boat—except when crossing a river (sexual misconduct)

Accepting robe-cloth from an unrelated bhikkhuni without giving her anything in exchange (right livelihood)

Eating staple or non-staple food in the period after noon until the next dawn (right livelihood)

Eating food that a bhikku formally received on a previous day (right livelihood)

Eating food that has not been formally given (right livelihood)

Obtaining gold or money through trade (right livelihood)

Causing a bhikkhu to be evicted from a dwelling belonging to the community, when one's primary motive is anger (community harmony)

Speaking or acting disrespectfully when being admonished by another bhikkhu for a breach of the training rules (community disharmony)

Giving a blow to another bhikkhu, when motivated by anger (community harmony)

Intentionally cutting, burning, or killing a living plant (etiquette of a contemplative)

Watching a field army, or similar large military force, on active duty, unless there is a suitable reason (etiquette of a contemplative)
Taking an intoxicant regardless of whether one is aware or not that it is an intoxicant (etiquette of a contemplative)
Tickling another bhikkhu (etiquette of a contemplative)
Jumping and swimming in the water for fun (etiquette of a contemplative)
Attempting to frighten another bhikkhu (etiquette of a contemplative)
Bathing more frequently than once a fortnight when residing in the middle Ganges Valley, except on certain occasions (etiquette of a contemplative)
Hiding another bhikkhu's bowl, robe, sitting cloth, needle case, or belt, or having it hid, either as a joke or with the purpose of annoying him (etiquette of a contemplative)
Entering a king's sleeping chamber unannounced, when both the king and queen are in the chamber (etiquette of a contemplative)

***Patidesaniya*** (acknowledgement)
Should any bhikkhu chew or consume staple or non-staple food, having received it himself from the hand of an unrelated bhikkhuni in an inhabited area, he is to acknowledge it: "Friends, I have committed a blameworthy, unsuitable act that ought to be acknowledged. I acknowledge it."

***Sekhiya*** (training)
All having to do with the deportment of monastics, such as:
If a lay person is not respectful, a monk is not supposed to teach Dharma to him or her

***Adhikarana-samatha*** (settlement of issues)
Seven rules having to do with the settlement of legal processes concerning monastics

# 4 Rituals/Ritual Objects/Symbols

## ALTAR / SHRINE

All Buddhist traditions make use of a personal or household shrine or altar as a reminder of Dharma practice and as a focal point for meditation. The shrine represents the body, speech, and mind of the Buddha, so traditionally certain objects have been determined as appropriate for this use. The most common characteristics have been included here.

### Where to locate an altar

The best place for an altar is in a separate room. If the building has more than one floor, the top floor is best. Otherwise, any room or space can be used; it is helpful if it is closed off or separated from any other activities of the room. It is of great help to the practice to set aside a space for meditation that is used only for that purpose, and that it is clean and comfortable. The altar should be positioned higher than one's head while seated.

If the altar is placed in the bedroom, it should be oriented towards the head of the bed rather than the foot of the bed. It should also be higher than the bed, and should be placed on a separate shelf or table, one which is not used for any other purpose.

The altar can be a table or a shelf (freestanding or wall-mounted). The size is not important as long as it is in as clean and respectful a place as possible. In maintaining an altar, one is trying to cultivate the qualities of the Buddha—his enlightened body, speech, and mind.

### Objects on an altar and what they represent

Buddhists should not place Buddha images or other similar objects as decoration in a living room or other rooms. All objects discussed here are

*Altar at Namgyal Monastery retreat, Ithaca, NY, 2007*

to be part of one's practice and respect for the Dharma. It is also proper and respectful to place the main object of the shrine, normally a Buddha image or image of your teacher, as the highest object in the room. When a Buddhist stands before a shrine, the objects he or she sees help to recall the qualities that are found in the Buddha, Dharma, and Sangha. This is to inspire him or her to work toward cultivating these qualities.

Objects on an altar would be those representing the enlightened body, speech, and mind. The three primary examples might be an image or statue of Buddha Shakyamuni or one's teacher (body), a Buddhist scripture (speech), and a stupa (mind). The minimum on an altar would be an image or statue of the Buddha. Other objects often seen on an altar would be a bell and dorje; a seven-bowl set for water offering; flowers; incense; pictures of teachers or respected spiritual leaders, especially His Holiness the Dalai Lama; candles or butter lamps; Buddhist books; ritual dagger or knife (*phurba*); a thangka on the wall above. Items on an altar are often placed on an altar cloth, usually of a brocade material (Tib. *tilden*).

*Pilgrims circumambulating stupas at Tashilhunpo Monastery, Shigatse, Tibet, 2005*

## Circumambulation

The word "circumambulate" (Tib. *kora gyahp*) literally means to "walk around." In the context of Buddhism, it is usually walking around a stupa (e.g., Dhamekh Stupa in Sarnath, India, where Buddha preached his first sermon), a Buddha image or shrine (e.g., the Jokhang Temple in Lhasa, Tibet), or a holy mountain (e.g., Mt. Kailash in Tibet). By circumambulating, you generate merit. Circumambulation in all Tibetan traditions (except Bön) is to go in a clockwise direction, often spinning prayer wheels as you walk, and reciting mantras. Quite often, many shrines have prayer wheels built into the walls for pilgrims to spin with their right hands as they circumambulate.

## Eight Auspicious Symbols

There are eight particular symbols that can be seen on the walls of almost every Tibetan monastery, shrine, on many private dwellings, and in many Buddhist publications. In Buddhism, these are considered good luck symbols. Some have been adapted from their use in India. Listed here in alphabetical order, these are known as the Eight Auspicious Symbols (Tib. *Tashitag Gya*; Sans. *Ashta-Mangala*).

***Dharma Wheel*** (Tib. *chos kyi 'khor lo*)—"wheel of doctrine." Symbolizes the teachings of Buddha. The Buddha's first sermon after his enlightenment is known as his First Turning of the Wheel of Dharma. The eight spokes point to the eight directions and also symbolize the Buddha's Eightfold Path

***Endless Knot*** (Tib. *apalbe*)—symbolizes the mutual dependence of religious doctrine and secular affairs; the union of wisdom and method; the inseparability of emptiness and dependent arising while on the path; the union of wisdom and compassion at the time of enlightenment; the endless wisdom and compassion of Buddha; and the interdependence of all things

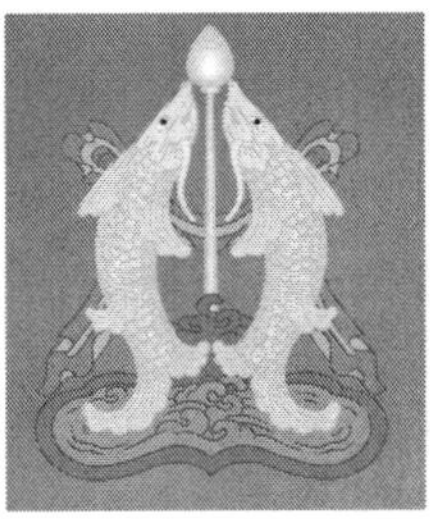

***Golden Fish*** (Tib. *gsernya*)—symbolic of beings saved from the ocean of earthly life and suffering; represents Buddha's eyes, hence transcendent wisdom; happiness and utility; the auspiciousness of all living beings in a state of fearlessness without danger of drowning in the ocean of sufferings

**Lotus Flower** (Tib. *padma)*—symbolizes purity; the complete purification of the defilements of body, speech, and mind; the blossoming of wholesome deeds; sometimes symbolizes awakening; often has eight petals corresponding to the Eightfold Path; colors may be white, red, blue, pink, or purple

**Right-coiled Conch Shell** (Tib. *dung gyas-'khyil*)—symbolizes the sound of Dharma, which can be heard in all directions, and a symbol believed to banish evil spirits and scare away harmful creatures

**Treasure Vase** (Tib. *gter-chen-po'i bumpa*)—the innumerable qualities of a Buddha's body; the treasury of all desires; it symbolizes long life and prosperity

**Umbrella (Parasol)** (Tib. *rinchen dug*)—symbolizes the protection of the Dharma; symbolically protects one from the heat of suffering, desire, illness, evil, and other harmful forces; denotes respect

**Victory Banner** (Tib. *gyaltsen*)—symbolizes the victory of body, speech, and mind over obstacles and negativities, both one's own and that of others. In early Buddhism, the banner represented Buddha's victory over Mara (hindrances and defilements) and his enlightenment. In Tibetan Buddhism, it represents the methods of overcoming Mara

## Empowerments / Initiations

Also sometimes called an initiation, an empowerment is a ceremony that enables a person to make a closer connection with a particular deity or Buddha. During the empowerment, the body, speech, and mind of the disciple are blessed and purified, and the disciple is empowered to practice by reciting the deity's mantra and to meditate on the nature of one's mind as if it were the mind of that deity. In this way, one's nature becomes closer to the nature of the deity or Buddha. Receiving an empowerment is like planting a seed. With the right conditions, this seed will sprout and grow into Buddhahood. By receiving an empowerment and practicing the appropriate *sadhana* (rituals), one can draw closer to the ultimate compassion and wisdom of a Buddha and realize our own Buddha nature. (Rameshori Buddhist Center)

Most empowerments are given to relatively small groups in a monastery, by a geshe or lama. On occasion, there will be mass empowerments or initiations given, such as the Kalachakra Initiation given at various times and places by His Holiness the Dalai Lama and by others. At some, more than 100,000 people attend. Examples of some of the more frequently given empowerments are White Tara and Chenrezig.

## Foods / Eating Meat / Vegetarianism

Most religions place some restrictions on food, beverage, and diet, and Buddhism is no different. Although the monasteries might have discouraged the killing of animals, because of the climate in most of Tibet, agriculture was only of limited use in feeding the population year-round. One yak might feed a nomadic family for a whole season. This would seem to agree with the Buddhist principle of trying to diminish as much as possible the harm we do. And because of the harsh conditions in much of Tibet, a vegetarian diet would not support the population. Tsampa, a staple made from roasted barley, had to be supplemented with meat from one of a number of animals that were raised in the country (yaks,q sheep, and goats, for example). As for the actual killing of the animals, there were often Muslim butchers in the larger towns and villages to butcher the animals; many nomads, however, had to butcher the animals themselves.

In general, Buddhism prohibits the killing of any animal. One of the most basic and important of Buddhist tenets is "do not kill"—do not take the life of another sentient being and deprive it of the opportunity to attain enlightenment. There is still room for interpretation in this. Do not personally kill anything to eat yourself? Or do not eat anything that someone else has killed for you? Or do not eat anything that someone else has killed not knowing who will eat it? Strict interpretation means that we do not eat anything derived from an animal. A looser interpretation says that actually eating the meat is not the issue—so if the animal was not killed by you, or specifically for you, you can eat the meat, with a prayer for the animal to receive a fortunate rebirth. One interpretation of the teaching of the Buddha was that it was not against the teachings to buy and eat meat if the animal was not killed for you personally. It has also been said that there are ten kinds of meat that the Buddha said should not be consumed by a monk or a novice—human flesh, elephant, tiger, yellow tiger, leopard, bear, lion, snake, dog, and horse. There are also those who say that eating a fish or small bird, which will only feed one or two people, is not as karmically correct as eating a larger animal, such as a yak or cow, which will feed many more people. It has also been said that it is acceptable to eat that which has not been killed specifically for you and has been killed at least a day earlier. This seems to be a matter of interpretation. It boils down to intention—right intention leads to right view which leads to right action.

## Vegetarian Diet

In the days when Buddha lived, monks and nuns begged for their food—that is, they were mendicants. According to the practice, you were obliged to accept whatever was put into your alms bowl, whether or not it was fresh or appealing, meat or vegetable. You ate what those who supported the teachings gave. As stated above, Buddha prohibited the consumption of flesh of any animal that was "seen, heard or suspected" to have been killed specifically for the benefit of monks. This would indicate that it was permissible to accept meat if that was what the giver offered. And it was to be accepted without discrimination or aversion; to reject such offerings would be inhospitable and might deprive the giver of the opportunity to gain merit by the offering.

"Killing and eating meat are interrelated, so do we have to give up eating animal products? I myself once tried to give it up, but health problems arose and two years later my doctors advised me to again use meat in my diet. If there are people who can give up eating meat, we can only rejoice in their noble efforts. In any case, at least we should try to lessen our intake of meat and not eat it anywhere where it is in scarce supply and our consumption of it would cause added slaughter."—His Holiness the Dalai Lama, *The Path to Enlightenment*

## Intoxicants

The Buddha also said that one should "refrain from taking intoxicants." In the time of the Buddha, this referred primarily to alcoholic drinks. Today, however, "intoxicants" can also be applied to recreational drugs such as heroin, cocaine, and marijuana; prescription drugs, to which one might become addicted; and to cigarettes and other tobacco products. Taken to another level, anything that intoxicates should be avoided. This could also be applied to activities in our culture such as television, shopping, gambling, and other activities which give us apparent pleasure but which distort the mind's view of reality and continue to support attachment.

## Tibetan foods

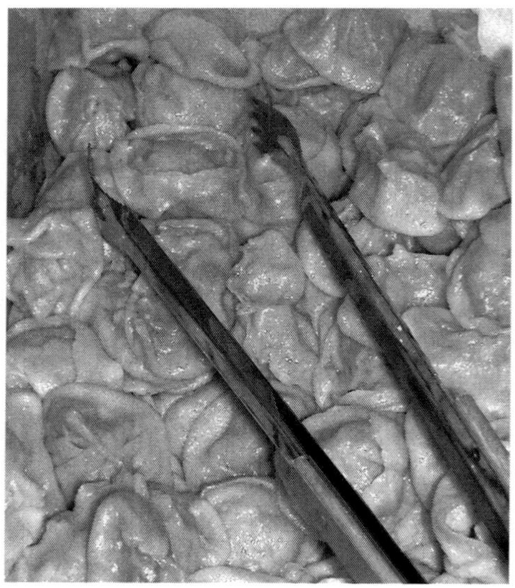

*Momos*

Foods traditionally eaten in Tibet include *tsampa* (roasted barley ground into flour and eaten as a paste moistened with tea), yak meat, mutton, momos (small dumplings filled with meat and/or vegetables), *thugpa* (soup, made with vegetables and with or without meat), breads, cheeses, yogurt, and tea (either yak butter tea or *chai*, a sweeter tea with milk and sugar). Because of the climate, vegetables were not usually available much of the year in most of the country. However, they are now grown in hothouses and are more readily available throughout the year.

## KALACHAKRA

*Kalachakra* is Sanskrit for "wheel of time;" it has also been translated as "cycle of time." Kalachakra is a deity, a tantric system, and a mandala. It is thought that Shakyamuni Buddha taught the Kalachakra toward the end of his life, perhaps the year before he attained parinirvana.

"The Kalachakra Tantra is one of the most advanced and complex teachings of the practice of Buddhism. Like all Buddhist teachings, Kalachakra serves as a path to enlightenment." (Bryant, *The Wheel of Time Sand Mandala*, Snow Lion, 2003) A further description of the Kalachakra can be found in the previously-mentioned book.

To date (February 2013), His Holiness the 14th Dalai Lama has given the Kalachakra Initiation 32 times, the first two of which were given at the Norbulingka in Lhasa, Tibet, in May 1954 and April 1956, prior to his going into exile. These two were among the largest attended, each estimated as having more than 100,000 participants. All counted, the 32 initiations add up to more than 1.7 million people. His first Kalachakra Initiation in the United States, in July 1981 in Madison, Wisconsin, numbered 1,500 (the smallest number). The largest Kalachakra Initiations, all with attendance of about 200,000, were in Bodh Gaya, India, in December, 1985; in Salugara, West Bengal, India, in December, 1996; in Bodh Gaya, India, in January, 2003; and again in Bodh Gaya in January, 2012. (www.dalailama.com)

## KHATA

A *khata* (Tib.; *kata, khatag*) is a prayer scarf, usually 12 to 14 inches wide and 4 to 11 feet long, often made of silk or silklike materials. They are used as an offering in greeting. As an auspicious symbol, it lends a positive feeling to the start of any enterprise or relationship and indicates the good intentions of the person offering it. Khatas may be offered to persons or to religious images and are often seen draped across the hands

*Dalai Lama presenting a khata to Muhammad Ali, Bloomington, IN, 2003*

of a statue or on a thangka, or to lamas or government officials prior to requesting their help in the form of prayers or other services. The offering of a khata indicates that the request is not marred by corrupt thoughts or ulterior motives. Khatas are usually in shades of white or ivory (although they are also made in blue, red, green, yellow/gold, and yellow) and are made in different qualities. Some khatas are imprinted with images, most often the eight auspicious symbols. When offering a khata, it should be held in both hands and offered with a bow. If offered in greeting to a monk or other religious person, he or she will then often drape the khata you offered around your neck.

## LOTUS

The lotus is a symbol of purity and enlightenment. It is reported that when Siddhartha Guatama (the future Shakyamuni Buddha) was born, he took his first steps immediately, and where he stepped, lotuses bloomed. The lotus has its roots in mud but blossoms into a beautiful flower. Similarly, though an individual may be impure, there is the potential to gain the perfect state of enlightenment. An open blossom (as many deities are seated on in thangkas) signifies full enlightenment; a closed blossom signifies the potential for enlightenment. The historical Buddha, Shakyamuni, is associated with a pink lotus. Avalokiteshvara (Chenrezig) is associated with the red lotus, which symbolizes love and compassion. The blue lotus is associated with Manjushri and symbolizes wisdom. In Tibetan, lotus is *padma*; Padmasambhava, also known as Guru Rinpoche, is known as being "lotus born," meaning he was born in purity.

## MALA

A mala (Tib. *treng ah*) is a device used in Buddhism (Hindus, Muslims, and Catholics also use a similar device) for counting repetitions of mantras. "Prayer beads date back to sometime around 500 BCE and according to most historians the point of origin was somewhere in India. . . . The mala was one of the main tools used to focus one's mind and devotional aspirations." (www.easternhealingarts.com) A mala used by Tibetan Buddhists traditionally is a string of 108 beads plus a larger bead, called the Guru or Root bead. A wrist mala traditionally has 9, 22, or 27 beads. Mala beads can be made of many materials and colors, including turquoise, sandalwood, amethyst, tiger eye, quartz, pearl, bone, or seeds. The beads come in various sizes, and you should choose a mala that feels comfortable to you, with the beads not too large or too small, with adequate space between the beads (not strung too tightly or loosely), and bead texture that is pleasing to your touch. Malas should not be worm as decoration, only as part of a practice. When wearing the mala around the neck, the Guru bead should be at the back of your neck. If worn around the wrist, it should be worn around the left wrist and wrapped as many times as necessary to keep it from slipping off (depending on the size of the beads). Keep the mala off the ground, as you would do for any sacred object.

Traditionally, the mala is held in the right hand and the beads are passed between the thumb and index finger as you count. One should start the count at the first bead past the Guru bead, and as you say a mantra, gently "pull" or draw each bead towards you for each mantra. One "round" of mantras would be 108, and you would start counting again for each round you do. Some say that when starting the next round of counting, you should "reverse" the counting on the beads, so that you don't go over the Guru bead. This would be accomplished by twisting the mala 180 degrees and starting again.

Malas have traditionally been blessed by monks or lamas when you ask them to do so. There is also a mantra that you can say for your mala that will multiply the results of saying mantras. (see Mantras on page 45)

## MANDALA

A mandala (Sanskrit for "circle"; Tib. *kyilkor,* for "center and surrounding environment") is a sacred diagram usually created in sand or paint or on a thangka. It symbolizes the pure, perfected universe and provides a visual framework for establishing feelings of peace, well-being, and wholeness. It is a cosmic diagram representing the symbolic dwelling place of a particular Tibetan Buddhist deity.

### Sand Mandala

Composed of millions of grains of dyed sand, the mandala is believed to have a positive effect on all who see it, as each particle personifies good-

*Monks from Drepung Loseling Monastery in India constructing a White Tara sand mandala at Berea College, Berea, KY, 2008*

*Left, Kalachakra sand mandala. Above, 3D representation of Kalachakra mandala, as created by Arjia Rinpoche, TMBCC*

ness. Created by Buddhist monks, the mandala is often part of initiation ceremonies—accompanied by other ritual objects, costumed dancers, music, and chanting—that grant the initiate the privilege to study and practice the teachings of a Sutra or Tantra—sacred texts that are guides to visualizing a particular deity.

The mandala is often illustrated as a palace—a two-dimensional representation of a three-dimensional object. It is a cosmic diagram which represents the symbolic dwelling place of a particular deity, each deity having its own particular, unique mandala. Tibetan Buddhists believe that the seed of enlightenment in each person's mind is nourished by the process of visualizing and contemplating the symbolic meanings contained within the mandala, as well as the actual process of creating it. In addition to serving as a tool for spiritual development, the mandala is also created to purify the environment and promote harmony in the world. In order to show impermanence, mandalas are ritually destroyed, or "deconstructed," after completion. Sand from a mandala is then ritually poured into a local body of water—a river, lake, or ocean—in order for the mandala to further benefit sentient beings. After some dismantlings, sand from the mandala is put in small envelopes for the attendees to take with them, to be placed on their home altar.

## Mandala-Offering Mudra

The mudra (hand gesture, or position of the hands) that is demonstrated in the following photograph represents the offering that is made in the Tibetan "mandala offering practice" and is the equivalent of the multi-

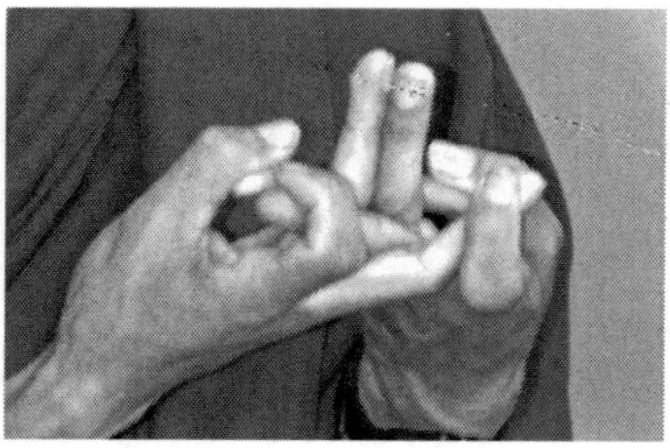

tiered structure that appears on the mandala offering-plate in the succeeding photograph. The ring fingers that extend upward in the middle of the configuration thus represent not only the nine-tiered "Mt. Sumeru" that forms the axis around which the mystical cosmology that is being offered is constructed but also the central channel (*shushumna*) in the energy system that permeates the body of the individual. The complex arrangement of all of the fingers in this mudra brings the two hands into a bowl-shaped arrangement that approximates the shape of the lower half of a lotus. And the manner in which the thumbs of each hand wrap around to connect with the little finger of the opposing hand, instead of thumb to thumb and little-finger to little-finger, is reminscent of a mobius-like "figure eight," suggesting that the three-dimensional figure that is being represented must have a non-linear surface, one that folds in on itself. (www.tap3x .net/EMBTI/j4selfcc.html)

These offerings are followed immediately with the short mandala offering. You may instead recite the intermediate or extensive mandala offering while either placing a mandala on your altar or performing the mandala-offering mudra with your hands.

*Short mandala offering:*

This earth anointed with incense and strewn with flowers,
And Mt. Sumeru, adorned by the four continents, the Sun and Moon,
I transmute into a Buddha-Field and offer:
May all beings partake of the Field of Supreme Purity.
*Idam Guru Ratna Mandalakam Niryatayami*

## Ritual Mandala

A ritual mandala is a tantric device, used as a visual aid for concentration and meditation leading to insight. It consists of a base, three rings, and a crowning ornament for the top, all usually made of a precious metal. During certain rituals, the monk making the mandala chants as he builds it, filling each ring with stone and small shells before continuing on to the next ring, then placing the ornament on top, which represents Mt. Sumeru.

## MANI STONES / MANI WALLS

A *mani stone* is a stone with the traditional Tibetan mantra *Om Mani Padme Hum* ("hail to the jewel in the lotus," referring to Chenrezig, the Buddha of Compassion) carved or painted on it. The practice of doing this brings merit to both the person who does it and to others who circumambulate collections of these stones, called *mani walls*. They can be seen throughout Tibet, from central population centers like Lhasa to the most remote regions of the country. A mani wall can be an actual "wall" or stone fence constructed over time, or just a random pile of mani stones, perhaps with a prayer banner at the top. The fact that so many mani walls are found in Tibet attests to the spiritual nature of the population. It has been said that it is extremely bad luck for anyone to take

*A mani wall with a slab of slate, with writing on it, at Lake Namtso, Tibet, 2007*

a mani stone from a mani wall. (A 1993 novel by Ken Mitchell, *Stones of the Dalai Lama*, recounts the travails of a family from the U.S. that brings back mani stones from Tibet and is then beset by bad luck.)

## MANTRAS

A mantra (Tib. *ngahk*, also *mani*, usually referring to the commonly used six-syllable mantra of Chenrezig) is a series of syllables designed as a tool to focus the mind through repetition and is often used during meditation; commonly used to invoke the power of a particular deity (such as the Buddha of Compassion, or Green Tara, or the Medicine Buddha). The most widely said mantra is: *Om Mani Padme Hum* (mantra of Chenrezig). Tibetan Buddhists believe that saying the mantra aloud, silently to oneself, or making use of it in a prayer wheel invokes the powerful and benevolent attention of Chenrezig, the embodiment of compassion. Mantras are generally recited three times, seven times, 108 times (the number of beads on a mala), or however many times they should traditionally be chanted. Many mantras begin with the syllable "Om"—this is because Om symbolizes one's impure body, speech and mind, and also the pure noble body, speech, and mind of a Buddha. "Buddhism claims that an impure body, speech, and mind can be transformed into the pure one of a Buddha, who was once impure, and later by removing negative attributes, achieved enlightenment on his path." (14th Dalai Lama) Some mantras end with the word "Soha," which means "may the meaning of the mantra take root in my mind."

**Mantra of Chenrezig** (also known as the Six-Syllable Mantra)
*Om Mani Padme Hum*

**Mantra of Padmasambhava (Guru Rinpoche)**
*Om Ah Hum Vajra Guru Padme Siddhi Hum*

**Mantra of Buddha Shakyamuni**
*Om Muni Muni Maha Muniye Soha*

**Mantra of Kalachakra**
*Om Ah Zar Ma La Wa La Yah Soha*

**Mantra of Tara**
*Om Tare Tutare Ture Soha*

**Mantra of the Medicine Buddha (short form)**

*Om Benkandzay Benkandzay Maha Benkandzay Radza Sumudgate Soha*

**Mantra of Manjushri**

*Om Ah Ra Pa Tsa Na Dhi* . . . . . (repeat *Dhi* as many times as possible)

**Mantra of Milarepa**

*Om Ah Guru Hasa Vajra Sarwa Siddhi Phala Hum*

**Mantra of Je Tsongkhapa**

*Mig Me Tse Way Ter Chen Chen Re Sig*
*Dri Me Khyen Pay Wang Po Jam Pel Yang*
*Du Pung Ma Lu Jom Tse Sang Way Dag*
*Gang Chen Ke Pay Tsug Gyen Tsong Kha Pa*
*Lo Zang Drag Pay Zhad La Sol Wa Deb*

**Mantra of Vajrasattva** (short form)

*Om Vajra Sattva Hum*

**Mantra of Prajnaparamita**

*Om Gate Gate Paragate Para Samgate Bodhi Soha*

**Multiplying Mantra** (it is said that if this is recited seven times, whatever virtuous actions one does that day will be multiplied by 100,000)

*Om Sambhara Sambhara Bimana Sara Maha Dzawa Hum*
*Om Mara Mara Bimana Kara Maha Dzawa Hum*

**Mala Blessing Mantra** (recite this seven times and then blow on the mala to increase the power of subsequent recitations)

*Om Rutsira Mani Prawa Taya Hum*

**Blessing the Feet Mantra** (by reciting this mantra three times in the morning, then spitting on the soles of your feet, it helps any living creature that dies beneath your feet that day to be reborn in the God Realm of the Thirty-three)

*Om Kraytsara Ghana Hum Hri Soha*

**Eating Meat Mantra** (recite this seven times over the meat to stop the fault of eating meat and to help the sentient being whose flesh it was to be reborn in a happy realm)

*Om Ahbirakay Tsara Hum*

## Merit

**Merit** (Sans. *punya*; Tib. *sonam*) is doing good deeds or actions, in an unselfish way, with no thought of reward or repayment. It is intimately connected with karma, in that the actions and deeds performed in one lifetime will determine the life circumstances in the next or future lifetimes. Positive imprints that are left on one's mindstream will ripen when conditions are right as positive karma. If one accumulates positive merit, then a good rebirth and favorable life circumstances will result; if negative merit (demerit) is accumulated, then a not so good rebirth is likely. Good intention in creating merit is more important than the actual act. Buddhism stresses that a good deed should be guided by good intention, mindfulness, and wisdom, so that the deed will result in a wholesome outcome. "To develop merit, it is necessary to perform positive actions, to make efforts of generosity, honesty, and concentration. . . . For this merit to be beneficial, it must be cultivated with wisdom, that is, positive actions should be performed with the intention to take care of and develop the [Dharma] (for one's own progress and that of others)." (www.dhammadana.org)

Among ways to gain merit are:

- giving to the needy
- dedicating merit to others
- pujas
- tsog offerings
- offering butterlamps at a monastery
- building stupas
- circumambulating holy places
- visiting holy sites
- supporting monastics and monasteries
- reciting and practicing Buddha's teachings
- seven non-material actions: gentle looks; smiling countenance; gentle words; unstinting physical labor; sincere work for others; giving others one's seat; and providing shelter for rest
- nine ways to perform good deeds: virtuous conduct; contemplative meditation; mutual respect to other beings; helping people around you; providing others an opportunity to make merit together; rejoicing at another's good deed; cultivating Dharma in oneself; propagating Dharma to others; possession of right understanding

## MONASTIC MUSICAL INSTRUMENTS

**Bell** (Tib. *drilbu*)—always used with the left hand and at the same level as your heart. Most often used in concert with the dorje during ritual, it is sometimes used for the sound the bell makes during ceremonies. It is used either continuosly or in short bursts. The sound of the bell is also very auspicious, and it is said that it drives away evil spirits. Bells are usually made from bronze, copper, or silver.

**Conch shell trumpet** (Tib. *dung dkar*)—the mouthpiece is made by cutting away the tip of the spiral of the conch shell. Many of these instruments have intricate engravings or engraved metal plates attached. Produces a deep vibrating tone—the sound is a symbol of purity and devotion, and is used as a ritual instrument in Hinduism and Jainism, as well as Buddhism

**Cymbals,** large (Tib. *rolmo/sil nyan*)—large cymbals held one above the other and brought together in a vertical movement

**Cymbals,** small (Tib. *tingsha*)—small hand-held cymbals, sometimes called finger cymbals, attached to each other with a string or cord. They create a clear sustaining sound when struck, usually striking the edges against each other. It is said that they "are used to summon 'hungry ghosts' to accept offerings. The belief is that in making an offering and relieving the hunger of these ravenous spirits, their suffering is diminished and enlightenment can thereby be reached." (www.tibetinfor.com.cn)

**Frame drum** (Tib. *dhyangro/tangdu/nga*)—circular wooden frame with a handle on the bottom, often carved, and with goatskin stretched across both sides resulting in two membranes. It is struck with a curved cane beater, shaped somewhat like a question mark

**Long horn** (Tib. *rag-dun/dungchen,* "great horn")—long horns are made from pieces of copper or brass that can telescope for portability and storage. They can be up to 20 feet long and produce a low bass sound. When played stationary, the end of the horn can be placed on a low wooden stand. When used in procession, the end of the horn can be put on the

*Touring monks from Drepung Loseling Monastery in India using (from left) wind instruments, large frame drum, bell, large cymbals, small cymbals, and long horns*

shoulder of a monk. "In order to get a continuous sound, the instruments are always used in pairs, and the two players must not simultaneously pause for breath." (www.erpmusic.com)

**Skull drum** (Sans. *damaru*)—a small, two-sided hand drum, originally each side of which was made from the top part of a human skull. Now usually made of wood with leather membranes. Two "clappers" attached by string or cord to the middle, each strike a membrane when the drum is quickly rotated side to side using the right hand. Used by both Buddhists and Hindus. "According to a Hindu belief, the universe was created by Shiva with the help of a damaru. . . . It is said that the dead whose skulls have been made into [the] drum speak to us in the language of the sounds of a damaru." (www.erpmusic.com)

**Thighbone trumpet** (Tib. *kangling/kang-dung*)—short horn that in the past was made using a human thighbone; today it is made of wood or metal and is similar to a trumpet. "Originally, this instrument was made of a thighbone of a young girl who had, preferably, died a virgin. This is because the sound of the kang-dung symbolizes purity; therefore, the instrument was to be pure." (www.erpmusic.com)

## MUDRAS

A mudra (Tib. *chagyah*) is the position that one sees the hands in, as shown in Buddhist statues, thangkas, other artwork, or by monks during ceremonies. Each hand has a particular meaning, or both hands together have a particular meaning. One or both hands might be holding an implement or weapon, and no mudra is then indicated. The mudras shown here are those seen most often.

**The Gesture of Turning the Wheel of Dharma (Dharmachakra)**—thumb and index finger of the right hand stand for wisdom and method combined. The other three raised fingers symbolize the teaching of the Buddhist doctrine, which leads sentient beings to the paths of the beings of three capacities. The position of the left hand symbolizes the beings of the three capacities, who follow the combined path of method and wisdom

**The Gesture of Pressing the Earth (Bhumisparsha)**—also called "touching the earth" or "calling the earth to witness," symbolizIng the Buddha's victory over Mara at his enlightenment under the Bodhi Tree. The right hand gestures pressing the earth. The position of the left hand symbolizes meditation. Together, they stand for the Buddha's overcoming of hindrances while meditating on emptiness

**The Gesture of Meditation (Dhyana)**—also called Samadhi; the nerve channel associated with the mind of enlightenment (Bodhicitta) passes through the thumbs. Thus, joining of the two thumbs in this gesture is of auspicious significance for the future development of the mind of enlightenment. "This gesture expresses overcoming the world of appearance through enlightenment." (www.urbandharma.org/udharma7/mudras.html)

**The Gesture of Teaching or Giving Instruction (Vitarka)**—also called "the gesture of debate" or "discussion." "This is the mystic gesture of Taras and Bodhisattvas, often used when explaining the Buddha's teachings." (www.buddhas-online.com) Similar to Abhaya, but with the thumb touching the forefinger.

**The Gesture of Granting Wishes or of Charity (Varada)**—also called "Gift bestowing Gesture of Compassion" or "conferring boon" or "grace" mudra. Sometimes used by the left hand, and sometimes by the standing Buddha. (www.buddhas-online.com) "It is the mudra of the accomplishment of the wish to devote oneself to human salvation." (www.urbandharma.org/udharma7/mudras.html)

**The Gesture of Fearlessness and Granting Protection (Abhaya)**—also called "Gesture of Protection" or "blessing." Sometimes also used with the left hand. "It is the gesture of the Buddha Shakyamuni immediately after attaining enlightenment. . . . It indicates not only the appeasement of the senses, but also the absence of fear; and it confers such absence of fear on others, which is a liberating factor." (www.urbandharma.org/udharma7/mudras.html)

## PHOWA

A *phowa* (Tib., powa) is a ceremony requested by a family member of a dying person. A trained lama or monk performs rituals and reads the *Bardo Thodol* (*The Tibetan Book of the Dead*) in order to guide the transference of consciousness at the time of death so as to successfully achieve a fortunate rebirth. Part of the success in death comes from the individual's own preparation and readiness during his or her life. A good attitude and acceptance of the process is said to make a significant difference in the consciousness's travels from the current body, through the *bardo* (transition or "in between") state, and into a new rebirth. This process, in most cases, is said to take 49 days.

## PRAYERS FLAGS AND BANNERS / FLAGS

### Prayer flags and Banners

Prayer flags (Tib. *lungta,* "wind horse") are seen throughout Tibet and the Tibetan diaspora. They can be seen hanging on the roofs of Tibetan homes, businesses, monasteries, mountain passes, and marketplaces. The concept is that the prayers printed on the flags are carried on the wind for the benefit of the one who hangs the flags and all other sentient beings. Prayer flags that are strung in a horizontal direction, such as between trees or across the front of a dwelling or business, are called *darding*. A prayer banner, which is in a vertical direction, is called *dar-chen.*

Tibetan prayer flags are usually individually printed from a woodblock which has been carved by a skilled craftsman, sometimes a monk or

*Prayer flags (dar-ding) across a small stream in Bhutan, 2007*

lama. They are printed on colored squares of cloth and strung together in groups of five (or two consecutive groups of five to make ten), and in this order (and representing the Buddha family and element): Blue (Akshobhya Buddha/space), White (Ratnasambhava Buddha/water), Red (Amitabha Buddha/fire), Green (Amoghasiddhi Buddha/air and wind), and Yellow (Vairocana Buddha/earth).

*Prayer banner (darchen)*

Among the more common images that are seen imprinted on prayer flags are: Wind Horse, Green Tara, Chenrezig, Amitayus (Long Life), Medicine Buddha, Padmasambhava (Guru Rinpoche), Vajrasattva, White Tara, Four Dignitaries (Garuda, Dragon, Snow Lion, Tiger), and Kalachakra. In addition to the images, prayers and mantras are imprinted on each flag.

There are certain days that are more auspicious to hang prayer flags. And there are some days, as listed in certain Tibetan Buddhist calendars as determined by Tibetan astrologers, that are inauspicious to hang flags. (see page 209) Prayer flags are meant to be hung out of doors; over time, sun, wind, and rain will fade and wear out the flags (also giving a reminder of the impermanence of all things). When they have been worn, they are often burned with the appropriate ceremony at a monastery so that their last use will release the final prayers.

## Tibetan flag

"...during the rule of His Holiness the Great Thirteenth Dalai Lama, this eminent spiritual and temporal ruler of Tibet enacted many modifications in administrative policies in accordance with international customs. Based on the formats of previous Tibetan military flags, His Holiness improved upon them and designed the present, modern national flag. With an official proclamation, He declared that this would be the uniform, standard flag to be adopted by all Tibetan military defence establishments [1912]. Since the time of that proclamation, all Tibetan regiments have likewise adopted this flag as their standard.

"The colour scheme of the Tibetan national flag gives a clear indication of all aspects of Tibet in its symbolism, such as the geographic features of the religious, snowy land of Tibet, the customs and traditions of Tibetan society, the political administration of the Tibetan government and so forth.

"History attests to the fact that Tibet is one of the most ancient nations of the world. Therefore, in all the three regions of Tibet, irrespective of caste and creed, this national flag inherited from our ancestors is universally accepted as a common, peerless treasure and even today still continues to be highly respected and esteemed as in the past." (www.tibet.net/about-tibet/the-tibetan-national-flag/)

***"An Explanation of the Symbolism of the National Flag of Tibet***—In the centre stands a magnificent thickly snow-clad mountain, which represents the great nation of Tibet, widely known as the Land Surrounded by Snow Mountains.

"Across the dark blue sky six red bands spread representing the original ancestors of the Tibetan people: the six tribes called Se, Mu, Dong, Tong, Dru and Ra which in turn gave the [twelve] descendants. The combination of six red bands (for the tribes) and six dark blue bands for the sky represents the incessant enactment of the virtuous deeds of protection of the spiritual teachings and secular life by the black and red guardian protector deities with which Tibet has had connection for a very long time.

"At the tip of the snow mountain, the sun with its rays brilliantly shining in all directions represents the equal enjoyment of freedom, spiritual and material happiness and prosperity by all beings in the land of Tibet.

"On the slopes of the mountain there proudly stand a pair of snow lions blazing with the manes of fearlessness, which represent the country's victorious accomplishment of a unified spiritual and secular life.

"The beautiful and radiant three coloured jewel held aloft represents the ever-present reverence respectfully held by the Tibetan people towards the Three Supreme Jewels (the Buddhist objects of refuge: Buddha, Dharma, and Sangha).

"The two-coloured swirling jewel held between the two lions represents the peoples' guarding and cherishing the self discipline of correct ethical behaviour, principally represented by the practices of the ten exalted virtues and the 16 humane modes of conduct.

"Lastly, the surrounding border of yellow adorning the perimeter represents the spread and flourishing in all directions and times of the purified gold-like teachings of the Buddha." (www.tibet.net)

## Buddhist flag

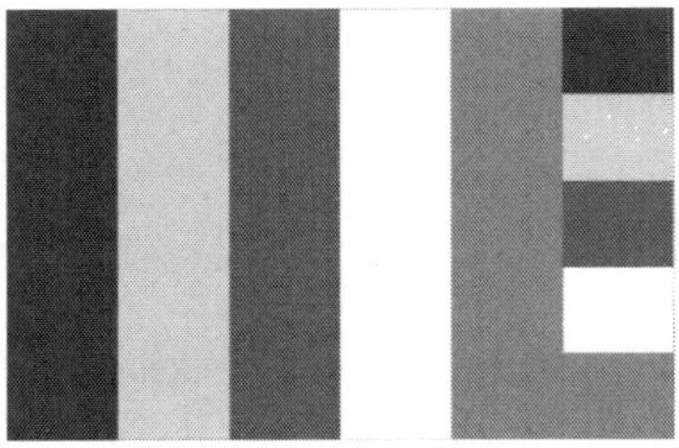

The flag symbolizing Buddhism was developed in Ceylon (now called Sri Lanka) in 1880, to mark the revival of Buddhism in that country. One of those helping in development and use of the flag was an American Buddhist in Ceylon, Col. Henry Steele Olcott. According to Olcott's diary, "Our Colombo [Ceylon] brothers had hit upon the quite original and unique idea of blending in the flag the colours alleged to have been exhibited in the aura of the Buddha" when he attained enlightenment (www.dhammaweb .net). It was accepted as the international Buddhist flag in 1952 by the World Buddhist Conference, which was held in Japan.

The colors represent the following:

- Blue: loving kindness and universal compassion
- Yellow: the Middle Path, a mind free from greed, anger, and ignorance
- Red: blessings, including wisdom, virtue, dignity, and fortune
- White: purity and liberation
- Orange: wisdom, the essence of Buddhism

## Karmapa "Dream" Flag

This flag was seen in a dream by the 16th Karmapa, H.H. Rangjung Rigpe Dorje (1924-1981). It was initially made into a flag in 1980 in Boulder, CO, where the Karmapa was visiting. He called it Namkhyen Gyaldar, "Victorious Flag of the Buddha's Wisdom." "The blue is the sky, symbolizing spiritual insight and wisdom, and the yellow is the earth, the actual world of our everday experience. The symmetry of the wave pattern shows how we come to understand their interdependence when we practice the Dharma." (www.dharma-haven.org)

## PRAYER WHEELS

Prayer wheels (Tib., *mani khorlo*, meaning "Wheel of the Law") are exclusively found in Tibetan Buddhism. The instrument is usually a cylinder mounted on a wooden or metal handle, allowing the cylinder to rotate. Most often, inside the cylinder, *Om Mani Padme Hum* (the mantra of Chenezig, the Buddha of compassion) is inscribed on paper many times. With each turn of the prayer wheel, merit is generated as if one were saying the number of mantras that are within the cylinder. The size of a prayer wheel can be as small as to be able to hang around the neck, or desktop, or hand-sized and carried by the user (the most com-

*Prayers wheels built into the wall at the back of the Main Cathedral, Dharamsala, India, 2005*

mon), or as large as being mounted in a small building of its own. Many monasteries and stupas have prayer wheels mounted on the outside walls, so that when pilgrims circumambulate, they are also able to spin the prayer wheels (with their right hands), thereby gaining merit. In addition to hand-powered, they can also be powered by water, wind, or the sun.

## PROSTRATIONS

Prostration (Tib. *chatsel*) is defined as being "stretched out with face on the ground in adoration or submission." Prostration is a practice done in many religious traditions. Among the reasons for doing prostrations in Tibetan Buddhism are: to express our deep veneration before an image of Buddha or a teacher (who is an emanation of Buddha's knowledge and wisdom); to purify negative karma from the past in which we did not respect another; to help us overcome and purify feelings of ego and pride that have accumulated through past lifetimes; to show respect for the qualities of a Buddha (such as compassion, wisdom, patience, and virtue), and to inspire us to develop these qualities.

*The Purpose and Benefits of doing Full Prostration*
By Sakya Pandita Kunga Gyaltsen

NAMO GURUBAE. The recitation of one mantra is transformed into 1,000 prostrations.
OM NAMO MANJUSHRI YE.
To Lord Manjushri I prostrate, NAMO SUSHRIYA.
To the incomparable glory I prostrate.
NAMO UDA DHARMA SHRIYE SVAHA.
To the most excellent glory I prostrate.
By prostrating to the most superior Triple Gems, defilements and obscurations of sentient beings and myself are purified.
By clasping the 2 palms, may methods and wisdom be attained.
Resting the clasped hands on the top of the crown, may one enter the celestial land of Akanishta.
Resting the clasped hands on the forehead between the eyebrows, may the defilements and obscurations of the body be purified.
Resting the clasped hands at the throat, may the defilements and obscurations of the voice be purified.

*Prostrations in front of the Jokhang Temple, Lhasa, Tibet, 2007 (one woman also using a prayer wheel)*

Putting the clasped hands at the heart, may the defilements and obscurations of the mind be purified.

Each time for unfolding the two hands, for the sake of all sentient beings may the two bodies be obtained.

When the two knees touch the ground, may the damnation of samsara be free.

When the ten fingers of the two hands touch the ground, may the ten bhumis and five stages be reached.

When the forehead touches the ground, may the eleven radiant rays shine everywhere.

By straightening and the bending of the arms and legs, may the four activities be all at once accomplished.

By straightening and bending the veins and sinews, all the knots at the veins are loosened without exception.

By bending the spine and central artery, may all the wind enter the central vein without exception.

To touch the ground and later to rise up, may liberation from samsara be attained.

After prostrating many times, may one become the guide of all sentient beings without attaching to personal calmness.

By the meritorious power of offering full prostration by oneself and others, may the conditions in this life be freed from sickness and blessed with three auspiciousness.

During the time of dying, one is reborn in the state of bliss and quickly attain the state of a Fully Enlightened Buddha.

This is a preparation of Lord Sakya Pandita. After doing this full prostration, if one reflects the reasons and purposes, immeasurable benefits and results will be received.

**Full Prostration**, as described above, is this:

1. Join hands together, with thumbs and opposing fingers all touching each other.
2. Bring the joined hands to the top of your head (the crown), then
3. Bring the joined hands to your forehead, then
4. Bring the joined hands to your throat, then
5. Bring the joined hands to your heart.
6. Then as gracefully as possible, drop to your knees and lay stretched out as completely as possible on the floor.

This is repeated a total of four times, but on the fourth time, stop when you have your hands joined at your heart, contemplate for a short few seconds, then continue your activities.

**Five-Point Prostration** is almost identical to full prostration, but instead of stretching out fully, one only goes down on hands and knees, touches forehead to the ground, and rises again (with five points—two knees, two hands, and one forehead touching the ground). This is also repeated a total of four times, and on the fourth time, stop when hands are joined at the heart, contemplate shortly, then continue with whatever one is going to do next.

## Protection Cord / Prayer Cord / Blessing Cord / Reminder Cord

A protection cord (Tib. *sungdu* [*sung*–protection, *du*–knotted string]) is a cord made out of colored string (usually red, sometimes yellow, sometimes both colors woven together), to be worn around the wrist, upper arm, or neck. It is made by lamas, who after making it and tying a knot or knots in it, pray over it and blow the power of a mantra into it and give it out to wear as a blessing. It is said that sometimes three knots are tied that represent the body, speech, and mind of a Buddha. It is meant to protect the wearer from obstacles, to give them long life, and bring them prosperity. Some say that one should wear the protection cord for at least three days; others say that one should wear it until it falls off on its own accord. Protection cords are often given out to participants when an initiation such as the Kalachakra or other deity empowerment concludes.

## PUJA

*Puja* (Pali; Tib. *mchod pa*) is a general term used for all forms of ceremonial worship. In Pali, the meaning is "honor, worship, and devotional attention." The ceremonies can range from individual daily offerings of flowers, candles (light), fruit, or water to the deities in homes or at temples to much larger rites performed by many people. A puja is a ceremony in which prayers and offerings are made to deities—the different manifestations of enlightened beings—to help bring down their blessings and help. Different schools, lineages, and monasteries have their own particular puja ceremonies. The puja is a traditional ritual and involves taking refuge (all pujas begin with refuge), then visualizing the particular deity, and offering praises.

### Types of pujas

**Chenrezig puja**—performed in order to cultivate great compassion, wisdom, and skillful means
**Funeral puja**—usually done for 49 days after a person has passed away
**Guru puja**—performed to pay homage to a spiritual teacher and to try to identify with his qualities
**Long Life puja**—performed to request long life for a particular lama, teacher, or the Dalai Lama
**Mahakala puja**—performed to help remove all kinds of obstacles in our practice and daily life
**Medicine Buddha puja**—performed to help improve one's health
**Shakyamuni Buddha puja**—homage and offering to Buddha, to encourage, cultivate, and develop devotion, morality, concentration, and wisdom
**Tara puja**—performed to help remove worldly fears

## RITUAL IMPLEMENTS

Many of these implements might be found on altars in the homes of many Tibetans. However, the actual use of some of them are restricted to monks and lamas, who are trained in their proper use. The exceptions on this list would be the water bowls and butter lamps.

**Bell** (Tib. *drilbu;* Sans. *ghanta*) and **Dorje** (Tib. meaning "thunderbolt," "diamond," or "indestructible hardness;" Sans. *vajra*, meaning "the hard or mighty one")—Used together, the bell and dorje are primary ritual objects used in Tantric Buddhism (Vajrayana). The bell is held in the left hand and represents the female principle of wisdom. The dorje is held in the right hand and represents the male principle of action or universe. Used together, they symbolize the inseparable union of method and wisdom in following the path Dharma lays out for us. The use of the bell and dorje together is also symbolic of the joining of wisdom and compassion.

The bell can be of varying height—8, 12, 16, 18, or 22 finger-widths in height. The base is round, above which is a vase with the image of the goddess Prajnaparamita. Above this are a lotus, a moon disc, and on top, a vajra. The hollow of the bell symbolizes wisdom that understands emptiness. The clapper in the bell represents the sound of emptiness.

A dorje (or vajra) can have three, five, or nine spokes. The spokes of a peaceful dorje meet at the tip, whereas those of a wrathful dorje are slightly splayed out at the end. The prongs of a five-spoked dorje are representative of five wisdoms: the mirror-like wisdom; the wisdom of equality; the wisdom of individual analysis; the wisdom of accomplishing activity; and the wisdom of the sphere of reality. It is also said that the five tapering prongs on one end of the dorje represent the Five Buddhas

(Akshobhya, Vairochana, Ratnasambhava, Amitabha, and Amoghasiddi) and that the five prongs at the other end represent the five female consorts of the Buddhas (Mamaki, Lochana, Bajradhatvishvari, Pandara, and Tara). Together, it is said the ten prongs symbolize the ten perfections (generosity, morality, renunciation, wisdom, energy, patience, truthfulness, resolution, loving kindness, and equanimity).

**Bumpa** (Tib.)—a ritual vase which represents the palace of the deities and is used in tantric practices for holding blessed water and dispelling obstacles. It is used as a vessel of purification, to bestow blessings, and to confer empowerments. Inserted into the top of the bumpa is an implement called a *flourish*, which is made from peacock feathers and used to sprinkle water from the vase during ceremonies.

**Damaru** (Tib.)—a ritual instrument used in tantric ceremonies; it is a two-headed hand drum, originally made with two top-halves of human skulls, covered with a leather membranes, with two "clappers" attached to the middle by cords which strike the drum heads when the damaru is rotated back and forth. (see picture on page 48)

**Phurba** (Tib.; *purba, phurpa, phurbu*) (Sans. *kila*) —a Tibetan ritual dagger used in ceremonies to exorcise demons or drive away evil spirits. With a three-sided blade, the phurba symbolizes overcoming or cutting through the three root poisons—ignorance, desire, and hatred. It is also known as *vajrakila*, which means thunder nail or magical dagger. Often, the head of the Tibetan deity Vajrakila appears at the top of the phurba. Phurbas have been made of wood, iron, or other metals.

*Iron phurba*

**Skull Cup** (Tib. *thod pa*; Sans. *kapala*)—ritual implement fashioned from the oval upper section of a human skull. It serves as a libation vessel for numbers of Vajrayana deities, mostly wrathful. The power of the skull cup comes to some degree from the "forces" of the original owner of the skull, which are still embodied within the bone as a spirit. As a benign symbol, the skull cup is seen as the begging bowl of an ascetic, serving as a constant reminder of death and impermanence in samsara. It is often used in concert with the curved knife, where the skull cup is the vessel that collects the blood and organs that are cut by the knife, and used ceremonially as the sustenance of a deity. Skull cups are now composed of man-made materials.

*Skull cup with lid, on stand*

**Curved knife / Chopping blade** (Tib. *tri gug*)—one of the most prominent weapons seen brandished by wrathful deities, used to chop up enemies of Dharma, or to cut through the fog of ignorance. Often seen in use with the skull cup.

**Water bowls** (Tib. *teeng*)—on altars, it is customary to offer seven bowls of fresh, clean water, which represent the seven-limb prayer: prostrating, confession, rejoicing in the good qualitities of oneself and others, requesting the Buddhas to remain in this world, beseeching them to teach others, and dedicating the merits. They are made of metal, sometimes with auspicious symbols on them.

*Monk at Samye Monastery, Tibet, cleaning water bowls, 2007*

**Butter lamps** (Tib. *chömay*)—lamps and candles symbolize wisdom, eliminating the darkness of ignorance. In Tibet, one way that pilgrims gener-

*Large butter lamp at Samye Monastery, Tibet, 2007*

ate much merit is by filling butter lamps in monasteries. It is not unusual to see Tibetans carrying containers of yak butter with them, spooning out some in each group of butter lamps they come to.

## Shrine Room Etiquette

**Shoes**—leave all shoes in the area near the door or outside the shrine area; never enter the shrine area with shoes on.

**Greetings**—place your palms together in front of your heart and bow slightly as a proper gesture of either greeting or farewell to a teacher or a monk. It is not mandatory, but it is very respectful and polite to do so.

**Teacher's entrance**—stand and bow slightly when the Lama enters the room. Remain standing while he prostrates to the Buddhas and his own teachers (visualized on the throne) and takes his seat.

**If late**—if you must enter the shrine room after meditation or teaching has begun, do so as quickly and as quietly as possible, so as not to disturb others.

**Appropriate dress**—wearing revealing clothing, such as tank tops, short skirts, shorts, and the like is considered inappropriate attire in temple and shrine room settings. Within Buddhism, appropriate attire is usually flexible and based on the polite and inoffensive social customs of each country.

**Legs outstretched**—it is considered impolite and disrespectful when seated on the floor or on a cushion to stretch the legs out and face the soles of the feet toward the shrine or teacher. Honor your teacher and shrine room by sitting as comfortably as you can without pointing your feet frontward.

**Prostrations**—you may notice some people doing three prostrations (either low bows or stretching out on the floor) when entering or leaving a shrine room or when a teacher arrives or leaves. This is extremely respectful, and a personal gesture of special respect when done by a practitioner. Anyone may do this if they wish, but it is certainly not required. After the Lama is seated, practicing Buddhists often perform three formal prostrations as a sign of respect to the Lama and to the teachings. Others may join in or stand quietly. For those wishing to participate, the form is: with palms together touch crown of head, forehead, throat, and heart; kneel on hands and knees, touching forehead to ground very briefly and rising quickly. Perform the entire act three times altogether. At the conclusion, once more touch hands to crown, forehead, throat, and heart, pausing very briefly at the end for contemplation. Then take your seat.

**Dharma materials**—because books on Buddhism contain scriptures considered sacred, one should never place them on the floor or rug. This is true for Dharma books, meditation texts, notes on the teachings, or prayer beads (malas). You may want to use a small table, shelf, pillow, handbag, or special cushion. Also, do not step over Dharma books and articles.

**Stepping over**—when moving through a crowded shrine room, make every effort not to step over the top of another person's body (e.g., leg or foot) or Dharma items. When seated, if others are passing by, raise the knees to afford a pathway so they are not forced to step over you in any way. Stepping over is considered disrespectful and rude.

**Turning pages**—when turning the pages of Dharma books, do not wet the fingers with the tongue.

**Mala beads**—do not place malas on the ground, the floor, or on a bed. During teachings and initiations, do not recite mantras or count beads unless told to do so as part of the teaching or initiation. Malas should not be worn when using the bathroom.

**Indicating** (pointing)—when pointing (to a teacher, monastic, thangka, etc.), indicate with the hand open and fingers extended and palm up, rather than pointing with the index finger, which is considered very rude.

**Incense**—when lighting incense, after the stick has ignited with a glowing ember, do not blow the flame out with the breath, but rather wave with the hand to extinguish. The same is true when blowing out candles and butter lamps: do not blow them out with the breath but rather use a candle snuffer or wave gently with the hand.

**Offerings**—having placed offerings such as fruit or cookies on a shrine or altar, it is appropriate when replacing them with newer offerings to give the first offerings away to others rather than eating them oneself.

**Teacher's exit**—as the teacher stands to leave, stand and bow slightly, until he or she is out of the room. Some students will again perform three prostrations, except at the last teaching session, where the omission conveys the wish for the teacher to return.

**Addressing a teacher or other monastic**—if the individual is a *Rinpoche* (a term of respect for incarnate lamas), he would be addressed as "Rinpoche." When referring to him, he would be called "Thrangu Rinpoche" (if his name was Thrangu). When *Tulku* appears in a name, it is also referring to an incarnate lama but is not used in addressing him. If the individual has a *Geshe* degree, it is proper to address him as "Geshe-la." The "la" at the end is an honorific. If the individual is a *Venerable*, that is, has taken vows as a monk, one may address him by his name, with an honorific. For example, if his name was Ven. Tenzin Deshek, you would address him as "Deshek-la."

When interacting with any monk or nun, it is appropriate to treat them with great respect. They have gone through many years of training and should be accorded treatment as if they were emanations of a Buddha.

## SKY BURIAL

Sky burial in Tibet is used to dispose of a body after the consciousness has left it. In Tibet, there is little wood, so cremation was reserved for the very few (high lamas and nobles). The ground was often frozen, so there could be no burial in the ground.

Sky burial in Tibetan is *jhator,* meaning "giving alms to the birds." After death, a person's body is prepared following rituals by monks. It is then taken to the site of the sky burial, on the outskirts of towns, away from everything else. Specific individuals, called *domdens* ("body-breakers"), are charged with this task. The cloth covering the body is unwrapped, and all flesh is carved off and thrown to the gathering flock of vultures and other birds to eat. The bones are ground up (and sometimes mixed with tsampa) and also fed to the vultures.

## SNOW LION

*Snow Lion as represented in a Snow Lion Dance presented by monks of the Drepung Loseling Monastery at Berea College, Berea, KY, 2008*

The snow lion is the symbol of Tibet, and appears in many Tibetan pieces of art, thangkas, and on the TIbetan flag (see page 52). The snow lion is "fearless and valiant and indicates the complete victory over all obstacles. They represent the strong vitality of the Tibetan people who revere the Three Precious Gems—the Buddha, Dharma, and Sangha. Elsewhere the lions appear supporting the thrones of various deities and symbolize the strength and fearlessness of those who have perfect wisdom and compassion." (www.snowlionpub.com) "They also represent unconditional cheerfulness, a mind free of doubt, clear and precise. The Snow Lion has a beauty and dignity resulting from a body and mind that are synchronized. The Snow Lion has a youthful, vibrant energy of goodness and a natural sense of delight." (www.viewonbuddhism.org)

The white Tibetan mastiff, a large dog often seen in Tibet, has also been called a Snow Lion, owing to its striking similarity to the mythical animal.

"Snow Lions are purely mythological creatures. However, there is information to be found in Tibet that these animals did exist in the snow mountains of the Himalayas, many thousands of years ago. . . . The Tibetan name of the Snow Lions is "Seng-Kyi". The little Lhasa Apso dogs are also called by this name because of the resemblance between Lhasa Apso and the Snow Lions." (www.friends-of-tibet.org.nz/flag.html)

## STUPA

*Stupa at Samye Monastery, Tibet, 2007*

*Stupa* (Sans.) or *chörten* (Tib.) meaning "the basis of offering" is used to describe a reliquary monument that would usually enshrine cremated remains of a spiritual being (lama, great teacher, and so on). After the historical Buddha Shakyamuni passed into parinirvana, there were two primary reasons that stupas were built:

1) to commemorate the eight great deeds he accomplished during his lifetime. These eight great deeds were:

1. Birth
2. Enlightenment
3. Turning of the Wheel (the first teaching)
4. Miracles
5. Descent from Tushita heaven
6. Reconciliation
7. Complete Victory
8. Parinirvana, and

2) to enshrine his relics after he passed away:

After he passed into parinirvana, his cremated remains were divided among certain of his disciples—often the number eight is thought to be correct, but other numbers have also been suggested. Stupas were built to contain the relics of the Buddha.

## THANGKA

*Thangka of Bhudda Shakyamuni*

A *thangka* (pronounced tong'-ka) (Tib. *tanka*) is a painted, appliquéd, or embroidered scroll painting. One meaning of thangka is "painting done on a flat surface;" another is "something that can be rolled up." Both are true. Thangkas are found in all Tibetan monasteries and in the shrine room of many private homes. Their size can range from the size of a postcard to the size of a building, although the most common sizes range from two to two-and-a-half feet in width by three to four feet high. The central image on a thangka, usually a Buddha, bodhisattva, or mandala, is affixed on a very elaborate brocade mounting; wooden rods are usually located at the top and the bottom, and metal or wooden decorative knobs often are placed at the ends of the bottom rod. The rods serve two purposes: one, to hang from the top one and to keep the thangka stretched out from the bottom one; and two, to help protect the thangka when it is rolled up for travel or storage.

Thangkas are created only for the spiritual value they bring to a practice or to a monastery and not for their decorative value, although many thangkas can be considered as works of art. They are created according to centuries-old standards, whereby certain proportions and certain colors are used for specific deities, who are identified by particular attributes, such as hand position (mudras), dress, clothing, jewelry, weapons, whether they are standing or sitting or riding, upon what they are standing or sitting or riding, and other elements. Thangkas have survived since the eleventh century and are being made to this day, created mostly in Nepal and India by both monks and laypersons trained in the art.

On March 17, 1959, His Holiness the 14th Dalai Lama escaped from

Tibet and went into exile in India. One of the few items he chose to take with him was a thangka of Palden Lhamo (the female protector deity of Tibet) that had belonged to the 2nd Dalai Lama. (Gill Farrer-Halls, *The World of the Dalai Lama*. Wheaton, IL: Quest Books, 1998)

### Refuge Tree

*Gelug Refuge Tree*

A special type of thangka is known as a Refuge Tree. Each of the four major schools, and some lineages within the schools, have a visual representation of the "geneology" of that school or lineage.

As the Dalai Lama explains it: "Within the context of Tibetan Buddhism, the importance of lineage extends far beyond the ordinary sense of a particular line of inheritance or descent. Lineage is a sacred trust through which the integrity of Buddha's teachings is preserved intact as it is transmitted from one generation to the next. The vital link through which the spiritual tradition is nourished and maintained is the profound connection between an enlightened master and perfectly devoted disciple. The master-disciple relationship is considered extremely sacred by all the major schools of Tibetan Buddhism." (www .khandronet/Tib Bud_refugetrees.htm)

## TSA TSA

A *tsa-tsa* (Tib.) is a small image (mostly in the two-inch-to four-inch-high range) of a Buddha, other deity, or important Buddhist figure that is impressed in clay. They can be dried in the sun or fired to hardness in a kiln. They may then be painted or varnished. Often a mantra is written on the back of the tsa tsa. As they are hollow, a small roll of prayers or mantras or other religious relic may be placed inside. Tsa tsas are made because it is considered an action which generates merit. They can be made for the following purposes:

- to use as offerings at shrines and holy places and to fill stupas
- to use as devotional relics for home altars
- to contain funeral ashes and kept as relics of deceased family members or teachers
- as part of a practice obligation
- for purification and to accumulate merit for oneself and others

Tsa tsas are holy objects and thus create positive imprints in the minds of all who see them. The actual making of these holy objects creates enormous merit, in addition to specific benefits:

- to achieve a perfect rebirth to benefit others
- to achieve perfect surroundings, to benefit oneself and others
- to generate devotion towards one's teachers and Buddhas
- to generate courage and perseverance to help others
- to achieve the path where delusions and defilements cease (one stops creating karma)
- in this life, one pacifies obstacles, achieves less disease, has a longer life, a good reputation, and increased joy
- to achieve the resultant three kayas in future life

(Adapted from "Images of Earth and Water: The Tsa-Tsa Votive Tablets of Tibet" by Juan Li, and from literature from Babette Teich-Visco, tsa tsa maker and teacher located in Manlius and Ithaca, NY.)

## Wheel of Life

The Wheel of Life (Sans., *Bhavacakra*; Tib., *srid pa khor lo*) is one of the more striking and important illustrations of Buddha's teachings, capturing the key elements of rebirth, karma, and dependent origination. Yama, the Lord of Death, is seen holding a wheel in his teeth and claws with numerous representations on it, among them:

The Three Poisons (Sans. *tri visa*; Tib. *dug-gsum*) (in the center), represented by:

- pig (delusion/ignorance; Sans. *moha*; Tib. *gti-mug* )
- rooster (greed; Sans. *raga*; Tib. *dod-chags*)
- snake (hatred; Sans. *dvesa*; Tib. *zhe-sdang*)

*The Wheel of Life thangka*

The first circle moving outward is divided into two areas:

- a light area of those beings ascending, who have lived good lives
- a dark area of those beings descending, who have not lived good lives

Next, moving outward, are the Six Realms of Existence (Tib. *rikdruk*) in samsara. They are:

- gods (Sans. *devas*; Tib. *lha*)

- titans or demi-gods (Sans. *ashuras*; Tib. *lha ma yin*)
- humans (Sans. *manushyas*; Tib. *mi*)
- animals (Sans. *tiryakas*; Tib. *dudo*)
- hungry ghosts (Sans. *pretas*; Tib. *yadik*)
- hell beings (Sans. *narakas*; Tib. *nyal kham*)

The outermost ring shows the twelve links of dependent origination, which, according to Buddha, is the process by which beings live, die, and are born again:

- a blind man (ignorance; Tib. *avidya*; cannot find his way)
- a potter (action/impulses; Tib. *samskara*; molds pots, as molding his own karma)
- a monkey (consciousness; Tib. *vijñana*; with no self-control, as monkey-mind in meditation)
- people in a boat (body/mind or name/form; Tib. *namarupa*; floating down the stream of samsara)
- a house with five windows and a door (the five senses plus mind; Tib. *shadayatana*; senses by which outer world is perceived, plus the faculty of thinking)
- lovers (contact; Tib. *sparsha*; symbolizing contact between world and mind)
- arrow in the eye (sensation/emotions; Tib. *vedana*; show feelings can be so strong they can blind us)
- a man drinking (craving; Tib. *trishna*; signifies desire, leading to grasping)
- a man picking the fruits off a tree (craving/entanglement; Tib. *upadana*; implies clinging)
- a pregnant woman (or a couple in bed or a bride) (becoming/ procreation; Tib. *bhava*; shows new life beginning)
- woman giving birth (birth/rebirth; Tib. *jati*; symbolizes birth)
- old man or corpse (old age and death; Tib. *jara-maranam*; inevitable old age and death for all)

# 5 Deities and Other Manifestations

Images of various deities and manifestations are used by most Tibetan Buddhists in their practice. They can be in the form of *thangkas* (scroll paintings usually hung on the wall), statues made of various materials and often placed on a personal altar, or visualized mentally during meditation. The purpose of the deity varies in function from practitioner to practitioner, but in general they are used as an aid to focus on a particular aspect (such as compassion), personified by that deity, during meditation, leading to transformation, and eventually liberation and enlightenment.

Deities come in a number of forms, and can be classified as *meditational* deities or *protector* (or guardian) deities. A subcategory, or aspect, of these would be *benign* or *wrathful,* and the activities or actions of each would be appropriate to the type. For example, Chenrezig is a peaceful meditational deity, the emanation of the Buddha of Compassion, while Palden Lhamo is a wrathful aspect, and the special protectress of the Dalai and Panchen Lamas and Lhasa, the capital of Tibet, and of Tibet itself. The "wrathful deities, though benevolent, are represented in visual arts as hideous and ferocious in order to instill terror in evil spirits which threaten the Dharma." (www.exoticindiaart.com) Dharmapalas are religious protectors; there are both worldly (*lokapala*) and beyond worldly (*jnanapala,* wisdom protector). The jnanapalas are enlightened Buddhas; the lokapalas have not yet reached enlightenment. There are eight great *Dharmapalas* that are known as special defenders of the Dharma. A *yidam* (also known as a tutelary deity) is another deity, one with whom one associates in a special relationship in one's practice.

**Aspects of a Buddhist Deity**—any Buddhist deity might manifest in four ways: benign, active, semi-wrathful, and wrathful; their activity can be pacifying, enriching, magnetizing, or subduing/destroying. (www.khandro.net)

**Bodhisattva**—being who aspires to relieve all suffering, postponing his or her own enlightenment to do so; examples are Chenrezig, Manjushri, and Tara.

**Buddha** (Tib. *sangye*)—"a fully enlightened being who has transcended the limits of this realm of suffering (samsara). He or she manifests for the benefit of all beings." (www.simhas.org) Shakyamuni Buddha is the Buddha of the current aeon; the future Buddha is Maitreya.

**Deva**—gods who live in the various realms of heaven as reward for their previous good deeds, but they are still subject to karma, and hence to samsara and rebirth.

**Guardian Deities/Dharma Protectors/Protector Deities**

**Dharmapalas** (Tib. *drag ched*) ("Dharma Defender," "Protector of the Doctrine")—bodhisattvas who are the eight Defenders of the Dharma, protectors of the teachings of the Buddhas. They are Begtse, Changpa, Hayagriva, Kubera, Mahakala, Palden Lhamo, Yama, and Yamantaka.

**Lokapalas (Digpalas/Dikpalas)** (Tib. *'jig-rtenskyong*)—the Four Guardian Kings defending the Dharma at the cardinal points of the compass, and seen at the entrance to monasteries: Virudhaka (south), Vaishravana (also called Jambhala and Kubera) (north), Virupaksha (west), and Dritarashtra (east).

**Heruka** ("blood-drinker")—a category of wrathful and semi-wrathful deities "representing the dynamic of compassion and skillful means, and . . . the ultimate expression of the radiantly selfless qualities of the mind." (www.khandro.net) An example is Chakrasamvara.

**Naga (**Sans., "snake;" Tib. *klu*)—a class of large serpent-like spirits that dwell in lakes, rivers, or underground streams. They are said to have magical powers, and are also known as keepers of terma, given to them by Padmasambhava. The Fifth Dalai Lama had a temple built on an island in a small lake behind the Potala Palace, called Lhukang, dedicated to the nagas.

**Trikaya**—the three bodies of Buddha (www.ship.edu):

**Nirmanakaya**—the earthly Buddhas; the intentional human embodiment of a reborn master.

**Sambhogakaya**—the Transcendent Buddhas—the five Buddha families; Buddhas in their heavens, the result of accumulated merit.

**Dharmakaya**—the teachings of the Buddha, and the true nature of the Buddha; Buddha mind (shunyata/emptiness).

| Five Transcendent Buddha Families (Dhyani Buddhas) and their Attributes | | | | | |
|---|---|---|---|---|---|
| **Head** | Akshobhya | Amitabha | Amoghasiddha | Ratnasambhava | Vairochana |
| **Family** | Buddha | padma (lotus) | karma (action) | ratna (jewel) | vajra (diamond) |
| **Direction** | center | west (top) | north (right) | south (left) | east (bottom) |
| **Color** | blue | red | green | yellow | white |
| **Element** | space | fire | wind | earth | water |
| **Hand Gesture** | earth-touching | meditation | protection | giving | teaching |
| **Syllable** | Om | Hrih | Ah | Tram | Hum |

**Yidam** (Tib. "firm mind")—an enlightened being (or tutelary or meditational deity) who is the focus of and aid to one's practice and with whom one identifies during meditation. They can be a lineage teacher, a guru, a dharma protector, or a dakini. A yidam is often suggested by one's lama, taking into consideration the student's personality and karma. Examples are Green Tara, Hevajra, and Kalachakra.

## Tibetan Buddhist Deities

No disrespect is intended to the many deities who have not been included in this listing.

**Akshobhya Buddha** (meditational) (Tib. *Mikyopa*) ("The Immovable," "The Unshakeable," "The Imperturbable," "The Mirror to Our Souls")—one of the five Transcendent Buddhas, representing the primordial cosmic element of consciousness; consort is Mamaki/Lochana.

**Amitabha Buddha** (meditational) (Tib. *Opame*) ("Infinite Light" or "Boundless Light")—the Buddha of Infinite Light in the Blissful Pure Land of the West; most ancient of the five Transcendent Buddhas; an essential aspect of Amitabha is that of meditation—his assocation with the setting sun (west) suggests the withdrawal of our external sense perceptions inwards, into higher states of meditative concentration; (www.kheper.net/topics/Buddhism) his cosort is Pandaravasin/Gokarmo.

**Amitayus Buddha** (meditational) (Tib. *Tsepagme*) ("Infinite Life")—the Buddha of Infinite Life, an aspect of Amitabha and the focus of practice that removes the possibility of untimely death; he is usually depicted sitting and holding in his hands a vessel containing the nectar of immortality; worshipped because of the faith of the believers in his powers to prolong life.

**Amoghasiddha Buddha** (meditational) (Tib. *Donyo Drupa*) ("Unerring Achiever")—one of the five Transcendent Buddhas, of all-accomplishing wisdom or unfailing accomplishment; consort is Green Tara.

**Avalokiteshvara**—see Chenrezig

**Begtse** (Dharmapala) (Tib.) ("hidden coat of mail") (Sans. *Prana Atma*)—god of war and special protector of the Gelug lineage; it is thought that Begtse is Mongolian in origin; last to join the 8 Dharma Protectors, in the 16th century, after the Mongolians had taken teachings from the Third Dalai Lama.

**Cakrasamvara** (Chakrasamvara) (yidam) (meditational) ("Wheel of Perfect Bliss," "Wheel of Union") (Sans.) (Tib. *Korlo Demchog, Korlo Dompa*)—also known as Heruka; usually portayed in yab-yum with Vajravarahi (Dorje Phagmo).

**Changpa** (Changpa Karpo) (Dharmapala) ("White Brahma," the Buddhist view of the Hindu deity Brahma)—consort is Saraswati.

**Chenrezig** (meditational) (Tib.) (Sans. *Avalokiteshvara*) ("Lord Who Does Not Look Away From Suffering," "He Who Looks with an Unwavering Eye," "One Who Sees all Sentient Beings Equally and Simultaneously and is Always Aware of Them and Their Needs")—the embodiment of compassion of all Buddhas and regarded by Tibetans as the guardian of their country. The Dalai Lamas and the Karmapas (Kagyu Karmapa lineage) are considered to be living manifestations of Chenrezig.

**Dorje Drakden**—see Nechung Choje

**Dorje Phagmo** —see Vajrayogini

**Dorje Phurba**—see Vajrakilaya

**Dorje Yudronma** (female dharma protector) (Tib.)—said to be one of the chief protectors of Tibet; associated with a divination practice using a mirror.

**Ekajati** (female Dharma protector) (Tib. *Tsechikma* or *Ralchikma*)—protectress of mantras, particularly in Nyingma, where she is also considered a protectress of Dzogchen.

**Ekajati** (female yidam/wrathful)—the wrathful form of Green Tara, also known as Black Tara.

**Hayagriva** (Pema Wangchen/Pema Sung) (Dharmapala) (protector/wrathful) (Sans.) (Tib. *Tamdrin*) ("The Horse-necked One")—"worshipped in Tibet particularly by horse-dealers because he is believed to frighten away demons by neighing like a horse. . . . His special ability is to cure diseases, especially skin diseases, even as serious as leprosy, which is said to be caused by the Nagas." (www.exoticindiaart.com)

**Jambhala** (bodhisattva of wealth) (Sans.) (Tib. *Dzambhala*)—a bodhisattva in the family of Ratnasambhava, and regarded by many as a god or bestower of wealth. The five different manifestations are green, yellow, black, white, and red. Jambhala's are always shown holding a mongoose, which when squeezed, spews jewels and other precious things out of its mouth. It is said that to most effectively realize Jambhala's beneficence, the statue should be located under a stream of water, falling directly over the crown of its head. Known as Kubera in Hinduism.

**Kalachakra** (yidam of the Highest Tantra) (meditational) ("The Wheel of Time") (Sans.) (Tib. *Dukyi Khorlo* or *Dukhor*)—both a deity and a Tantra. ". . . this sytem of Tantric practice uses a developed view of time to arrive at the Timeless. It is usually classified as a Mother Tantra, and both as deity and Tantra is hightly regarded by all Tibetan schools. It is an exceedingly complex system of thought and practice, which has outer, inner, and secret levels. The outer teachings . . . are concerned with astronomy, astrology, and mathematics. The inner deal with the body and its energy channels. The secret teachings are the actual instructions for meditating on the Kalachakra mandala." (Vessantara, *Meeting the Buddhas*, p. 275)

**Machig Labdrön** (female yidam, dakini, and historical figure)—founder of the chöd practice; considered an incarnation of Yeshe Tsogyal.

**Mahakala** (Dharmapala) (protector/wrathful) (Sans.) (Tib. *Nagpo Chenpo*) ("the Great Black One," "the Great Dark One")—the manifestation of the awakened mind, destroying mind chatter and bringing the mind back into attentive focus; symbolizes cutting through the five poisons. Different lineages portray Mahakala in different situations and different contexts. The Panjarnata aspect of Mahakala is the main protector of the Sakya school.

**Maitreya Buddha** (meditational) ("The Buddha of the Future") (Sans.) (Tib. *Jampa*)—the future Buddha, the last of the five Buddhas to gain supreme enlightenment in this aeon. He presently resides in the Tushita realm.

**Mandarava** (female yidam and historical figure)—one of two consorts of Guru Rinpoche (the other being Yeshe Tsogyel) is known as a deity of long life..

**Manjushri** (Sans. "sweetly glorious") (bodhisattva of wisdom) (Tib. *Jampel Yang*)—confers mastery of the Dharma and destroys ignorance; bestows intelligence, wisdom, eloquence, and memory; represents discrimination (*prajna*) borne of knowledge and learning; he is the principle guardian of astrologers and revered as the patron of arts and sciences. (www.tsl.org/masters) All four schools of Tibetan Buddhism do Manjushri practices.

**Mara** (deva)—". . . associated with death and hindrances to enlightenment. It was Mara who tempted Buddha under the Bodhi Tree" on the night of his enlightenment. (www. ship.edu) Stephen Batchelor (*Living with the Devil*) concludes that "'Buddha' stands for a capacity for awareness, openness, and freedom, [and] 'Mara' represents a capacity for confusion, closure, and restriction."

**Medicine Buddha** (meditational) (Sans. *Bhaisajyaguru*) (Tib. *Sangye Menla*) ("The Healing Master of Lapis Lazuli Radiance")—"practice of the Medicine Buddha is . . . invaluable in counteracting any sort of illness arising out of excessive desire, including addiction or addictive behavior: relationship, drug, alcohol, over-eating addictions, etc. . . . If one meditates on the Medicine Buddha, one will eventually attain enlightenment, but in the meantime one will experience an increase in healing powers, both for oneself and others, and a decrease in physical and mental illness and suffering." (Khenchen Thrangu Rinpoche, *Medicine Buddha Teachings*, Snow Lion Publications, 2004)

**Nechung Choje** (Pehar Gyelpo, Dorje Drakden) (Nechung Oracle)—protector of the Dalai Lamas and Tibet. One of five emanations of the Gyelpo spirits (Indra, Monbuputra, Shingjachen, Kyechikpu, and Pehar). Pehar was first invited to Samye Monastery as its guardian by Guru Rinpoche in the 8th century. One tradition says he was a student of Tsongkhapa, and that Nechung Monastery was constructed in 1416. Another says that he moved to Nechung Monastery, near Drepung, during the reign of the 5th Dalai Lama. Pehar manifests through the kuten to give advice to the Dalai Lamas. (see page 146)

**Padmasambhava** (Guru Rinpoche)—while not a deity in the same way many of the others are recognized, Padmasambhava has eight different emanations that are associated with him.

- ***Padmavajra,*** Vajra of the Lotus, severed the roots of the five poisons
- ***Padmaraja***, King of the Lotus, provided mundane and ultimate benefits to sentient beings
- ***Padmasambhava,*** the Lotus-born, blessed beings endowed with faith (see right)
- ***Dorje Drolo,*** tamed the Yakshas and haughty beings
- ***Suryaprabha***, the Rays of the Sun, taught the essence of secret mantra
- ***Sakyasimha***, the Lion of Sakyas, guided beings towards the path of liberation
- ***Simhanada***, Roar of the Lion, defeated the outside aggressors of non-Buddhists
- ***Dhimanvaruchi***, the Supremely Wise Love, showered the teaching of Sutra and Tantra

**Palden Lhamo** (Dharmapala) (protector/wrathful) (Tib.; "Glorious Goddess") (Sans. *Sri Devi*)—the only female deity among the Dharmapalas. Palden Lhamo is the personal protector of the Dalai and Panchen Lamas and is also associated with the protection of Lhasa and of Tibet. Unlike other dharmapalas who are often shown on a lotus, Palden Lhamo is usually atop or surrounded by the Himalayas. Her wrathful form shows her riding a mule, and she has flaming red hair, three red eyes, and sharp fangs. Due to her wrathful look, her image is sometimes kept covered in an out-of-the-way place in some monasteries. She is the only female dharma protector common to all four schools of Tibetan Buddhism. Consort of Mahakala.

**Pehar Gyelpo**—see Nechung Choje

**Prajnaparamita** (scripture deity/yidam) ("Perfection of Wisdom") (Tib. *Yum Chenmo*, Great Mother)—embodies perfect discriminative awareness; sometimes referred to as Mother of all the Buddhas.

**Ratnasambhava Buddha** (meditational) (Tib. *Gyalwa Rinjung*) ("Jewel-born")—Transcendent Buddha presiding over the pure land in the south; represents the primordial wisdom of equality; believed to transform the negative trait of pride into the widsom of equality; consort is Vajradhatvishvari/Mamaki.

**Samantabhadra** (dharma protector) ("All Good") (Tib. *Guntu Sangpo*)—the primordial Buddha associated with compassion; mainly associated with Nyingma and Dzogchen. His consort is Samantrabhadri.

**Sarasvati** (Saraswati) (yidam) (Sans.)—goddess of learning and the arts, sometimes considered to be a counterpart to, and a consort of, Manjushri.

**Shakyamuni Buddha** (historical Buddha of the current era) (meditational)—Shakyamuni (sage of the Shakya clan) attained enlightenment after six years of searching for the end to suffering, and became known as Buddha, one who is awakened.

**Tara** (meditational)—the most popular female deity in Tibetan Buddhism, the goddess of universal compassion represents virtuous and enlightened activity. A legend has it that Tara was born from the compassionate tears of Chenrezig, one tear becoming White Tara and another becoming Green Tara.

*White Tara*

***White Tara*** (yidam) ("she who grants long life and wisdom") (Tib. *Drolkar*)
***Green Tara*** (yidam) ("beloved saviouress," "she who saves") (Tib. *Drolma*)
***Cittamani Tara*** (highest yoga tantra meditational practice of Green Tara in Gelug)

**Red Tara** (yidam of bountifulness) (Tib. *Yeshe Dawa, Kurukulla*) primarily practiced in Nyingma and Sakya

**Yellow Tara** (yidam) (Tib. *Norgyuma*) practice of the gift of wealth and physical and spiritual abundance

***Praise to the 21 Taras*** is a prayer that encompasses the 21 emanations of Green Tara. Because Tara is so important to the Tibetan Buddhist pantheon of deities, following are three different versions of the 21 Taras, from different traditions/translations/aspects.

Protection against carnivore
Protection against earthly disaster
Protection against elephant
Protection against evil spirit
Protection against famine
Protection against fire
Protection against flood
Protection against lion
Protection against politics
Protection against sickness
Protection against snakes
Protection against thief
Protection against untimely death
Protection against war
Protection against weapons
Protection against wind disasters
Indestructibility protection
Increasing harmony
Increasing activities
Increasing power
Source of all 20 emanations

The Swift Heroine
Saraswati, the Great Pacifier
The Giver of Supreme Virtue
The All Victorious
The Giver of Intelligence
The Terrifier

The Invincible
The Conqueror of Others
The Savior of the Scented Forest
The Conqueror of the Three Worldly Realms
The Giver of Wealth
The Auspicious
The Destroyer of Opposing Forces
The Wrathful
The Very Peaceful
The Blazing Light
The Subduer of Countless Harmful Forces
The Peahen
The Invincible Queen
The Mountain-dwelling Mendicant
Rays of Light

The Green Tara, Goddess of Goddesses, the source of the other 20 emanations/aspects
The Tara who averts disasters
The Tara who averts earth-born calamities
The Tara who averts destruction wrought by water
The Tara who averts destruction wrought by fire
The Tara who averts destruction wrought by wind
The Tara who increases wisdom
The Tara who averts heaven-born calamities
The Tara who averts destruction wrought by armies
The Tara who averts hell-born calamities
The Tara who averts evil caused by robbers
The Tara who increases power
Tara who averts evil caused by demons
Tara who averts evil effecting cattle
Tara who averts evil caused by wild beasts
Tara who averts the evil effects of poison
Tara who subdues demons
Tara who heals sickness
Tara who bestows longevity
Tara who bestows prosperity
The wish-fulfilling Tara

**Vairocana (Vairochana)** (primordial Buddha) ("radiant") (Tib. *Namnang*) —one of the five Buddha families; represents the cosmic element of form; consort is Lochana.

**Vaisravana (Vaishravana, Jambhala)** (Dharmapala) (Tib. *Kubera*)—the protector of wealth, "who are believed to manifest in order to help those in need of money. . . . These wealth deities [statues] are believed to be most effective in bringing wealth to the home when they are properly placed under falling water." Also the guardian of the north.

**Vajrabhairava** (wrathful) (yidam) ("diamond terror" or "terrifying thunderbolt") (Tib. *Dorje Jikje*)—dharma protector, keeping away that which hinders the practitioner on his path; wrathful emanation of Manjushri.

**Vajradhara** (primordial buddha) ("bearer of the thunderbolt," "the Vajra Holder," "Enlightened One") (Tib. *Dorje Chang*)— "primordial Buddha, personification of the dharmakaya—truth body of enlightenment— and progenitor of the Vajrayana system of Buddhism." (www.himalayanart.org) He is "the embodiment of all the Buddhas of the three time periods, and the essence of the three kayas, or bodies, of the Buddha. . . . He represents the Dharmakaya Buddha and therefore, the ultimate aspect of Enlightenment." (www.drukpa.org)

**Vajrakilaya (Vajrakila)** (wrathful) (Tib. *Dorje Purba*)—a wrathful form of Padmasambhava; he is a Tantric deity who is embodied in the phurba.

**Vajrapani** (wrathful tantric buddha) ("holder of the diamond thunderbolt") (Tib. *Chakna Dorje*)—fights ignorance, craving, and samsara; the heroic embodiment of spiritual energy and power.

**Vajrasattva** (meditational) ("the diamond or adamantine being") (Tib. *Dorje Sempa*)—Tantric buddha available to all practitioners for purification of faults and negative karma; the "priest" of the five transcendent buddhas.

**Vajrayogini** ("diamond practitioner")/**Vajravarahi** ("diamond sow") (yidam) (tantric female buddha) (Tib. *Dorje Naljorma/Dorje Phagmo*)—queen of the Dakinis; represents the combined aspects of the union of method and wisdom.

**Yama** (Dharmapala) ("the Lord of Death") (Tib. *Shinje*)—king of the 21 hells; often shown grasping the Wheel of Life in his fangs and claws. (see page 71)

**Yamantaka** (Dharmapala) (protector/wrathful) (Sans.; "Remover of the Obstacle Yama," "Defeater of Death") (Tib. *Dorje Jikche* or *Shinjeshe*)—the wrathful form of Manjushri, the embodiment of all the Buddha's wisdom and the overcoming of hatred. Depicted with as many as thirty-four arms, sixteen legs, and nine heads, the central one of which is that of a bull. Usually appears as black or midnight-blue.

**Yeshe Tsogyal** (yidam, historical figure) (Kuntuzangmo)—consort of Guru Rinpoche; emanation of the goddess Sarasvati.

## Deities in Tibetan Buddhist Practice

"Some might think that praying to the Buddha of Compassion is idol-worship or relying on external forces. However, Buddhism is not in favor of idol-worship. It believes that the only source of real spiritual attainment is our own mind. Only our own mind is the ultimate source of power, as it possesses the enlightened mind, which is the Buddha. However, Buddhists do use images, among other things, as the source of spiritual teachings, inspiration, and support. This is called skillful means. If we see something as positive, and use it in a positive manner, positive results will ensue. When the image used has spiritual significance, it can greatly help us to generate spiritual benefits. Notwithstanding this, we ultimately receive benefits because of our own mind, our mental attitude and view, not because of the external phenomena." (Tulku Thondup, *Enlightened Journey*, 1995, Shambhala, p. 26)

## Meditational Deities

The Tibetan Buddhist Library
Deity Yoga Meditation

All four schools of Tibetan Buddhism identify themselves as followers of Vajrayana Buddhism. The heart of Vajrayana Buddhist meditation is a system of practice that primarily involves a complex process of visualization and identification of oneself with an enlightened form that is portrayed as a meditational deity. This meditative practice is known as *Lhai naljor*, or "Deity Yoga." The Kalachakra practice is one such example. It is on the basis of an initiation ceremony that an individual is authorized to engage in a deity yoga meditation. Tibetan Buddhists will often have, as part of a daily religious practice, deity yoga meditation associated with a chosen meditation deity. The most popular practices are that of Yamantaka, Guhyasamaja, and Chakrasamvara in the Gelug School, Guhyagarbha and Hayagriva in the Nyingma School, Vajrayogini and Chakrasamvara in the Kagyü School, and Chakrasamvara and Hevajra in the Sakya School. In addition, there are practices for deities such as Chenrezig, Manjushri, and Tara, which are popular amongst the followers of all four schools, especially the laity.

The "Offering to the Five Deities of the Individual" by the Fifth Dalai Lama (1617-1682) discusses the deities that reside with a person. They are called the *gowe lha* and are believed to take birth at the same time as a child. They are comprised of (www.khandro.net):

1. a *Dralha*, the personal protector or "enemy" god that resides on the right shoulder
2. a *Soglha* or life deity, whose seat is in the heart
3. a *Molha* or female god, in the left armpit
4. a *Pholha* or male lineage god, in the right armpit

There is also a *Yul-lha*, the local god, whose position is at the crown of the head (Samuel, *Civilized Shamans*, 1993, 187)

## WRATHFUL MANIFESTATIONS

| Deity/Vehicle | Wrathful Manifestations |
|---|---|
| Amoghasiddha | Garuda |
| | Heruka |
| | Chakrasamvara |
| Chenrezig (Avalokiteshvara) | Hayagriva |
| | Palden Lhamo (female) |
| | Mahakala |
| | Vajrakilaya |
| | Vajrapani |
| Buddha Shakyamuni | Demchok |
| Gadong Oracle | Shinjachen |
| Green Tara | Ekajati/Black Tara (female) |
| Manjushri | Kalarupa |
| | Nagaraksha |
| | Yamantaka |
| | Vajrabhairava |
| Nechung Oracle | Pehar |
| Padmasambhava | Dorje Drolo |
| | Sengdongma (female) |
| | Vajrakiliya |
| Sarasvati | Palden Lhamo (female) |
| Vairocana | Trailokya-vijaya |
| Vajrasattva | Vajrakilaya |
| Vajrasattva Akshobhya | Vajra-Heruka |
| Vajrayogini | Tromo Nogma |

# 6 Buddhist Profiles

**Ananda** (contemporary of Shakyamuni Buddha)—cousin to Buddha, and one of Buddha's closest disciples, who also served as his personal attendant for the last twenty-seven years of his life. Along with Mahaprajapati, helped to persuade the Buddha to create an order of nuns

**Anuruddha** (Aniruddha) (contemporary of Shakyamuni Buddha)—first cousin to Shakyamuni Buddha, and one of his main disciples

**Aryadeva** (3rd century CE)—main disciple of Nagarjuna

**Asanga** (c. 310-390)—founder of the Yogacara school, precursor to Buddhist Tantra

**Ashoka** (Asoka) (c. 272-236 BCE)—Indian king and supporter of Buddhism. Known for his edicts throughout India written on rocks and pillars, some of which still survive

**Atisha** (Atisa) (982-1054)—Indian Buddhist teacher who helped reestablish Buddhism in Tibet at the start of the second great infusion. Atisha combined the Sutra and Tantra teachings, resulting in his writing *Lamp for the Path to Enlightenment*, the original Lam Rim text, which serves as the model for all subsequent Lam Rim teachings. Although Atisha was supposed to have remained in Tibet only three years, he remained for twelve years, teaching, and died before he could return to India. Followers of Atisha's teachings are known as Kadampa's

**Stephen Batchelor** (1953- )—British-born author and lecturer. Ordained as a novice in 1974 and received full ordination in 1978. Trained in Tibetan Buddhism in India, Switzerland, and Germany, and in Zen in South Korea. Disrobed and married Martine Fages in 1985. Among his books is the bestselling *Buddhism Without Beliefs* (1997)

**Sir Charles Bell** (1870-1945)—British civil servant born in Calcutta, posted in India, and served posts as political officer in Sikkim, Bhutan, and Tibet. He first met the 13th Dalai Lama in 1910, and maintained a personal and professional relationship with him during and after his political career. Much of what the 13th Dalai Lama learned about the rest of the world came through Bell, who assisted the Tibetan leader in doing what was best for Tibet. He wrote a number of books about his experiences, including an excellent biography of the 13th Dalai Lama, *Portrait of a Dalai Lama* (1946, 1987)

**Bodhidharma** (c. 470-543)—Indian master who traveled to China and is credited with bringing the Dharma (Ch'an) to China

**Chandrakirti** (c. 600-650)—Indian master and author of *Introduction to the Middle Way*

**Alexandra David-Neel** (1868-1969)—French Buddhist and explorer. Most known for her trips in the early years of the 20th century to Tibet and to Lhasa, both of which were for all intents and purposes closed to foreigners. She twice met the 13th Dalai Lama and once met the 9th Panchen Lama. Disguised as a pilgrim, with Tibetan monk Lama Yongden (whom she later adopted), she crossed all of China and reached Lhasa in 1924, spending two months there. She wrote many books describing her journeys, most notably *Magic and Mystery in Tibet* (1929) and *My Journey to Lhasa* (1927). A biograply, *The Secret Lives of Alexandra David-Neel*, was published in 1998

**Trisong Detsen** (754-797)—second of the three great Dharma Kings of Tibet, who brought Padmasambhava and Shantarakshita to Tibet and established Samye Monastery

**Dharmakirti** ("Famous Dharma") (c. 530-600)—Indian philosopher best known for his *Commentary on Compendium of Valid Cognition*. His main concept is that of direct experience and the reasoning based on that experience

**Songsten Gampo** (617-650)—first of the three Dharma Kings of the Yarlung Dynasty; built the Jokhang and Ramoche temples in Lhasa, along with other monasteries throughout his kingdom, including at least twelve demoness-suppressing temples

**Gampopo** (Gampopa) (1079-1153)—student of Milarepa; founder of Karma Kagyu lineage

**Gendün Drup** (1st Dalai Lama) (1391-1474)—founded Tashilhunpo Monastery in 1447, subsequently home to the Panchen Lamas. One of the main disciples of Tsongkhapa

**Gesar of Ling** (King Gesar)—epic of the Tibetan culture similar to the *Il-iad* and *Oddysey* in Greek literature and the Arthurian legends in England. As with most literature of this type, it started as an oral tradition, with the stories being passed down from one generation of bards and storytellers to another. In its written form, it is said that the Gesar epic is much longer than any other of its type in the world. There is no definitive version, and the stories and details vary from one region to another

**Guru Rinpoche**—see Padmasambhava

**Ngawang Gyatso** (5th Dalai Lama) (1617-1682)—usually referred to as the Great Fifth. The first Dalai Lama to hold both temporal and secular authority over Tibet. Built the Potala Palace

**Tenzin Gyatso** (14th Dalai Lama) (1935-     )—born Lhamo Dhondup in Takster, Kumbum region in Amdo, eastern Tibet. The Dalai Lama, though forced into exile in 1959 after his country was invaded by Chinese in 1949 and occupied since, brought knowledge of Tibet and Tibetan Buddhism to the world. Won the Nobel Peace Prize in 1989 for his non-violent struggle for independence for the Tibetan people. Often describes himself as "a simple monk"

**Tubten Gyatso** (13th Dalai Lama) (1876-1933)—often referred to as the Great Thirteenth, he tried to bring Tibet into the 20th century, but was stymied by opposition from the monastic hierarchy and Tibetan nobility. He did manage to bring more order to the monastic way of life, to some degree formed an army, and predicted that Tibet would see dark times ahead. He was twice forced to go into exile due to incursions, once to Mongolia (when invaded by the British in 1903) and once to India (when invaded by the Chinese in 1910).

**Heinrich Harrer** (1912-2006)—Austrian mountain climber, captured by the British in 1939 while climbing in the Himalayas and put into a prisoner-of-war camp in northern India. He escaped later the same year, and after crossing the Himalayas with companion Peter Aufschnaiter, reached Lhasa, becoming the only two foreigners there at the time. Befriended and became a mentor to the young 14th Dalai Lama, explaining things about the world outside of Tibet. One of Harrer's books, *Seven Years in Tibet*, was made into a movie, exposing more people to the circumstances and history of Tibet

**Jeffrey Hopkins** (1940- )—Professor Emeritus of Religious Studies at the University of Virginia, where he taught Tibetan studies and the Tibetan language from 1973-2005. Served as chief translator for His Holiness the 14th Dalai Lama from 1979 to 1989. Has written, edited, and translated many books on Tibetan Buddhism

**Ven. Kalu Rinpoche** (1905-1989)—a major figure in the Kagyu school, born in the Kham region of Tibet. He was instrumental in bringing these teachings to the west, establishing 70 Dharma centers and 20 retreat centers worldwide, and building 20 stupas. In 1955, the 16th Karmapa asked Kalu Rinpoche to go to India and Bhutan to prepare for what was thought to be the inevitable exile from Tibet. In 1965, he established his own monastery in India, at Sonada, near Darjeeling

**Altan Khan** (1507-1583)—Mongol leader and descendant of Genghis Khan. He was so impressed with the Gelug tradition of Tibetan Buddhism that he bestowed the title "Dalai" Lama (meaning "ocean-wide" or "ocean of wisdom") on Sonam Gyatso (1543-1588), who became the Third Dalai Lama, and who posthumously named his two predecesors as first and second Dalai Lamas. This established a priest-patron relationship between the Gelugs and the Mongols

**Dusum Khyenpa** (1110-1193)—the first Karmapa (in the Kagyu lineage)

**Langdharma** (b.?–846?)—brother of King Tri Ralpachen; Langdharma killed the king (or had him killed) in 841 because of his support of Buddhism, while Langdharma supported the indigenous Bön tradition. Langdharma persecuted monks, made them disrobe, closed monasteries, etc. In 846, during a ceremony, a former monk shot and killed Langdharma with an arrow. This ended the persecution of Buddhism, but also ended the time of the religious kings in Tibet. A more decentralized time re-emerged, to last for more than 100 years until the second major dissemination of Buddhism in Tibet

**Jigme Lingpa** (1729-1798)—Nyingma lineage Dzogchen master and tertön best known for his terma revelation called Longchen Nyingtig, but also for his work *The Excellent Path of Omniscience*

**Longchenpa** (Longchen Rabjampa) (1308-1363)—major scholar of the Nyingma tradition. He was a prolific writer and a noted tertön

**Losang Drakpa**—see Tsongkhapa

**Mahaprajapati** (contemporary to Shakyamuni Buddha)—aunt (or foster mother?) to the Buddha, who helped persuade him, with the help of Ananda, to create an order of nuns

**Marpa Lotsawa** (Marpa the Translator) (1012-1096)—co-founder of the Kagyu lineage; disciple of Naropa and teacher to Milarepa. Revered for having translated numerous Indian texts into Tibetan

**Maudgalyayana** (contemporary to Shakyamuni Buddha)—one of the Buddha's ten major disciples

**Maya** (Queen Maya, Mahamaya, Mayadevi)—mother of Buddha Shakyamuni, who died seven days after his birth. Buddha was thought to have been raised by his aunt, Mahaprajapati

**Jetsun Milarepa** (1040-1123)—second great guide of the Kagyu lineage and major saint and poet of Tibet. Practiced black magic in his youth, and after studying for years under Marpa, spent years repenting for his earlier activities. After years of teachings and meditating in caves, Milarepa achieved enlightenment in one lifetime

**Nagarjuna** (c. 150-250)—born to a Brahmin family in south India. Attended Nalanda University, where later, after much study and practice, he was appointed abbot. It is said that Nagarjuna retrieved the *Prajna-Paramita Sutra*, which had been left in the care of the Nagas. Nagarjuna formulated the Middle Path of voidness (emptiness [*sunyata*]), which came to be called the Madhyamika school, writing, among other texts, *Fundamental Verses on the Middle Way* (*Mulamadhuamakakrika*)

**Naropa** (1016-1100)—main disciple of Tilopa

**Thich Nhat Hanh** (1926-    )—Vietnamese Zen monk, ordained in 1942. Credited with coining the phrase "engaged Buddhism." Forced into exile by the Vietnamese government in 1966 due to his anti-Vietnam War activities, based on the non-violent principles of Gandhi. Moved to France and in 1982 established Plum Monastery and retreat center. Travels world-wide teaching and lecturing. Has authored more than 80 books, including *Living Buddha, Living Christ* and *Old Path White Clouds*

**Ogyen Drodul Trinley Dorje** (17th Karmapa) (1985-    )—enthroned as the 17th Karmapa in 1992, and authenticated by His Holiness the 14th Dalai Lama. Another candidate (Tenzin Khyentse, b. 1982) is believed by some in Karma Kagyu to be the authentic reincarnation

**Pabongka (Pabonka, Phabongka) Rinpoche** (1878-1941)—root lama to Trijang Rinpoche and Ling Rinpoche, both tutors to the 14th Dalai Lama. In 1921, he gave a 24-day teaching on the Lam Rim, the Stages of the Path, attended by both monastics and laypeople. It was later translated, edited, and published as *Liberation in the Palm of Your Hand*, a book widely used to teach Buddhism in the west

**Padmasambhava** ("The Lotus Born") (c. 730-805)—great tantric master who brought Buddhism to Tibet during the reign of Dharma King Trisong Detsen. Among his other feats, he tamed the spirits and demons in Tibet and made them Dharma Protectors. Also known as Guru Rinpoche. His birth was prophesized by the Buddha

**Paltrul Rinpoche** (1808-1887)—great teacher in the Rimé (nonsectarian) movement. He is known for his famous *The Words of My Perfect Teacher* (his perfect teacher was Jigme Gyalwai Nyugu)

**Sakya Pandita** (1182-1251)—major Sakya figure, recognized as an incarnation of Manjushri. Established a patron-priest relationship with the Mongol court of Godan Khan in 1244, which passed on to his successors, but was replaced by that of the Gelug school in the 16th century. Author of *Treasury of the Knowledge of Valid Cognition*

**Ven. Pema Chodron** (1936-     )—born in the U.S., she taught elementary school until her mid-thirties. She went to Europe, where she received novice vows in 1974; she received full ordination in 1981 in the Chinese lineage in Hong Kong. She is currently the director of Gampo Abbey in Cape Breton, Nova Scotia, an affiliate of Shambhala International. She teaches and has written numerous books, including *When Things Fall Apart* (2002)

**Purna** (contemporary to Shakyamuni Buddha)—one of Buddha's main disciples, who was pre-eminent in preaching the Dharma

**Longchen Rabjampa** (1308-1364)—Nyingma scholar and one of the great codifiers of Dzogchen teachings

**Tri Ralpachen** (806-841)—third of the three great Dharma Kings; killed by, or on order of, his brother Langdharma. After his reign, Buddhism greatly declined for more than 100 years, until the second major dissemination in the late 10th century

**Rahula**—the only child of the historical Buddha. Siddhartha Gautama, the future Buddha, was married to Princess Yasodhara. The night he left his palace to renounce the world and find an end to suffering, the Princess gave birth to their only child, Rahula (meaning love or burden or tie). Buddha was not to see his son until seven years later

**Thonmi Sambhota** (7th century)—minister of King Songsten Gampo of Tibet. He was sent to India (or some think Kashmir) to study languages, and came back to Tibet and devised the Tibetan written language with which to translate the teachings of Buddha

**Sariputra** (Sariputta) (contemporary to Shakyamuni Buddha)—one of two main disciples of the Buddha

**Shakyamuni Buddha / Siddhartha Gautama** (563-483 BCE)—Buddha of this era who was born a prince into a royal family in the area that is now Lumbini in southern Nepal. After seeing the four sights, he renounced his position, and went searching for an end to suffering. He eventually discovered the Middle Way, after discarding the extremes of worldly pleasures and of ascetism, and gained enlightenment under the Bodhi Tree in Bodh Gaya, India. He spent the remainder of his life teaching—turning the Wheel of Dharma

**Shantarakshita** (Santaraksita) (contemporary to Padmasambhava, 705-762)—Indian monk who responded to the invitation of King Trisong Detsen to establish Buddhism in Tibet. It is said he wasn't able to establish a monastery because of the interference of local deities. He returned to India, Padmasambhava came, subdued the deities, turned them into Dharma protectors, and then, with Shantarakshita, began the first diffussion of Buddhism from India into Tibet

**Shantideva** (Santideva) (7th-8th century CE)—Indian master born of a royal family; took ordination at Nalanda University. He is credited with the discourse *The Bodhisattva's Way of Life* (*Bodhichary'avatara*)

**Sogyal Rinpoche** (1945- )—born in Kham, Tibet, and recognized early as an incarnation. He went to England in 1971 to study comparative religion at Cambridge University, and has also studied with masters of all Tibetan traditions. In 1993 he founded the Spiritual Care Program, and has Rigpa centers in eleven countries around the world. He travels and lectures widely and is the author of *The Tibetan Book of Living and Dying* (1993)

**Gampopa Sonam Rinchen** (1079-1153)—main disciple of Milarepa; author of *The Jewel Ornament of Liberation*

**Suddhodana**—king, and father to Siddhartha Guatama. He tried to stop his son, Prince Siddhartha, from seeing the four sights, which led him to renounce his princely life and seek an end to suffering for all beings

**D.T. Suzuki** (1870-1966)—considered to have popularized Zen in the United States, opening the door to the teachings of other Buddhist traditions

**Lodrö Thayé, the First Jamgön Kongtrül** (1813-1899)—born in Kham, eastern Tibet. Studied all subjects from every school, and was the founder and important proponent of the Rimé movement of non-sectarian teachings. His writings are incorporated into *The Treasury of Knowledge*, a compendium of volumes containing the wisdom of Tibet

**Ven. Thubten Chodron** (1950- )—educated in the U.S., Thubten Chodron took novice ordination in 1977, and full ordination in 1986. She studied and taught in India, Nepal, Italy, France, and Singapore, and continues to travel widely to teach. She was involved in the founding of Sravasti Abbey near Spokane, Washington. Among her books are *Open Heart, Clear Mind* (1990) and *Buddhism for Beginners* (2001)

**Robert A. F. Thurman** (1941- )—Thurman first met the 14th Dalai Lama in 1964, through Geshe Wangyal, and in 1965 became the first westerner to be ordained as a Tibetan Buddhist monk. He gave back his robes in 1967 to return to the U.S. and to what he considers to be the "modern" monastery—the university. He currently holds the first endowed chair in Tibetan Buddhist studies, as the Jey Tsong Khapa Professor of Indo-Tibetan Buddhist Studies, at Columbia University in New York. In 1987, with actor Richard Gere (another student of the Dalai Lama), he founded Tibet House in New York City, a nonprofit institution dedicated to preserving Tibetan culture. He has written, edited, and translated many books on Tibetan Buddhism

**Tilopa** (988-1069)—Indian master and teacher of Naropa. He is said to have received teachings directly from Vajradhara, the primordial Buddha

**Chögyam Trungpa Rinpoche** (1939-1987)—11th in a lineage of tulkus in the Kagyu school. Trungpa was also trained in the Nyingma tradition, and was an adherent of the Rimé movement of non-sectarian teaching. After escaping from Tibet in 1959, he served in India, then went on to attend Oxford University in England, at which time he founded a meditation center, gave up his monastic vows, and married. He moved to the United States, where he was eventually to form Shambhala International, an organization that includes more than 100 worldwide meditation centers. He also founded what is now known as Naropa University in Boulder, CO

**Tsongkhapa** (Losang Drakpa) ("The Man from the Land of Onions" or "The Man from Onion Valley") (1357-1419)—born in Tsongkha in Amdo province; Kumbum Jampaling Monastery is built at the spot where a sandalwood tree grew at Tsongkhapa's birthplace. At the age of three, he was given lay ordination and the name Kinga Nyingpo; at seven, he was given novice vows and the name Losang Drakpa. Tsongkhapa traveled extensively, taking teachings and empowerments from masters of all traditions existing at that time. His inspiration in founding the Gelug school was in Atisha and the Kadampa tradition. Tsongkhapa's view of the Gelug was the union of Sutra and Tantra, and the emphasis he placed on the Vinaya, the monastic code of discipline for monks. There are four specific activities of Tsongkhapa's that were considered especially beneficial: 1. the renovation of a statue of Maitreya at Dzingji (Dzinchi) Temple (east of Lhasa, near Lhama Lhatso); 2. an extensive teaching on monastic discipline, thereby revitalizing monasticism; 3. founding the Monlam Chenmo (Great Prayer Festival) held during Losar, starting in 1409 and continuing to the present day; and 4. the construction of Ganden Monastery (1409). Added to this should be his work *The Great Exposition of the Stages of the Path* (*LamRim Chenmo*), and the fact that among his direct disciples, one founded Drepung Monastery, one founded Sera Monastery, and one founded Tashilhunpo Monastery and became the First Dalai Lama (posthumously)
**Giuseppe Tucci** (1894-1984)—Italian explorer, and one of the earliest of the modern Tibetologists. Among his many books are *The Religions of Tibet, To Lhasa and Beyond: Diary of the Expedition to Tibet in the Year 1948*, and *The Theory and Practice of the Mandala*

**Geshe Ngawang Wangyal** (1901-1983)—Gelug teacher of Mongolian descent. Fled Tibet in 1951, and moved to the United States in 1955, where he founded the first Buddhist monastery in North America, the Lamaist Buddhist Monastery of America in New Jersey (renamed the Tibetan Buddhist Learning Center in 1986). Geshe Wangyal is also known for his students Robert Thurman and Jeffrey Hopkins, both of whom went on to become renowned Tibetan Buddhist scholars

**Yasodhara**—wife of Siddhartha Gautama, whom he left, along with his newborn son Rahula, to find an end to suffering for sentient beings
**Yeshe Tsogyel** (777-837)—disciple of and consort to Padmasambhava
**Ven. Lama Tupden Yeshe** (1935-1984)—born in Tibet, and entered Sera

Monastery at age six, where he remained until 1959. He went to India, where he became teacher to Lama Tupden Zopa. His first students from the west came in 1965; in 1971, he founded Kopan Monastery near Kathmandu, Nepal. Lamas Yeshe and Zopa began touring and teaching in the west in 1974. The Foundation for the Preservation of the Mahayana Tradition (FPMT) was founded by Lama Yeshe in 1975; it now has 142 centers, study groups, and projects worldwide. His reincarnation, Lama Tenzin Ösel Rinpoche, was born to Spanish parents in 1985

**Ven. Lama Tupden Zopa** (1946- )—born in the Mount Everest region of Nepal; became a student of Lama Yeshe, and then spiritual director of FPMT after Lama Yeshe passed away in 1984

# 7 Significant Buddhist Sites

## INDIA

**Ajanta** (Maharashtra)—location of an intricate cave system overlooking the Waghora River; the 28 caves contain an immense number of preserved paintings, sculptures, and murals going back to the second century BCE. Uncovered by British soldiers in 1819.

**Bodh Gaya** (Bihar)—location of the enlightenment of the historical Buddha after meditating for 49 days under a tree that has come to be called the Bodhi Tree. The tree that now exists in Bodh Gaya is actually a cutting from a tree that was grown in Sri Lanka, which was itself grown from a shoot from the original Bodhi Tree. Many Buddhist monasteries and temples from different countries have been established here.

**Dharamsala** (Himachal Pradesh)—home to the 14th Dalai Lama and the Tibetan government-in-exile. This former Indian hill station was provided to the Tibetans by the Indian government in 1960. There are currently more than 8,000 Tibetans and an additional 2,000 or more Tibetan children living in the immediate area. There are many monasteries and nunneries that have been established or re-established here.

**Kushinagar** (Uttar Pradesh)—location where the historical Buddha passed into parinirvana

**Ladakh** (Jammu & Kashmir)—region in far northwest India, bordered by Pakistan and Tibet. The appeal of this area is that it still maintains the traditions and lifestyle that Tibet had prior to the invasion by the Chinese. Site of many monasteries that are in the condition that they have been for many centuries. The two schools that are most predominant are the Gelug and the Drukpa Kagyu.

**Nalanda Monastic University** (Bihar)—Buddhist monastic university founded in the fifth century CE; scholars attending included Nagarjuna, Asanga, Atisha, and Padmasambhava, who then went to Tibet and spread Buddhist doctrine. Nalanda was destroyed during an invasion in the late twelfth century.

**Rajgir** (Bihar)—location of the second turning of the Wheel of Dharma by the Buddha

**Sanchi** (Madhya Pradesh)—location of the Great Stupa, dating from c. 3rd century BCE

**Sarnath** (Deer Park, Uttar Pradesh)—location of the first sermon of the historical Buddha—the first turning of the Wheel of Dharma. Also located here is a Bodhi Tree from the cutting of the original cutting in Sri Lanka.

**Sravastri** (Uttar Pradesh)—location of the third turning of the Wheel of Dharma by Buddha

## NEPAL

**Lumbini**—birthplace of the historical Buddha; located nearby is where Kapilavastu was, the town where King Suddhodana, Siddhartha Gautama's father, ruled from.

**Kathmandu**—site of stupas said to have been built during the reign of Ashoka. The Swayambhunath Stupa (also known as the Monkey Temple, and important to both Tibetans and Hindus) is particularly striking, as is the Bodhnath Stupa, around which many Tibetan Buddhist monasteries have been built. Many Tibetan refugee communities have been established in the Kathmandu area.

## TIBET

**Lhasa** (central Tibet)—site of numerous temples, monasteries, and nunneries, including the Jokhang and Ramoche temples, Sera, Drepung, and Nechung monasteries, and the Potala Palace and the Norbulingka (formerly the winter and summer residences, respectively, of the Dalai Lamas). Ganden Monastery, built by Tsongkhapa, and the first of the Gelug lineage, is located not far east of Lhasa.

**Mt. Kailash/Lake Manasarovar** (western Tibet)—mountain sacred to four religions (Buddhist, Hindu, Jain, and Bön); many thousands of pilgrims circumambulate both the mountain and the lake every year, which usually takes three days each.

**Samye Monastery** (south central Tibet)—considered to be the first Buddhist monastery built in Tibet (founded somewhere between 765 and 780 CE), southeast of Lhasa, on the north shore of the Yarlung Tsangpo River

## BHUTAN

Himalayan kingdom bordered by Tibet and India, where Tibetan Buddhism of the Drukpa lineage of the Kagyu school is the official state religion, and where the majority of the monasteries and monks are supported by the kingdom. Taktsang Lhakhang ("Tiger's Lair"), located northwest of Paro, is set on the side of a mountain, and is one of the most venerated pilgrimage locations in Bhutan. It is said that Padmasambhava, riding on the back of a tiger flying through the air, landed at this location, meditated for three months in a cave, converted the Paro valley to Buddhism, then returned to Tibet to continue giving teachings. Kyerchu Lhakhang, also located in Paro, is one of the Yandral (demoness-supressing) Temples constructed by Tibetan King Songsten Gampo in the mid-8th century CE.

# 8 The Dalai, Panchen, and Karmapa Lamas

## THE DALAI LAMAS

*14th Dalai Lama*

The term "Dalai Lama" first came into use in 1578, when Mongol king Altan Khan bestowed the title "Dalai" (which means "ocean" or "ocean of wisdom" in Mongolian) on Sonam Gyatso, who sat on the Golden Throne of Drepung (as Abbot). This came about when Sonam Gyatso visited the Mongol ruler, who was so taken by the wisdom and spirituality of the lama that he reintroduced the Tibetan form of Buddhism to his people and began a priest/patron relationship with the Buddhist lama. Sonam Gyatso then was known as the Third Dalai Lama, as he named his two previous incarnations posthumously as the First and Second.

Ngawang Lobsang Gyatso, the Fifth Dalai Lama (known widely as the Great Fifth), was the first to have a unified Tibet to rule. He came to hold both spiritual and temporal power in the country, partly with the help of another Mongol, Gushri Khan, who helped prevent an uprising from within Tibet. He also initiated the building of the Potala Palace as it is now, although it was completed after his death—his regent, Desi Sangye Gyatso, hid the fact of the Fifth Dalai Lama's death for 15 years while the Potala was completed, saying that the Dalai Lama was in retreat.

Tsangyang Gyatso, the Sixth Dalai Lama, is one out of the first fourteen who came from a completely different mold. He rejected the monastic lifestyle, and lived most of his shortened life as a "free spirit" and a poet, writing love poems still very popular with Tibetans.

Thupten Gyatso, the Thirteenth Dalai Lama (called the Great Thirteenth), ruled during a turbulent time in Tibet's history. The British invaded in 1903 and the Chinese in 1910, and both times the Dalai Lama went into exile, the first time to Mongolia and the second to India. Part of his legacy was the attempt to modernize Tibet and bring it more into the outside world and out of the isolation it had been in for virtually its entire history. However, much of what he tried to do was resisted by the monastic heirarchy and the upper class nobility. He also predicted dark times ahead for Tibet.

Tenzin Gyatso, the Fourteenth Dalai Lama, was born in northeast Tibet, in the province of Amdo, not far from where Tsongkhapa was born. At the age of two he was recognized as the reincarnation of his predecesor, taken on a three-month-long trip to Lhasa, and enthroned at the age of four. He was given full authority at age fifteen, due to the invasion of the army of the People's Republic of China in 1949. He escaped into exile to India in 1959, and has resided in the India hill station of Dharamsala since 1960, traveling, giving teachings, acting as a proponent for his people both inside and outside of Tibet, and strongly standing for the principles of non-violence, for which he was awarded the Nobel Peace Prize in 1989.

Each Dalai Lama is the reincarnation of his predecessor (and some think that the reincarnations can be traced back further than the First Dalai Lama; see Mullen, *The Fourteen Dalai Lamas*). The Dalai Lamas are considered to be an emanation of Chenrezig, the Buddha of Compassion (Avalokiteshvara).

Other names that are accorded to the Dalai Lama include: *Kundun* (The Presence), the Inmost One, Precious Presence, Precious Conqueror, Precious Protector, Wish-granting Jewel, Yeshe Norbu (the Wish-fulfilling Jewel), and His Holiness. At birth, the 14th Dalai Lama was named Lhamo Dhondup; when recognized as Dalai Lama at the age of two and later enthroned, his name became Jetsun Jamphel Ngawang Lobsang Yeshe Tenzin Gyatso—Holy Lord, Gentle Glory, Compassionate, Defender of the Faith, Ocean of Wisdom.

**Reigns of the Dalai Lamas**—Listed here are the fourteen Dalai Lamas to date, and the years they lived. It should be noted that a number of them, notably the ninth through twelfth, did not have very long lives. When a Dalai Lama is first enthroned as a youngster, a Regent—a position of great power—is appointed to handle his affairs until his majority. And a position that the Regents in those years seemed not to want to give up if a Dalai Lama reached his majority.

| | |
|---|---|
| 1391-1474 | Gendun Drubpa, First Dalai Lama (83 years)* |
| 1575-1542 | Dendun Gyatso, Second Dalai Lama (68 years)* |
| 1543-1588 | Sonam Gyatso, Third Dalai Lama (45 years) |
| 1589-1617 | Yonten Gyatso, Fourth Dalai Lama (28 years) |
| 1617-1682 | Ngawang Lobsang Gyatso, Fifth Dalai Lama (65 years) |
| 1683-1706 | Tsangyang Gyatso, Sixth Dalai Lama (23 years) |
| 1708-1757 | Kalsang Gyatso, Seventh Dalai Lama (49 years) |
| 1758-1804 | Jampel Gyatso, Eighth Dalai Lama (46 years) |
| 1805-1815 | Lungtok Gyatso, Ninth Dalai Lama (10 years) |
| 1816-1837 | Tsultrim Gyatso, Tenth Dalai Lama (21 years) |
| 1838-1855 | Khedrub Gyatso, Eleventh Dalai Lama (18 years) |
| 1856-1875 | Trinley Gyatso, Twelfth Dalai Lama (19 years) |
| 1876-1933 | Thupten Gyatso, Thirteenth Dalai Lama (57 years) |
| 1935- | Tenzin Gyatso, Fourteenth Dalai Lama |

*Named posthumously

## THE PANCHEN LAMAS

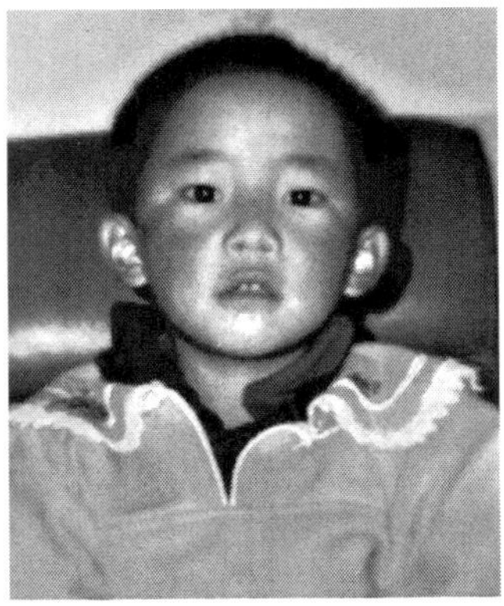

*11th Panchen Lama as a child (current whereabouts unknown)*

The institution of the Panchen Lama was established during the 17th century, when the Fifth Dalai Lama, in 1642, honored his tutor with the title *Panchen*, which means "great scholar." The Panchen Lamas, who were the abbots of Tashilhunpo Monastery (and sometimes referred to as the Tashi Lama), are thought to be the emanation of Amitabha, the Buddha of Infinite Light. As did the Dalai Lama, the Panchen Lama traced his reincarnations back, and named his three predecessors at Tashilhunpo posthumously as the First, Second, and Third Panchen Lamas.

It has been traditional that the elder of the two Lamas (Dalai and Panchen) would act as a tutor and mentor to the younger, and assist in finding the other's reincarnation. The Panchen Lama is considered to be the most revered figure in Tibetan religion and culture after the Dalai Lama. As seen in the dates, the reincarnations of the Panchen Lama go back a little farther than that of the Dalai Lama.

**Reigns of the Panchen Lamas**

| | |
|---|---|
| 1365-1438 | Kedrup Geleg Pelzang, First Panchen Lama (73 years)* |
| 1439-1504 | Sonam Choglang, Second Panchen Lama (65 years)* |
| 1505-1566 | Lobsang Dondrup, Third Panchen Lama (61 years)* |
| 1567-1662 | Lobzang Cholyi Gyaltsen, Fourth Panchen Lama (95 years) |
| 1663-1737 | Jetsun Lobzang Yeshey, Fifth Panchen Lama (74 years) |
| 1738-1780 | Panchen Rinpoche, Sixth Panchen Lama (42 years) |
| 1782-1854 | Lobzang Tenpai Nyima, Seventh Panchen Lama (72 years) |
| 1854-1882 | Tenpai Wangchuck, Eighth Panchen Lama (28 years) |
| 1883-1937 | Lobzang Chokyi Nyima, Ninth Panchen Lama (54 years) |
| 1938-1989 | Choekyi Gyaltsen, Tenth Panchen Lama (51 years) |
| 1989- | Gedun Choekyi Nyima, Eleventh Panchen Lama (current whereabouts unknown) |

*Named posthumously

## THE KARMAPAS

*17th Karmapa*

"'Karmapa' means 'the one who carries out Buddha-activity' or 'the embodiment of all the activities of the Buddhas.'" (www.kagyuoffice.org) The Karmapa is the spiritual head of the Karma Kagyu school of Tibetan Buddhism, one of Kagyu's four main lineages. The Karmapa is generally accepted to be the head of the entire Kagyu school, as the predecessor of the current Karmapa was thus named while he was in exile. After the Dalai Lama and the Panchen Lama, the Karmapa is generally recognized as being the next most venerated reincarnated lama of Tibetan origin. Like the Dalai Lama, the Karmapa is regarded as an emanation of Chenrezig, the Bodhisattva of compassion. "The line of the Karmapa's is self-announced; each incarnation leaves a letter predicting his next rebirth." (www.rumtek.org) And in noticing the years of the holders of the Karmapa incarnation, it goes back further than that of either the Dalai or Panchen Lamas. There has, however, been a question about the legitimacy of the naming of the most recent incarnation. Although validated by both the Dalai Lama and the Chinese authorities, and many in the Karma Kagyu school, some in the lineage believe another candidate to be the legitimate 17th Karmapa.

**Reigns of the Karmapas**

| | |
|---|---|
| 1110-1193 | Dusum Khyenpa, First Karmapa (83 years) |
| 1203-1283 | Karma Pakshi, Second Karmapa (80 years) |
| 1284-1339 | Rangjung Dorje, Third Karmapa (55 years) |
| 1340-1383 | Rolpe Dorje, Fourth Karmapa (43 years) |
| 1384-1415 | Dezhin Shegpa, Fifth Karmapa (31 years) |
| 1416-1453 | Thongwa Donden, Sixth Karmapa (37 years) |
| 1454-1506 | Chodrag Gyatsho, Seventh Karmapa (52 years) |
| 1507-1554 | Mikyo Dorje, Eighth Karmapa (47 years) |
| 1555-1603 | Wangchuk Dorje, Ninth Karmapa (48 years) |
| 1604-1674 | Choying Dorje, Tenth Karmapa (70 years) |
| 1676-1702 | Yeshe Dorje, Eleventh Karmapa (26 years) |
| 1703-1732 | Changchub Dorje, Twelfth Karmapa (29 years) |
| 1733-1797 | Dudul Dorje, Thirteenth Karmapa (64 years) |
| 1798-1868 | Thegchog Dorje, Fourteenth Karmapa (70 years) |
| 1871-1922 | Khakhyab Dorje, Fifteenth Karmapa (51 years) |
| 1924-1981 | Rangjung Rigpe Dorje, Sixteenth Karmapa (57 years) |
| 1985- | Ogyen Trinley Dorje, Seventeenth Karmapa |

## How High Lamas are Identified

Soon after a high lama (including the Dalai and Panchen lamas) has passed away, the search begins for his reincarnation. Some have left behind instructions as to where to look, or names of people to look for (such as the Karmapa lineage as noted above). Other methods include consulting the State Oracles (the Nechung Oracle and the Gadong Oracle), looking for signs, listening for tales of children born under certain conditions and with certain physical characteristics, and consulting a special oracle lake, Lhamo La-tso, where visions have been seen on the surface of the water. Once candidates have been identified by various means, they are tested in different ways by those who knew the previous lama. This usually happens when the child is between two and four years old. A successful search concludes when all have agreed on a child who meets all the conditions; in the past, he and his family were taken to the monastery where the lama resided (the Potala in Lhasa in the case of the Dalai Lama and Tashilhunpo in Shigatse in the case of the Panchen Lama), where the child would be enthroned and his education begun.

# 9 Monasteries, Nunneries, Oracles, and Demoness-Subduing Temples

## Monastic Terminology

| | |
|---|---|
| Ani | nun |
| Ani Gompa | nunnery |
| Barkhang | middle or second floor |
| Barkhor | intermediate circumambulatory passage |
| Chikhor | outer circumambulatory passage |
| Chökhang | offering hall |
| Chömay | butter lamp |
| Chöpa | offerings |
| Chöra | debating courtyard |
| Chörten | stupa; reliquary for the remains of high lamas |
| Darchen | flagpole used for banners or prayer flags |
| Dhensa | main monastery of a high lama |
| Drubkhang | meditation hermitage |
| Duchen | large assembly hall |
| Dukhang | assembly hall |
| Dungkhor | large prayer wheel usually fixed in place on a wall, spun by pilgrims |
| Dzong | fort or fortress |
| Geshe | highest monastic degree attainable |
| Gompa | monastery |
| Göngkhang | chapel where protective deities are worshipped |
| Götshang | mountain hermitage |
| Gyaltsen | victory banner mounted on a monastery roof |
| Khang | house; sometimes an abbreviation for lhakhang |
| Khangtsen | house in a monastic college; residential quarters of monks |

| | |
|---|---|
| Khenpa | abbess |
| Khenpo | abbot |
| Khata | offering scarf |
| Kora | circumambulatory route, going clockwise for Buddhists |
| Khorla | Dharma wheel |
| Kudung khang | reliquary room |
| Kumbum | large multi-level, multi-chapel chörten |
| Kusho | monk |
| Labrang | residence of an abbot; sometimes a palace |
| Lhakhang | chapel; temple |
| Lingkhor | external circumambulatory circuit |
| Lungta | prayer flag |
| Mudra | hand position of a deity, indicating something specific |
| Nangkhor | inner circumambulatory passage |
| Nekhor | pilgrimage circuit (kora) around a holy site |
| Pecha | religious text |
| Puja | religious offering or prayer ceremony |
| Stupa | chörten |
| Sungkhang | chapel of the guardian protector |
| Thangka | painted religious image, which can be rolled up for travel |
| Tratsang | monastic college |
| Tsamkhang | hermitage; meditation room |
| Tshokchen | great assembly hall |
| Tshokhang | assembly hall |
| Tsuglag Khang | Jokhang Temple in Lhasa; also main temple in Dharamsala |
| Ütse | topmost structure of a monastic complex |
| Vinaya | monastic code of conduct |
| Zimkhang | hermitage |
| Zimphuk | cave retreat |

## MONASTERIES

**Mon´-as-ter-y.** n. 1. a community of persons, especially monks, bound by vows to a religious life and sometimes living in partial or complete seclusion. 2. the dwelling place of such a community.

Over time, three great monasteries evolved in Tibet—Sera, Ganden, and Drepung (all of the Gelug lineage and all in the Lhasa area). Each was started by Je Tsongkhapa or a direct disciple in the early 15th century. Their purpose was to provide education, training, and a place for spiritual seekers. People would travel from all over Tibet to enroll at these monastic universities in order to receive spiritual training. A total of more than 20,000 lived, studied, prayed, meditated, and practiced at these three monasteries prior to 1959.

Classes in a monastery are conducted on a personal level. Unlike the university system in the west, at monasteries there are no rosters of regularly scheduled classes that students sign up to attend. Each monk must seek out a teacher and ask to be taught the subjects that he needed to learn. If the teacher accepted the student, the teacher became responsible for caring for all of the needs of the student—emotional, financial, and spiritual. The teachers support the students completely, and no fees are charged. However, it has been said that any money the student receives should be turned over to the teacher.

Outside of their personal studies, the monks meet regularly and spend long hours debating, thereby demonstrating and proving what was learned in their individual studies. (A much greater emphasis is placed on debate, called dialectics, in the Gelug tradition; the other three traditions—Nyingma, Sakya, and Kagyu—place more emphasis on traditional learning and less on debate.) If a monk completes the full course of studies, defends his knowledge by debating successfully, and is able to memorize and recite extensively from scripture, he then qualifies to receive a Geshe degree. The rank of geshe is said to be roughly equivalent to a Doctor of Theology degree in the west, although it often takes much longer to earn.

## Organization of a Monastery

*Laji*—oversees monastery; includes all *dratsang khenpos*; presided over by Abbott (*khenpo*)
- Monk officials who handle property, financial affairs (*changzod*)
- Monk responsible for discipline (*gesko; dobdob*)
- Monk responsible for chanting (*budsad; omzod*)

*Dratsang*—headed by a *khenpo*, who serves a term as chief administrator and religious and financial officer
- Composed of a number of *khangchens*

Each *dratsang* has its own housing, prayer hall, kitchen, and library, and often owns land, which produces income
Chief monk officials manage the *dratsang*'s assets
Monk responsible for discipline (*gesko*)
Monk who leads chanting (*budsad*)
Monk in charge of study, debating, and exams (*shunglapa*)

*Khangchen*—lowest level of organization, usually grouped by the monks' place of origin (where they were from)
Consists of about 100 monks, with senior-most monk as leader (*jigen*)

## Tibetan Buddhist Monasteries

The alphabetical listing of monasteries that follows comprises only a small number of institutions from small to very large that ranged throughout Tibet prior to 1959, with some surviving to the present. This listing is to give a sense of some of the information still available, and if, where, and when the monastery has been relocated, if known. According to the Tibetan government-in-exile, in 1959 there were 6,260 monasteries and nunneries, and by 1976, only 8 monasteries remained that were undamaged. Many have been rebuilt to some degree, mostly from the 1980s onward. No disrespect is meant if a monastery has not been included. These monasteries, and many others, were the foundation of society and Buddhism in Tibet. As with other named Tibetan institutions, there are often multiple spellings; some listed below have alternate spellings given.

**Chakpori (Chakpo Ri) (Iron Mountain)**—located in Lhasa south of the Potala Palace. Original site of the Tibetan Medical School, founded in 1695 by Desi Sangye Gyatso, regent of the Fifth Dalai Lama. The Menpa Tratsang combined the study of medicine and Buddhism, and was the only institution in Tibet to do so. The school was destroyed in 1959, and was not rebuilt. A large antenna now stands on Chakpori.

**India—Chagpori Tibetan Medical College**, Darjeeling
**India—Tibetan Medical and Astrological Institute** (Men-Tsee-Khang), Dharamsala, reestablished March 23, 1961

*Chakpori as seen from the Potala Palace, Lhasa, Tibet, 2005*

**Chimphu (Chimpu) Caves**—located in the upper Chimphu Valley 10 mi/16 km northeast of Samye Monastery. More than 100 hermits inhabit the caves, the use of which goes back to the eighth century and included Guru Rinpoche and Longchen Rabjampa as their inhabitants.

**Chiu Monastery** ("Little Bird"; **Jiu Gompa**, "Sparrow Monastery)—near Darchen, western Tibet, of Drukpa Kagyu lineage and one of a number of monasteries on the Lake Manasarovar kora, on the northwest side of the lake. Beneath the temple is a small cave in which Padmasambhava is said to have lived during the last seven days of his life.

**Chögar Gong (Chögar Ghong)**—Karma Kagyu monastery founded in Tsurphu, central Tibet, by the lineage of Goshir Gyaltsabpa

**India—Palchen Chökhor Ling** founded in Ralang, Sikkim, by H.E. 12th Goshir Gyaltsapa Rinpoche

**Chökorgye Monastery**—founded in 1509 by the Second Dalai Lama, about 100 mi/161km east of Lhasa. It is the closest monastery to Lhamo La-Tso (Oracle Lake), the sacred lake where some have reported seeing omens of the future on the surface of the water. These visions have been important in discovering reincarnations of the Dalai Lamas.

**Chuku (Chukku, Choku, Chogu, Nyenri) Monastery**—Drukpa Kagyu monastery founded in the 13th century on the west side of Mt. Kailash. It was one of the first monasteries destroyed during the Cultural Revolution, and one of the first to be rebuilt. It is reported that a lama and six monks are housed there.

**Dira-puk (Drira Phuk) Monastery** ("Cave of the Female Yak Horn")—monastery in western Tibet on the north side of the circumambulation route around Mt. Kailash. Of Drukpa Kagyu tradition, it was founded in the 13th century.

**Dorje Drak Monastery (Thubten Dorje Drak)**—located along the north bank of the Yarlung Tsangpo River, west of Samye Monastery. Founded by Godemchen Ngodrub Gyeltsen (1337-1409), who is thought to be an incarnation of Guru Rinpoche. It is the main monastery of the Northern Treasures order of the Nyingma school. Relocated from Tsang to its present location in 1632.

**India**—founded in 1984 near Shimla, Himachal Pradesh, with 100 monks

**Drak Yerpa**—cave and temple complex located c. 18 mi/30 km northeast of Lhasa. Among those associated with the 80 or so caves are Guru Rinpoche, Atisha, King Songsten Gampo, and Lhalung Peldor, who meditated here for many years after his assassination of Langdharma (c. 842), ending the first dissemination of Buddhism in Tibet. During Guru Rinpoche's stay here, he is reputed to have secreted many *terma* objects. Yerpa Drubde, an 11th century Kadampa monastery, was located here. After converting to a Gelug monastery, it was the summer residence of the Upper Tantric College of Lhasa. At one time, it is said that 300 monks were in residence.

**Drepung Monastery** ("The Rice Heap")—founded in 1416 by Jamyang Choje (a main disciple of Tsongkhapa) on the north side of Lhasa; home of the Dalai Lamas (in Ganden Palace) until the Potala was built by the Fifth Dalai Lama; once the worlds's largest monastery, with more than 10,000 monks in residence; one of the Three Seats (three great monasteries in the Lhasa area, *densasum*, along with Ganden and Sera). About 250

*Drepung Monastery, Lhasa, Tibet, 2007*

monks initially escaped into exile in 1959. It is thought about 300 monks now reside there.

Deyang College

Gomang College—oldest of the four colleges; Gomang means "many doors"

Loseling College—largest of the colleges; means "the hermitage of the radiant mind"

Ngagpa College

**India**—Starting in 1969, Drepung was rebuilt on land given in Mundgod, Karnataka, in the south of India. More than 5,000 monks are now in residence between Gomang and Loseling colleges.

**United States**—Geshes and monks from Drepung Loseling are located in Atlanta, Georgia, at the **Drepung Loseling Institute Center for Tibetan Studies**, which is affiliated with Emory University. In February, 2007, His Holiness the Dalai Lama was named a presidential distinguished professor at Emory University.

In Louisville, Kentucky, the **Drepung Gomang Institute** was established in 2001, and currently has two Geshes in residence.

**Drigong Til Monastery**—Founded mid to late 12th century by Drikhung Kyopa Jikten Sumgön. Located northeast of Lhasa, this was the seat of the Drigung Kagyu school. This tradition, rooted in the ascetic practices of Milarepa, has also included many of the characteristics of the Nyingma. Another famous site here is Drigung Dundro—the sky burial site of Drigong Til.

**India—Drikung Kagyu Institute** (Jangchub Ling) was founded in 1985 by H.H. Drikung Kyabjon in Sahastradhara, Dhera Dun

**Druk Sang-ngak Chöling**—founded in southern Tibet by Kunkhyen Pema Karpo (1527-1592), one of two principal seats of the Drukpa Kagyu.

**India—Druk Thubten Sangag Choeling** was founded in 1971 by Thukse Rinpoche and H.H. Drukchen Rinpoche in Darjeeling

**Dzogchen (Rudam Orgyen Samten Chöling) Monastery**—founded in 1684 in eastern Tibet in the Rudam Valley by Dzogchen Pema Rigdzin (the first Dzogchen Rinpoche and a disciple of the Fifth Dalai Lama) and Ponlop Namkha Ösel, the first Dzogchen Ponlop Rinpoche. It is one of the six major seats of the Nyingma lineage. At its peak, there were more than 500 monks in residence, 13 retreat centers, and an estimated 288 branches. It is estimated to have about 300 monks there currently.

**India**—inaugurated in 1992, Dzogchen Monastery is located at the Dhondening Tibetan Settlement in Kollegal, south India, and is the official seat of the Seventh Dzogchen Rinpoche.

**Gadong Monastery**—founded by Zingpo Sherapa in the 11th century northwest of Lhasa. Once home to more than 200 monks, it is also the location of a meditation cave used by Tsongkhapa. It had also been the seat of the Gadong Oracle, second in importance behind the Nechung Oracle.

**India**—seat of the Gadong Oracle was re-established in Dharamsala in 1976. Gadong Monastery has fifteen monks and is largely supported by its restaurant and guest house.

**Ganden (Gaden) Choekhorling (Chokhorling) (Tsethang Gompa)**—Kagyu monastery founded in 1351 in Tsethang, at the foot of Mount Gonpori. It was converted to a Gelug Monastery during the reign of the Seventh Dalai Lama. Destroyed during the 1960s, it has since been under reconstruction.

**Ganden (Gaden, Gadan) Monastery** ("The Joyous," "Place of Bliss")—the first Gelug monastery, established in 1409 by Tsongkhapa (founder of the Gelug school) 24 mi/40 km east of Lhasa. Tsongkhapa was buried here, and most of his remains were destroyed during the Chinese Cultural Revolution. Prior to 1959, the monk population has been estimated at 7,500; presently there are about 300 monks. Since its founding, Ganden had been the seat of the Ganden Tripa (abbot), the Holder of the Golden

*Ganden Monastery, Tibet, 2005*

Throne of Ganden and the head of the Gelug tradition. One of the Three Seats (along with Drepung and Sera).

Jangtse College—"North Peak"

Shartse College—"East Peak"

**India**—re-established in 1969, and located in southern India, in Mundgod, Karnataka State. There are more than 3,000 monks between the two colleges, and it is the seat of the Ganden Tripa.

**Gongkar Chöde Monastery**—monastery of the Sakya tradition, and head monastery of the Gongkar school, founded during the 16th century by Dorje Denpa Kunga Namgyel. Decorated with beautiful wall paintings by Jamyang Khyentse Wangchuk (born 1524), founder of the Khyenri school of Tibetan painting. More than 160 monks were housed at one time; currently there are about thirty. Located south of Lhasa, near Gongkar Airport.

**Gossul (Gotsuk) Monastery**—monastery on the Lake Manasarovar kora, in western Tibet. Famous for meditation spot of Kargyu saint Gotsangpa Gonpo Dorje (1189-1258).

**Gyandruk (Gyangdrak) Monastery**—in far western Tibet, at 5000m (16,437 feet), this is the largest monastery near Mt. Kailash. It is a branch of the Kagyu Drigung Til Monastery north of Lhasa. It is thought to have been founded in the 13th century, on the spot where Shenrab Miwoche (founder of Bön) stayed when he first came to Tibet thousands of years ago. Gyandruk is located on the inner kora (*nangkor*) of Mt. Kailash, which one is supposed to undertake only after completing 12 circuits of the mountain itself.

**Gyantse Kumbum**—see Pelkor Chöde Monastery

**Gyudmed (Gyume) Tantric Monastery (Lower Tantric College of Lhasa)**—founded in Lhasa in 1433 by Je Sherab Sengey, a disciple of Tsongkhapa. One of five major learning monasteries of the Gelug. The monks from Gyudmed were trained in the Tantric knowledge of Buddhist philosophy and spiritual practice and the esoteric fields of sacred art: thangka painting, butter sculpture, and sand mandalas. They are known for their specialized prayer rituals, blessings, and healing ceremonies. In Tibet they were the monks designated as the monastic scholars to go into the homes of the lay people and provide blessings and ritualized ceremonies.

**India**—In 1959, 150 monks from Gyudmed fled to India, following His Holiness the Dalai Lama into exile. These original 150 monks survived in Dalhousie, Northern India, by weaving carpets, farming, and providing prayer rituals for local families. In 1972, the main Gyudmed Tantric Monastery was re-established in Hunsur, Karnataka, southern India.

**Gyuto Tantric University (Upper Tantric College of Lhasa)**—founded in 1474 as Palden Toegyu Monastery by Je Kunga Dhondup (a main disciple of Tsongkhapa) in eastern Tibet. Sometime thereafter, it was relocated to the north side of Lhasa, with 32 monks, using the Ramoche Temple as a meeting hall. They specialized in Tantric meditations, Buddhist philosophy, and ritual arts. Principal tantric deity is Ghuyasamaja, the King of Tantra. 900 monks were in attendance in 1959.

**India**—re-established in 1974 in Bombdila, Arunachal Pradesh; newlocation, **New Ramoche Monastery** in Sidhbari, Himachal Pradesh, near Dharamsala, opened in 1996. More than 500 monks are in residence.

**United States—Gyuto Vajrayana Center** opened in 2001 in San Jose, California. There are a geshe and four monks in residence.

**Jokhang Temple (Tsuglag Khang/Tsug Lha Khang/Tasa Trulnag Tsuklak Khang; Central Temple)** ("Chapel of the Jowo" or "House of the Lord")—built in the heart of Lhasa sometime between 637 and 647 CE, the Jokhang is more a temple than a monastery. It is the central focus for spiritual life in Lhasa, and Tibet. King Songtsen Gampo (618-649 CE) took two wives, one Nepalese, Princess Bhrikuti, and one Chinese, Princess Wengchen. Each brought with her as part of her dowry a statue of the Buddha. The Nepalese Buddha, Akshobhya, was housed in the Jokhang, the gates of which face southwest toward Nepal. Another temple, Ramoche, was built to house the Chinese Buddha, Jowo Sakyamuni, which purports to show the Buddha at age 12 (or age 8, depending on the source). After King Gampo's death, Princess Wengchen had the Jowo moved to the Jokhang for its protection. Prior to the moving of the Jowo Buddha, the temple was called the Trulnang Temple. During the Cultural Revolution, in August, 1966 when the Jokhang was sacked, it is thought that the Jowo statue was not desecrated to show a historical connection between Tibet and China. In front of the Jokhang stands a stone pillar with the inscriptions of the Chinese-Tibetan Treaty of 822/823, the only remaining one of three pillars erected.

**India**—Tsuglag Khang (Central Cathedral) was established in 1968 in McLeod Ganj opposite the residence of His Holiness the Dalai Lama

*Jokhang Temple, Lhasa, Tibet, 2007*

and is in the care of the monks of Namgyal Monastery. It is known to the locals as the Main Temple. It houses three main images—Shakyamuni Buddha, Padmasambhava, and Chenrezig. The principal image is that of Shakyamuni Buddha, measuring three metres high and made of gilded bronze. To its right are the images of Padmasambhava and Avalokitesvara, which are both facing Tibet. In addition, Tsuglag Khang houses the entire set of the Buddhist canons, the Kagyur and the Tengyur. In 1992 a new prayer hall was added to the Tsuglag Khang complex with frescoes of the Kalachakra tantra cycle. The Central Cathedral is the site of public prayers, sermons, and religious festivities, including monastic dances.

*Stone pillar in front of Jokhang Temple, Lhasa, Tibet, 2005, inscribed with 822/823 CE treaty between Tibet and China*

**Kachu (Keru) Monastery**—located in the upper Yarlung Valley, perhaps 10 mi/17 km miles north of Tsethang. Some think it pre-dates Samye, and it is the only Yarlung-era temple known to have survived. It is said the gompa is now shared by Nyingma and Gelug monks.

**Kathok (Katok) Dorjeden (Kham Kathok) Monastery**—Nyingma monastery established in 1159 by Katok Kadam Deshek near Pelyul in the area of Derge in Kham, eastern Tibet. It is thought to be the oldest Nyingma monastery surviving in Tibet other than Samye. For hundreds of years, the Kathok Nyingma had monasteries all over Tibet, Bhutan, India, Sikkim, and Mongolia, as well as China; during ancient times, there were more than 300 monasteries. Earlier in the 20th century, more than 400 monks were reported to be at Kathok; there are said to be more than 180 resident monks currently. Presided over my H.H. Lhoga Rinpoche, Nyingma Kathok 84th lineage throne holder.

**India—Kham Kathok Tibetan Society** was established in 1965 in Sauton, Himachal Pradesh

**Katsel (Katsal) Monastery**—7th century Drigung monastery located 41 mi/66 km northeast of Lhasa near the Kyi Chu River. One of the original demoness-subduing temples built by King Songsten Gampo.

**Korja Monastery**—Sakya monastery located in western Tibet southeast of Purang and on the Karnali River, just inside the border with Nepal. Korja was founded by Khor, an early king of Ngari. An important Jowo statue is reported to be located here.

**Kumbum Jampa Ling Monastery** ("100,000 Buddha Images")—located in the northeast Tibetan region of Amdo, near Lake Kokonor, Kumbum was founded in 1583 by Sonam Gyatso, the Third Dalai Lama. It was built at the site of the birthplace of Tsongkhapa, founder of the Gelug school. The first Throne Holder of Kumbum was Duldzin Ozer-Gyatso. Before going into exile to India, Thubten Jigme Norbu, eldest brother of the 14th Dalai Lama, was abbot at Kumbum. The 14th Dalai Lama, prior to his journey as a child to Lhasa to be enthroned, lived at Kumbum for a short period in 1938-1939. Prior to 1959, it was estimated there were more than 3,600 monks at Kumbum. Currently, there are about 600 monks in residence.

Debate College founded in 1612
Tantric College (Sangngag Dechenling Dratsang) founded in 1649
Tantric College (Ngagpa Dratsang) founded in 1711
Kalachakra College (Dukor Dratsang Rigden Loseling) founded in 1820

**United States—Kumbum Pande Ling** (The Tibetan Center for Compassion and Wisdom) was founded in 2001 in Oakland, CA by Arjia Rinpoche, former Abbot at Kumbum in Tibet. He fled Kumbum in 1998 due to Chinese repression of Tibetan culture and religion. Rinpoche is a Tibetan high lama of Mongolian descent, and as a boy was recognized as the reincarnation of Lumbum Gye, father of Tsongkhapa.

**Kumbum Chamtse Ling Temple**—dedicated in 2003 at the Tibetan Cultural Center founded in 1979 by Taktser Rinpoche, eldest brother of the 14th Dalai Lama (now called the Tibetan Mongolian Buddhist Cultural Center) in Bloomington, IN, for the promotion of world peace and harmony. Presided over since 2006 by Arjia Rinpoche.

**Kundeling Monastery**—located in Lhasa, to the west of the Potala Palace, and one of the four Regency Monasteries (*Ling Shi*). Supplied regents for the 8th, 9th, and 13th Dalai Lamas.

**Labrang Tashikyil Monastery**—founded in 1709 by the First Jamyang Zhepa Ngawang Tsondru (a disciple of the Fifth Dalai Lama and an emanation of Tsongkhapa's teacher, Umapa Pawo Dorje). Located in Amdo, Labrang is considered to be one of the six largest Gelug monasteries in Tibet (the others being Drepung, Sera, Ganden, Tashilhunpo, and Kumbum [in Amdo]). At its height, there were an estimated 4000 monks and 500 incarnate tulkus in residence, and there were more than 100 branch monasteries of Labrang throughout Tibet. There are many buildings, and it is one of only a handful of monasteries to survive the Chinese Cultural Revolution with little damage. There are reported to be 1,000 monks currently in residence.

**India—Tashi Kyil Monastery** was established in 1965 in Clement Town, Dehra Dun, Uttaranchal, with more than 200 monks

**Langbona (Langpona) Monastery**—of the Kagyu school, one of a number of monasteries in western Tibet on the north side of the Lake Manasarovar kora. Monastery is dedicated to Shakyamuni Buddha.

***Ling Shi***—collective name of the four Regency Monasteries in Lhasa that supplied most of the regents for the Dalai Lama's while they were still in their minorities. They were given this designation by the Fifth Dalai Lama. They are: Kundeling, Tengyeling, Tsomonling, and Drib Tsechokling.

**Lukhang Temple**—temple located in the lake behind the Potala Palace in Lhasa. "During the time of the Fifth Dalai Lama (1617-1682), great amounts of earth were dug from the Chingdröl Chiling to construct the Potala. The resulting cavity became a pond known as the Lake of the Naga King. According to legend, Regent Sangye Gyatso was able to utilize this earth and successfully complete the Potala by making a pact with Luyi Gyalpo, the Naga King. In exchange for the earth, he promised to build a shrine to honor the dragon-like subterranean denizens.

After the regent's death, the Sixth Dalai Lama (1683-1706), a pleasure-loving poet, fulfilled the promise and built the jewel-like chapel." (Victor Chan, *Tibet Handbook*, 1994)

**Menri Monastery** (Bön)—located northeast of Shigatse and built in 1405 by Nyame Sherab Gyeltsen. Replaced Ensakha Monastery, which was founded in 1072 and destroyed by floods in 1386. Menri was the most important center of Bön in Tibet. Prior to 1959, there were more than 400 monks; currently the number is about 50.

**India—Pel Shenten Menri Ling Monastery** was re-established in 1969 near Solan, Himachal Pradesh by the 33rd Throne Holder of Menri, Khenchen Lungtok Tempai Nyima. There are currently about 120 monks.

**Meru Nyingba Monastery—**located along side the Jokhang Temple in Lhasa. It was founded in the 7th century as a Nyingma monastery, and was the site where Thonmi Sambhota, minister to King Songsten Gampo, completed his work on the Tibetan alphabet. It was destroyed during the reign of Langdharma, and was reconstructed by Atisha and converted to a Gelug monastery during the reign of the 3rd Dalai Lama.

**Mindroling (Mindrolling) Monastery** ("Place of Perfect Emancipation") **(Og Min Ogyen Mindroling Monastery)**—founded at the end of the 10th century and rebuilt in 1676 by Terdak Lingpa ("Minling Trichen"—Great Treasure Finder Terton of Mindroling), a tutor to the Fifth Dalai Lama. The most renowned of the Nyingma monasteries in Tibet and head monastery of the Nyingma Southern Treasures School. At the end of the 10th century, Lumé Tsuyltrim Shenrab built a small chapel here, likely the earliest foundation of what was to become Mindroling. Partly destroyed during the Cultural Revolution, but much has been restored. Marriage is allowed at Mindroling; the throne of the abbot is passed from father to son or son-in-law. The head of the Mindroling lineage is His Holiness Minling Trichen Rinpoche.

**India**—Mindrolling Monastery was begun in 1965 in Dehra Dun, Uttaranchal. In October, 2002, the Great Stupa was inaugurated—the world's largest stupa at 185 feet tall and 100 feet square. Currently more than 300 monks in residence.

Ngedon Gatsal Ling

Primary and Secondary Buddhist School

Ngagyur Nyingma College, Institute of Advanced Buddhist Studies
Drubde Ödsal Ling Retreat Center

**Namdruk Monastery (Druk Gompa)**—one of two principal seats of the Drukpa Kagyu, founded in 1206 in central Tibet by Drupchen Lingrepa and Tsangpa Gyare. It was totally destroyed during the Cultural Revolution, and some re-construction has been done.

**Namgyal Monastery (Namgyal Phende Lekshey Ling Monastery)**—founded in 1575 by Gendun Gyatso, the Second Dalai Lama, to assist the office of the Dalai Lama in its public religious activities and in the performance of ritual prayer ceremonies for the welfare of Tibet. The monastery was subsequently located in the Potala Palace and was also known as Namgyal Dratsang (Victorious Monastery).

**India**—Namgyal Monastery is located in Dharamsala, Himachal Pradesh, home to the Tibetan government-in-exile; it currently has more than 180 monks who serve the Dalai Lama.

**Gaden Phelgay Ling/Namgyal Monastery** is located in Bodh Gaya. It was started in 1938, and became affiliated with Namgyal in 1998.

**Phuntsok Choephel Ling/TIbetan Temple** is located at Kushinagar, and became affiliated with Namgyal in 1967.

**United States**—**Namgyal Monastery Institute of Buddhist Studies** was founded in 1992 in Ithaca, NY. This monastery was start-

*Monks quarters, Namgyal Monastery, Dharamsala, India, 2005*

*Nechung Monastery, Lhasa, Tibet, 2007*

ed with a geshe and five Namgyal monks to serve as the North American seat of the personal monastery of His Holiness the 14th Dalai Lama. Construction on a new monastic center, **Dü Khor Choe Ling**, was begun in 2007. One monk had been serving as the first Buddhist chaplain at Cornell University.

**Narthang (Nartang) Monastery**—founded in 1153 as a Kadampa monastery 12 mi/20 km southwest of Shigatse. The texts of the Tibetan Buddhist Canon were collected during the 14th century at Nartang and organized by Büton Rinchen Drup into *Kanjur* (the Buddha's Words) and *Tanjur* (the commentaries by Buddhist masters). Only a small chapel, built in 1987, is in use, among extensive ruins.

**Nechung Monastery**—on the advice of the Great Fifth Dalai Lama, Nechung (*Ne*, place, and *chung*, small), was expanded from a small monastic community in 1683 to the monastery that became the seat of Tibet's State Oracle, Dorje Drakden (Pehar) (see page 146). Major decisions of the Tibetan government, both prior to 1959 and in exile, have been made in consultation with the Nechung Oracle. In 1959, six of the 115 monks in residence were able to escape into exile, following His Holiness the 14th Dalai Lama to India. (The Thirteenth Dalia Lama had determined that 115 monks was the correct number of monks for the Nechung Monastery.) Nechung Rinpoche, head of the monastery, escaped and was able to join them in 1962; he passed away in 1982. It is thought that there are now about 16 monks at Nechung.

**India**—located in Dharamsala, Himachal Pradesh. Construction of this new monastery in exile was completed in 1984. The 14th Dalai Lama and the Nechung Oracle mutually recognized the reincarnation of the present Nechung Rinpoche in 1993. Thubten Ngodrup was born in Lhasa on May 20, 1985. He went to school in Tibet for some years, and in September 1993, some monks and members of the Nechung Monastery went to Tibet and literally smuggled him to India. After reaching Dharamsala, he began his studies in earnest at the Nechung Monastery. On March 15, 1995 he was officially enthroned.

**United States—Nechung Dorje Drayang Ling**, a non-sectarian Buddhist temple and meditation center, was established in 1973 in Wood Valley, Ka'u, HI, and is Nechung's headquarters in the West.

**Ngor Monastery**—founded in 1429, Ngor is south of Shigatse, and is the head monastery of the Ngor Sakya tradition. Prior to 1959, 400 monks resided here. It is regarded as being second in importance to the Sakyas after Sakya Monastery itself.

**India**—established in 1978 as **Ngor Ewam Tcheu Den** in Manduwala, Dehradun, Uttaranchal; it houses more than 200 monks, many of whom are young.

**India**—established as **Palsa Ngor Tsar Sum Monastery** in Mundgod, Karnataka, with more than 100 monks.

**Norbulingka** (*Norbu*, "Jewel" or "Treasure," and *Lingka*, "Garden" or "Park")—the initial structure was built in west Lhasa in the mid-18th century by the 7th Dalai Lama as a summer palace, and has since been the summer residence of the Dalai Lamas. The Dalai Lama and the Tibetan government would relocate to the Norbulingka from the Potala on the 18th day of the third lunar month, with a large and elaborate procession. The complex is a collection of palaces and other buildings constructed during the reigns of subsequent Dalai Lamas. It was from the Norbulingka that the 14th Dalai Lama escaped into exile on March 17, 1959.

**India—Norbulingka Institute**, a complex of Tibetan-style buildings, was built in 1985, 5 mi/8 km from Dharamsala, and dedicated to preserving Tibetan culture. Within the complex is the Deden Tsuglakhang

*Sitting room of the 14th Dalai Lama at the Norbulingka, Lhasa, Tibet, 2007*

*Norbulingka Institute, near Dharamsala, India, 2005*

Temple, peaceful Japanese gardens, many classrooms, a gift shop, and two guest houses.

**Pabongka (Pabonka, Pawangka) Monastery**—located northwest of Sera Monastery in Lhasa. It is thought that Pabongka was built before either the Jokhang or the Ramoche. It is the site of a cave that King Songsten Gampo meditated in, and it was here, it is thought, that the King and his two wives meditated and were given the guidance to build the demoness-suppressing temples throughout Tibet (see page 147). The monastery is built on a huge rock that some liken to a female turtle. A visit to Pabongka is thought by some pilgrims to bring as much merit as a trip to Kushinagara in India, the site of the Buddha's parinirvana. Also located here is the original stone inscription of the six-syllable mantra *Om Mani Padme Hum* made by Thonmi Sambhota, who created the Tibetan alphabet in order to translate the Sanskrit teachings of Buddha.

**Palpung Monastery (Palpung Thupten Choekor Ling)** ("pal," glorious; "pung," to gather)—founded in 1727 by the eighth Tai Situpa Chökyi Jungney (1700-1774) in the Derge region in eastern Tibet; one of the most important Karma Kagyu monasteries in Kham.

- **India—Palpung Institute (Thupten Choekor Ling)** founded in Bir, Himachal Pradesh, by H.E. the 12th Tai Situ Rinpoche
- **United States**—centers located in California, Kansas, Texas, Virginia

**Palyul (Pelyul) Monastery (Palyul Namgyal Jangchub Ling)**—built in 1665 in eastern Tibet by Lhachen Jampa Phuntsog, the first Dharma King of Dege (Derge); the first throne holder of the Palyul lineage (Nyingma) was Vidyahara Kunszang Sherab (1636-1699).

- **India—Thek-chok Namdrol Shedrub Ling Monastery**, located in Bylakupp, Karnataka State; 1,600 monks
- **India—Palyul Chokhor**, Bir, Himachal Pradesh
- **United States**—Centers located in NY, CA, Washington, DC, MA, MT, OH, and TX

**Pelkor Chöde (Palchor Choide) Monastery** and **Gyantse Kumbum**—founded in 1418 in Gyantse, southwest of Lhasa, and affiliated with both Gelug and Sakya traditions. Gyantse Kumbum (Pangmo Chorten) was completed in 1427. There are at least 75 chapels on the nine stories,

*Pabongka Monastery, Lhasa, Tibet, 2007*

*Gyantse Kumbum, Tibet, 2005*

*Potala Palace as seen from the roof of the Jokhang Temple, Lhasa, Tibet, 2005*

and this Kumbum (large chorten; "100,000 Buddha images") is said to be the largest in Tibet. When viewed from above, the Kumbum represents a mandala.

**Potala Palace** ("The Place where Avalokiteshvara Lives")—the Potala Palace has been home to the Dalai Lamas and the seat of the Tibetan government since the 5th Dalai Lama, who moved there in 1649 from his quarters at Drepung. The original structure on Marpori (Red Hill) was built c. 637 by King Songsten Gampo, and destroyed by lightening during the reign of King Trisong Detson. The current structure was begun in 1645 and completed in 1694. There are eight Dalai Lamas whose tombs or chortens are located in the Potala. The building is 13 stories high and has an estimated 1,000 rooms. It is composed of the White Palace (seat of the Tibetan government and winter residence to the Dalai Lamas) and the Red Palace (consisting of temples and tombs of the Dalai Lamas). Namgyal Monastery is also located here. It is one of the most imposing buildings in the world, a World Heritage site, and can be seen from most parts of Lhasa.

**Ralung Monastery**—founded in 1180, Ralung is the primary seat of the Drukpa Kagyu tradition. It is located west of Gyantse, in the vicinity of some of central Tibet's highest (more than 7100m) peaks. Home to about 15 monks.

*Monks at Ramoche Temple, Lhasa, Tibet, 2007*

**Ramoche Temple** ("minor Buddha" or "minor Jokhang") (Gyuiaka Ramo Chezolhakang)—built in Lhasa (c. 637 to 647 CE), with its gates facing eastward towards China, around the same time as the Jokhang. Originally built to house the Jowo Buddha statue brought to Tibet by Princess Wencheng, the Chinese wife of King Songtsen Gampo. Following the king's death, the Jowo was moved into the Jokhang, where it still remains, while the statue that started out in the Jokhang, brought by Nepalese Princess Bhrikuti, was transferred to the Ramoche. It became the assembly hall for the Upper Tantric College in 1474; the college abbot also served as the abbot of the Ramoche.

**India—Gyuto Ramoche Monastery** was re-established in 1996 at Sidbhari, Himachal Pradesh

**Rato Dratsang Monastery**—founded in the 14th century in Lhasa Valley as a Kagyu monastery, primarily to preserve the teachings of Indian logicians Dharmakirti and Dignaga. Approximately 500 monks attended in 1959. Only a few were able to escape to India in 1959. It is currently a Gelug monastery with about 50 monks.

**India**—Re-established in 1983 in Mundgod, Karnataka. Monk population has grown to more than 70. Plans include increasing the size of the monastery to accommodate 200 monks.

**Rechung-puk Monastery**—located south of Tsethang, this was once a large Kagyu monastery, with more than 1,000 monks. Located here is a meditation cave (*puk*) which was used by Rechungpa Dorje Drak (12th century), the most accomplished disciple of Milarepa. The *Life of Milarepa* and the *Hundred Thousand Songs of Milarepa* were said to have been written here in the late 15th century by Sangye Gyeltsen.

**Reting Monastery**—founded in 1056 by Dromtompa (founder of Kadampa, the root of Gelug) in the Rong Chu Vally north of Lhasa. It was initially associated with Atisha, who led the second infusion of Buddhism in Tibet in the 11th century. When Tsongkhapa visited Reting in the late 14th century, he had a vision of Atisha, which inspired him to write *The Great Treatise on the Stages of the Path to Enlightenment* (*Lamrim Chenmo*), which he completed in 1402. Reting Rinpoche served as the first regent for the 14th Dalai Lama during his minority. The 14th Dalai Lama has said that if he were ever to return to Tibet, he would like to spend his days at Reting Monastery. (Craig, *Kundun*, p. 368)

**Rongbuk (Rongphuk, Rongphu, Dzarongpu, Dzarong, Do-Ngak Chöling) Monastery**—located south of Tingri (Dingri) and on the way to Everest base camp (Tibet side). Built in 1902 by Zatul Rinpoche, the Rongbuk Lama, this is said to be the highest monastery in the world, at about 5,000m (16,400 feet). At its height, there were about 500 monks and nuns in the area. Nuns of the Nyingma tradition had been in the region since the late 18th century. The area has many hermitage meditation caves, including one said to have been used by Guru Rinpoche.

**Sakya Monastery** ("Grey Earth")—located in the province of Tsang, and head of the Sakya tradition, two monasteries were erected: one on the north side of the Trum River was founded in 1073 by Kön Könchag Gyelpo; the second was built on the south side of the river in 1268. The head of Sakya is the Throne Holder (Sakya Trinzin)

- **India—Sakya Centre** in Rajpur, Uttar Pradesh, was founded in 1964 and is the main Sakya monastery outside of Tibet. His Holiness Sakya Trizin resides here; there are currently about 250 monks.
- **India—Sakya College** was established in Dehra Dun, Uttar Pradesh in 1972, currently with about 100 monks.
- **United States—Sakya Monastery of Tibetan Buddhism** was found-

ed in 1974 in Seattle, WA, by H.H. Jigdal Dagchen Sakya, as a non-sectarian religious center (seen during remodeling in the film *LIttle Buddha*).

**Samding Monastery**—founded in the 12th century by Khetsun Zhonudrub, and reputed to follow both Sakya and Nyingma teachings. Located south of Lhasa and the Yarlung Tsangpo River, between the two "pincer arms" on the western side of Yamdrok Yum-tso. One legend has the establishment of the monastery where it is to prevent a flood from the lake from destroying Tibetan lands. Another legend has the abbess of Samding, the only incarnate female lama in Tibet, turning herself and the nuns of the monastery into sows when invading Mongols attacked in 1716. One version has the invaders so shocked by the sight of the sows that they fled without causing any damage; another has the sows turning back into nuns in front of the Mongols, who were so overcome that they made offerings to the monastery. The abbess, named Samding Dorje Phagmo (Thunderbolt or Diamond Sow), was accorded great honor by the government. Apparently the current (12th) Samding Dorje Phagmo has disrobed (given back her monastic vows) and is working for the government as the vice-chairman of the standing committee of the Tibetan Autonomous Region People's Parliament. There was much damage to Samding during the Cultural Revolution, and some has been rebuilt. Currently about 30 monastics.

**Samye Monastery** ("Unimaginable")—Samye is located southeast of Lhasa, on the north side of the Yarlung Tsangpo River, and its lineage is Nyingma. It is considered by most to be Tibet's first monastery, founded sometime between 765 and 780 CE by Padmasambhava and Shantarakshita (the two Indian masters invited to Tibet to direct the spread of Buddhism and to translate the great Buddhist scriptures), under the patronage of King Trisong Detsen. It was the location of the Great Debate of 792-794, during which the Indian model of Buddhism and the Chinese model of Buddhism were challenging each other for "supremacy" in Tibet. The Indian tradition consisted of study, ethical rules, and a gradual path that led to enlightenment (Mahayana); the Chinese tradition (Ch'an, or Zen) focused on direct, sudden advances leading to the understanding of the ultimate nature of reality. Both sides apparently claimed success, but the Indian tradition held out, and the Chinese influence lost. It was also at Samye that the first seven Tibetans were ordained as monks by Shan-

*Samye Monastery, Tibet, 2007*

tarakshita, who examined them closely to make sure they were appropriate candidates to be monks; they are known as the Seven Examined Men (*misedun*). Samye is constructed to represent the structure of the Buddhist universe: the central Monastery represents Mt. Sumeru; around it, at the four cardinal compass points, are four temples, called *ling*, which represent the four continents; on either side of each *ling* are smaller temples representing the sub-continents. Between each of the four *lings* are built four great stupas, each in a different color, facing the corners of the main Monastery (see page 67). The entire monastery complex is surrounded by an oval wall, on top of which sit small stupas.

Akatoje College

**Selung Gompa**—located on the southwestern side of Mt. Kailash in western Tibet. It was a branch of Drigong Til Monastery, which is located northeast of Lhasa.

**Sera Monastery** ("The Merciful Hail")—Established in 1419 just north of Lhasa by Jamchen Choje Sakya Yeshe, a disciple of Tsongkhapa. It housed more than 5,000 monks prior to 1959. Several hundred monks still live at Sera Monastery between Jey and Mey Colleges. One of the Three Seats.

Mey College founded in 1419 by Sakya Yeshe
Ngagpa College built in 1419 by Sakya Yeshe
Jey College founded in 1435 by Gungyal Lodro Rinchen Senge

*Debating courtyard at Sera Monastery, Lhasa, Tibet, 2005*

**India**—re-established in 1979 in Bylakuppe, Karnataka. It now has more than 4,500 monks divided between the two colleges of Sera Mey and Sera Jey. Ngagpa College was not re-established.

**Seralung Monastary** ("Hailstone Valley")—one of a number of monasteries in western Tibet on the Lake Manasarovar kora. The original monastery housed up to 100 monks before the Cultural Revolution; a one-room temple was rebuilt in 1980.

**Shalu Monastery**—located south of Shigatse, Shalu was founded sometime between 1000 and 1040 by Jhetsun Sherab Jungnay during the major resurgence of Buddhism in Tibet. Early in the 14th century, under Butön Rinpoche, it became an important center of learning. Rinpoche had brought together the 108 volumes of the Kanjur, the fundamental Buddhist texts, and the two hundred volumes of the Tanjur, the commentaries on the Buddhist texts. A most prominent external feature of Shalu are the four Chinese-style tiled roofs which rise above the main building. Shalu had 100 monks at various times during the last century, and there are still a handful of monks in attendance.

**Shechen Monastery**—founded in 1695 in Kham, eastern Tibet, by Rabjam Tenpai Gyaltsen. The Great Fifth Dalai Lama had sent him to found this Nyingma monastery, and it is known as one of the six main monasteries of the Nyingma school. It was destroyed during the Chinese occupation, and is being restored

**India**—in 1996, a monastery complex in Bodh Gaya was built. **Shechen Monastery** houses about 50 monks.

**Nepal**—building was completed in 1990 near the Boudnath Stupa in Kathmandu, Nepal, under the direction of Dilgo Khyentse Rinpoche. More than 300 monks are in attendance.

**Sheldrak Monastery/Sheldrak Drubpuk (Drubphuk) Cave**—early Nyingma monastery southwest of Tsethang. Up the hill from the monastery is Sheldrak Drubpuk Cave, the first meditation cave in Tibet of Guru Rinpoche. It was from here that he first subdued the demons that were plaguing Tibet at the time and converted them into Dharma protectors. One of the more revered pilgrimage sites.

**Tabo (Tabo Chos-Khor) Monastery**—located in Spiti Valley, Himachal Pradesh, India, only 18 mi/30km from the Tibetan border. This monastery has remained virtually untouched by the ravages of civilization since it was founded by Rinchen Zangpo in 996 CE. It is located on the extended Tibetan plateau, at 3050m (10,006 feet), and is one of the few monasteries in the Tibetan Buddhist world that was not destroyed or damaged by either the Muslim armies in the 12th century or the Chinese in the 20th century. The collection of art, sculpture, scriptures, and thangkas is unmatched. Within the mud-brick wall that encloses the monastery are 7 temples (*lakhangs*) and 24 stupas. Both monks and nuns are in residence. There are currently about 45 monks. In 1996, His Holiness the Dalai Lama gave a Kalachakra Initiation in honor of the monasteries' 1000-year anniversary.

**Tangboche (Tangpoche) Monastery (Solnak Tang)**—located south of Tsethang, originally a Kadampa monastery founded in 1017 and visited by Atisha. Following a visit by Tsongkhapa during the 14th century, Tangboche began to follow the Gelug tradition.

**Tashilhunpo Monastery** ("Mount of Blessing" or "Mass of Glory")—seat of the Panchen Lama (often called the Tashi Lama), second most venerated spiritual leader of Tibet. It was founded in 1447 in Shigatse by

*Tashilhunpo Monastery, Shigatse, Tibet, 2005*

Gyalwa Gendun Drup (posthumously named as the First Dalai Lama). By 1959, there were estimated to be 5,000 monks in residence; only about 250 were able to initially escape into exile. It is thought that 400-500 monks are currently at Tashilhunpo.

**India**—re-established in 1972 at Bylakuppe, Karnataka, by 20 elderly monks who had followed the Dalai Lama into exile; by 2012 there were more than 300 monks in residence.

**Tengyeling Monastery**—located in Lhasa, and one of four Regency Monasteries (*Ling Shi*). It is currently an important shrine of the Nyingma school, and associated with Samye Monastery. In 1912, Tengyeling was sacked by the Tibetan government due to its support of the 1910 Chinese invasion. It was subsequently stripped of it's Regency designation by the 13th Dalai Lama.

**Tholing (Toling) Monastery**—founded between 1014-1025 by Rinchen Zangpo, in far western Tibet, about 100 mi/160km northwest of Mt. Kailash. The temples that remain in the complex are some of the only existing of the Guge style in western Tibet. Zangpo, along with Atisha, was among those responsible for the beginnings of the second dissemination of Buddhism in Tibet.

**Three Seats ("Three Pillars")** *(densasum)*—Ganden, Drepung, and Sera, the three large Gelug monasteries in the Lhasa region, are known collectively as the Three Seats.

**Trandruk (Tradruk) Monastery** ("roc conquering a dragon," or "falcon [*tra*] dragon [*druk*]")—located in Tsethang, just south of the Yarlung Tsangpo River. One of 12 demoness-subduing monasteries built during the reign of King Songsten Gampo, and built during the same time as the Jokhang and Ramoche temples. According to one legend, the King transformed into a roc (a mythical bird of prey having enormous size and strength) or a falcon and conquered an evil dragon. Only then could the monastery be built. This was also one of King Trisong Detsen's three royal temples (along with the Jokhang and Samye). In an upstairs chapel there is exhibited a thangka made entirely of 30,000 pearls and other precious jewels, depicting Princess Wengchen (the Chinese wife of Songsten Gampo) as an emanation of Tara. New buildings were consecrated in 1988.

**Trugo (Trugolho) Monastery** ("Bathing Head," "Head-washing South Gate Monastery")—one of a number of monasteries on the Lake Manasarovar kora, located on the south side; the only Gelug monastery in the Manasarovar/Kailash region. Destroyed during the Cultural Revolution and rebuilt in 1984.

**Tsandra Rinchen Drak**—hermitage retreat founded in 1860 by Jamgön Kongtrül the Great (1813-1899) in the Derge region of eastern Tibet, not far from Pelpung. It is revered as one of 25 power places in the region.

*Monks at Trandruk Monastery, Tsethang, Tibet, 2005*

**Nepal—Pullahari Monastery and Retreat Center** was completed in February 1992 by H.E. 3rd Jamgön Kongtrül Rinpoche (1954-1992) in Kathmandu. There are about 200 monks in residence.

**Tsechokling Monastery**—located in the village of Dip, south of Lhasa. Founded after 1775 by Kachen Yeshe Gyaltsen while he was in Lhasa after becomg a tutor to the 8th Dalai Lama. One of the four Regency Monasteries (*Ling Shi*).

**India**—Re-established in Dharamsala in 1987, Tsechokling Monastery supports and educates approximately fifty monks. General education is provided, including philosophy, Tantric studies, English, history, and Tibetan.

**Tsomonling Monastery**—located in Lhasa, south of the Ramoche, and one of the four Regency Monasteries (*Ling Shi*). Regents for the 8th, 10th, and 11th Dalai Lamas were from Tsomonling.

**Tsuglag Khang**—see Jokhang Temple

**Tsurphu Monastery**—founded in the 1180s northwest of Lhasa by the first Karmapa, Dusum Khyenpa, Tsurphu is the seat of the Karmapa branch of the Kagyu order and of the Gyalwa Karmapa. There were more than 1,000 monks in residence in 1950. In 1959, the 16th Karmapa, Rangjung Rigpe Dorje, fled Tibet and eventually relocated in Sikkim, India, where he founded a new seat in Rumtek. After passing away in 1981, his reincarnation, Trinlay Thaye Dorje, born in Lhasa, Tibet, was recognized as the 17th Karmapa. During the period of December 28, 1999 to January 5, 2000, the Karmapa left his monastery in Tibet and escaped, through Nepal, to India. The Karmapa is currently awaiting permission of the Indian government to return from his temporary headquarters near Dharamsala, India, to his seat in Sikkim.

**India**—Tsurphu was re-established as **Rumtek Monastery** and **Rumtek Dharma Chakra Center** in 1966, in the Indian state of Sikkim.

**Yangonpa Monastery**—located on the shores of Lake Manasarovar. The main hall is dedicated to the deity of the lake, Hlabsen Dorje Barvas. (mentioned on p. 116 of *Travelers' Tales Tibet*, story by Sven Hedin, *The Holy Lake*, 1907)

**Yangpachen Monastery**—founded in 1490 in central Tibet, northwest of Lhasa, by Muran Jampa Thukje Pal. It was the main seat of the Sharmapas, a sub-sect of the Karmapas, who were located nearby at Tsurphu. It was rebuilt in 1986, with approximately 100 monks currently in attendance. The sect is headed by the Shamar Rinpoche.

**Yerngo Monastery**—ruined monastery on the southern side of Lake Manasarovar kora; visited by and dedicated to Guru Rinpoche.

**Yumbu** ("mother deer") **Lakhang (Lagang)**—the monastery located here is the reconstruction (since 1982) of what is considered to have been the oldest building in Tibet. Thought to have been constructed in 127 BCE, Yumbu Lakhang is located south of Tsethang, and sits atop Tashi Tshe Ri, overlooking the Yarlung Valley.

**Zongkar Choede Monastery**—established in western Tibet in 1270 by King Tribum de gon. Prior to 1959, there were 500 monks in residence; 50 monks initially managed to escape into exile.

**India**—130 monks reside at Zongkar Chodede, re-establshed in 1992 in Mysore, Karnataka. A new temple was dedicated in December,

*Yumbu Lakhang, Tsethang, Tibet, 2005*

2004, by His Holiness the Dalai Lama. Geshe Thupten Jinpa, long a translator for the Dalai Lama and a revered scholar, received his early education and training here.

**Zutul Phuk (Zutrulpuk)**—located on the southeastern side of the Mt. Kailash kora. This gompa is associated with Milarapa, and it was here that he had a contest with Bön practitioner Bönchung for possession of Mt. Kailash. Milarepa won, and a nearby mountain, Bönri, was given as a consolation prize.

## Tibetan Buddhist Nunneries

Nunneries (*ani gompas*) have existed in Tibet for almost as long as monasteries; one of the oldest dates from the 7th century. It has been reported that prior to the Chinese invasion in 1949, there were 618 nunneries and 12,398 nuns in Tibet. (Council for Religious and Cultural Affairs, NIBWA Bulletin, #10, 1987) The nunneries suffered the same destruction as a result of the Chinese invasion that the monasteries did. However, unlike the monasteries in traditional Tibet, many nunneries did not receive the same support that the monasteries did. "In traditional Tibet, the position of nuns was inferior to that of their male counterparts. Only in recent times have steps been taken to bring their education and meditation training up to the standard of monks. There is still a long way left to go." (Berzin, *Relating to a Spiritual Teacher: Building a Healthy Relationship*) As was more true for nuns, many of their families provided their support. "Because the nunneries [usually] have so little endowment, they cannot afford to feed their member nuns on a daily basis, nor sponsor the extensive rituals that the monastery can. As a result, [many] nuns . . . seek their own subsistence by domestic and agrarian work." (www.gadenrelief.org) In addition, nuns seemed to be treated as second-class monastics—there were teachings that were not offered to them, they were not eligible [until recently] for the advanced geshe degrees that the monks were, the teachers (mostly monks) available to the nuns were limited, the facilities that they had available were often substandard, and, according to monastic hierarchy, the lowliest monk was accorded more respect than the most educated nun. Still, thousands of Tibetan girls and women sought out the teachings of the Buddha, and the nunneries, in their own way, flourished. Procedures have been completed within the Department of Religion and Culture of the Tibetan Central Administration in Dharamsala to make it possible for nuns to work towards obtaining a geshe degree, to be geshema. (see page 22)

**Ani Sangkhung (Tsangkung, Tshamkhung) Nunnery**—established in Lhasa in the 7th century, not far from the Barkhor; the main temple is dedicated to Chenrezig; located at the nunnery is a cave said to have been used for meditation by King Songsten Gampo; reported to currently house about 100 nuns.

*Nuns at Ani Sangkhung working on the rolls of prayers that go inside prayer wheels, Lhasa, Tibet, 2007*

*Entrance gate at Geden Choeling Nunnery, Dharamsala, India, 2005*

**Chu Hara Nunnery**—nunnery in ruins in the Everest region, prior to reaching Rongbuk on the way to the north side of Everest.

**Chupsang (Chubsang, Chubzang) Nunnery** ("good waters")—Gelug nunnery, formerly a monastery, located in Lhasa, north of Sera Monastery and near Pabongka Monastery; there are an estimated 130 nuns.

**Geden (Gaden) Choeling Nunnery** ("Home of the virtuous ones who devote their lives to the Buddha Dharma")—officially opened in McLeod Ganj, Himachal Pradesh, India, in 1973, and is now the oldest nunnery in the Tibetan exile community. Among the founding nuns were several who had been at Nechung Ri Nunnery in Tibet, which was destroyed.

**Garu (Gari, Ghari Ani Gompa) Nunnery**—one of the older nunneries in the Lhasa area, located northwest of Sera; currently home to about 100 nuns.

**Jamyang Choling Institute**—was founded in 1988 to educate Himalayan Buddhist nuns and laywomen who would otherwise have no opportunity to receive any formal secular or spiritual education. It is located in Dharamsala. India. Currently there are 103 students and seven teachers. The students range in age from 11 to 53 and come from various parts of the Himalayan region, including Tibet, Nepal, Bhutan, Ladakh, Zanskar, Lahaul, Spiti, Kinnaur, Garhwal, Darjeeling, Sikkim, and Arunachal Pradesh. The Institute has a program that requires more than 17 years of intense study to complete and is equivalent to the program of study required for a doctorate in Buddhist philosophy. (www.jamchoebuddhistdialectics.org/)

**Jangchub Choeling Nunnery** ("The Abode of Dharma")—is a Tibetan Nunnery located in Mundgod, southern India. It is located between two of the largest monasteries in India, Drepung and Ganden. Venerable Thupten Lhatso La was the founder and the abbess. In 1986 a small prayer hall was built with the help of the Tibetan government-in-exile. This prayer hall was used for schooling 18 young and eager nuns, who also used it for Dharma practice in the evenings. (www.jangchubchoelingnunnery.org/) There are now more than 180 nuns.

**Khachoe Ghakyil Nunnery**—located near Boudhanath, Kathmandu, Nepal, and affiliated with Kopan Monastery. It was officially founded in 1986 by Lama Zopa Rinpoche, and in 1994, 80 nuns moved in. A geshe study program has been established here for the nuns. There are currently about 390 nuns in residence.

**Reting Samtenling Nunnery**—north of Lhasa, about three miles from Reting Monastery, currently estimated to have 150-200 nuns.

**Samten Tse Retreat Center**—a branch of Mindroling established for nuns and retreatants; located in Mussoorie, Uttarkhand, India.

**Sangak Samtenling Nunnery**—established in Tsethang in the 18th century during the reign of the Seventh Dalai Lama, in conjunction with the Tsedong Monastery (Kadam) converting to Ganden Chokhorling (Gelug).

**Shugseb (Shuksep) Nunnery**—Nyingma nunnery southwest of Lhasa

**India—Shugseb Ogyen Dzong Nunnery and College** founded in Garoh Village near Dharamsala in the early 1990s for nuns, many of whom were former political prisoners in Tibet, and who follow the Nyingma school. About 100 nuns currently undertake nine years of study in Buddhist philosophy.

**Thukche Choling Nunnery**—founded around 1865 in the Keydong Mangyul region of southern Tibet, by Drugpa Lama Sherab Dorje.

**Nepal**—Thukche Choling Nunnery was re-established in Kathmandu in 1982. Fifteen of the original nuns from Tibet were able to escape; there are currently about 120 nuns, five of whom are from the original 15. It is affiliated with Zongkar Choede Monastery in Mysore, India.

**Tsogyal Shedrup Dargyeling Nunnery**—More than 400 nuns study in this nunnery established as a complement to the Namdroling Monastery in Bylakuppe, south India. The study program here qualifies graduates to become *ani khenpos*.

# ORACLES

> "Old Asia is the cradle of the world religions, and in this hermit Kingdom [Tibet] in the heart of Asia there are many strange survivals of an age that has long passed elsewhere. You will find oracles, as of old in Greece. . . . These oracles foretell public events, whether the crops will be good or bad, whether the year will be one of war or peace, and so on. They will also enlighten you on your private concerns, whether your wife will recover from her illness, and whether your next year's trading will be successful or the reverse. Among these oracles are two chief ones which helped in the finding of the last [13th] Dalai Lama; one at Nechung, . . . and the other at the Samye Monastery [Abbot Prophet]."—Sir Charles Bell, *Portrait of a Dalai Lama: The Life and Times of the Great Thirteenth,* 1946, pp. 43-44

An oracle in the tradition of Tibetan Buddhism is a spirit that enters a human body to use it as a medium between the natural world as we know it and the spiritual realms. The mind of the human host (called a "kuten" or "kuden," meaning "the physical basis") goes into an unconscious state or trance; the deity then communicates with and consults those in attendance. It is thought that at one time there were hundreds of oracles throughout Tibet. If the deity is a being solely driven by bodhicitta (the desire to help sentient beings), and has the proper perception of events, it can be of immense value to both individuals and the Tibetan government (in the case of the two oracles discussed here). The ceremonial garments worn by the kuten while serving as a medium, as well as all the other accessories (including headdress, jewelry, weapons, etc.), would be similar to that associated with the deity that is taking possession of the kuten.

**Nechung Oracle**—The State Oracle, the Nechung Oracle, is said to have been a deity from pre-Buddhist Tibet who was overcome by Padmasambhava and compelled to serve Tibet as a protector. The deity that manifests through the kuten is Dorje Drakden (an aspect of Pehar Gyalpo), and the primary function is to protect Tibet, the Dalai Lamas, and Buddhist Dharma and its practitioners. It was in 1544 that the spirit of Nechung was first projected through a human medium. In 1642, after the Great Fifth Dalai Lama had gained both temporal and secular power in Tibet, he named Pehar Gyalpo as protector of the Tibetan government. At that time, there were about 50 monks in the Nechung Monastery. In March, 1959, the thirteenth Nechung Oracle, through kuten Ven. Lobsang Jigme, indicated very clearly the route the Dalai Lama should take in his escape to India.

The current Nechung Oracle kuten is Ven. Thupten Ngodrup, born in Tibet in 1957. He came to India with his family in 1969 after three years in Bhutan, and joined Nechung Monastery in 1971. He was officially enthroned as the 14th Nechung State Medium on September 4, 1987, in Dharamsala, India.

*Current Medium (Kuten) of the Nechung Oracle Ven. Thupten Ngodrup, 2007*

**Gadong Oracle**—Gadong is the Tibetan government's second oracle, now located in Gangchen Kyishong, Dharamsala, India. The Gadong kuten is possessed by Shinjachen, a wrathful spirit, so it is possible the kuten might experience a more painful trance experience. The Gadong Oracles, unlike those of the Nechung, are not monks, but lay people; the medium of this oracle is hereditary, passed from father to son.

## Demoness-Subduing Temples

King Songtsen Gampo (617-650 CE) took two wives, Nepalese Princess Bhrikuti, in 632, and Chinese Princess Wencheng, in 641. Each brought to Tibet as part of her dowry a statue of the Buddha. Sometime around 647, King Gampo started to build a temple, the Jokhang, to house the Nepalese Buddha, the Akshobhya. However, work that was completed on the new temple during the day was somehow undone during the night. Through divination, it was determined that an enormous demoness (Srinmo) was situated under the entire country of Tibet. And that the temple that was to be built was directly over her heart, which was located underneath a lake in the center of Lhasa. The lake first had to be drained and filled in with dirt, and then the temple could be built. In addition, twelve (or 108, depending on the source) additional "demoness-subduing temples" were built, in three groups of four at varying distances from

Lhasa, corresponding to aspects of the demoness's body—shoulders and hips first, then elbows and knees, and finally, farthest away, hands and feet. These temples would "pin down" and subdue the demoness. The symbolism is that first the demoness (that is, Tibet) needed to be tamed before being inhabited and civilized (brought the teachings of Buddha). Listed below are the temples that are identified with subduing the specific aspects of Srinmo's body.

**Main temple**—Jokhang, Lhasa, located over the demoness' heart

**Runo (Runon) Temples** (inner ring)

1. Trandruk Monastery (Yarlung Valley, Tibet)—left shoulder
2. Katsal Monastery (Tukdam Tsuklakhang) (Maldro Valley, Tibet)—right shoulder
3. Drampa Gyang (Rulak Drompagyang) (Tanakpo Valley, Tibet)—left hip
4. Tsang Dram (Yeru Tsangdram) (Tobgyal district, on banks of Phari Tsangchu River, Tibet) (unlocated)—right hip

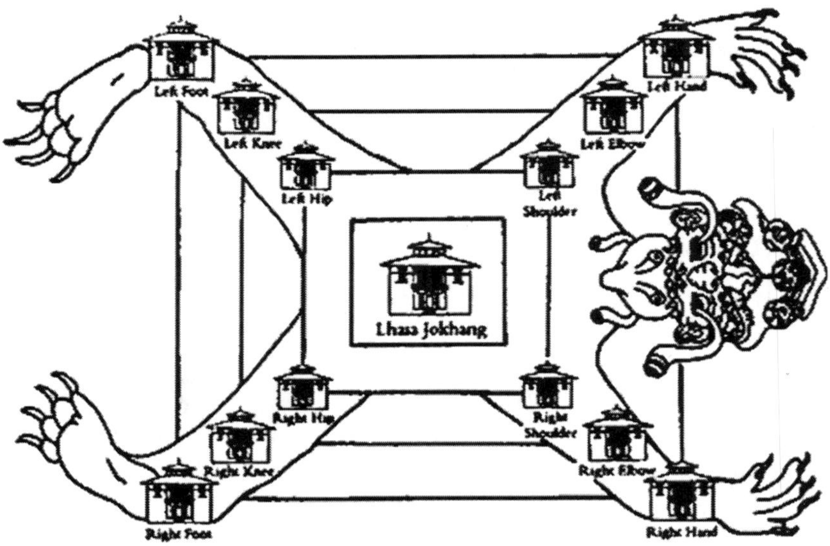


*Srinmo and the demoness-suppressing temples pinning down various aspects of her body*

**Tandrul (Thandul) Temples** (middle ring)
1. Khothing (Khomting) (Lhodrak, Tibet)—left elbow
2. Purchu (Buchu) (Kongpo, near Bayi, Tibet)—right elbow
3. Jampe-Lhakhang Temple (Mon Bumthang) (Bumthang, Bhutan)—left knee
4. Pradun Tse (Jang Traduntse) (west of Saga Dzong, Tibet)—right knee

**Yandrul (Yangdul) Temples** (outer ring)
1. Jang Tsangpa Lungnon (Tshangpa) (unlocated)—left hand
2. Dokham Longtang Dronma (Den Langtang Dronma) (Kham, Tibet)—right hand
3. Paro Kyerchu-Lhakhang Temple (Paro, Bhutan)—left foot
4. Mangyul Jamtrin (Kyirong Valley, Tibet)—right foot

*Kyerchu Lhakhang, Paro, Bhutan, 2007; left foot*

*Trandruk Monastery, Tsethang, Tibet, 2005; left shoulder*

# 10 Sacred Lakes and Mountains

## INTRODUCTION

Lakes and mountains have been considered sacred throughout history for many reasons. Lakes are seen as having healing powers: they are a source of water for crops and for drinking; they symbolize the primordial waters that humans arose from; and they are sometimes seen as the abodes of deities and spirits, that if appeased, bring about good. A mountain, as the highest point in the surrounding area, can be seen as a protector; it can be seen as the abode of gods or deities, also as protectors if they are treated with reverence and respect; it can be venerated for its beauty; if it is high enough to be snow-capped, it can be seen as the source for water, necessary for crops to thrive and the continuation of life.

Many lakes and mountains in Tibet are associated with specific deities or historical figures, and some with Tibet itself. The lakes and mountains listed here are some of the major geographic and spiritual features in Tibet that are venerated.

*tso* (Tib.)—lake
*latso* (Tib.)—soul lake

*ri* (Tib.)—mountain
*lari* (Tib.)—soul mountain
*la* (Tib.)—mountain pass

## LAKES

**Draksum Latso** (Basong Tso) (Kongpo) (3540m/11,614 ft)—soul lake of King Gesar of Ling. Padmasambhava and 14th century Nyingma lama Sangye Lingpa are also associated with this lake, thought by the local people to resemble the shape of a dragon. Lingpa built a monastery on the island in the lake.

**Lake Kokonor** (Mongolian; Tib. Tsongon) (Kangtsa, northeast Amdo) (3205m/10,515 ft, 1733 sq mi)—the largest lake on the Tibetan plateau. While not considered a sacred lake, there are a number of monasteries located on its shores.

**Lhamo Latso** (Oracle Lake) (Gyatsa) (5150m/16,896 ft)—soul lake of the Dalai Lamas is located about 160km/99 mi southeast of Lhasa. Consulted by Dalai Lamas and to aid in finding the reincarnation of the next Dalai Lama and Panchen Lama when one passes away. Letters and images are said to have been seen on the surface of the water, leading to the location of or information about the next incarnation. It is said that sitting Dalai Lamas were obliged to come to Lhamo Latso at least once during their lifetimes, and that they also might be able to see the timing and nature of their deaths in the waters of the lake.

**Lake Manasarovar** (Mapham Yutso, "unconquered," "lake conceived from the mind of God," "lake of consciousness and enlightenment") (Ngari) (4588m/15,052 ft, 412 sq km, max. depth 81m, freshwater)—located in western Tibet, just south of Mount Kailash. Source of four major Asian rivers: the Brahmaputru (Yarlung Tsangpo), the Sutlej (Langchen Tsangpo), the Karnali/Ganges (Mapcha Tsangpo), and the Indus (Senge Tsangpo). A portion of Mahatma Gandhi's ashes were reported to have been brought here and cast into the lake. Hindus consider Lake Manasarovar to be the "female energy" of the universe and the nearby Mount Kailash to be the corresponding "male energy." "Bathing in the icy sapphire water of Lake Manasarovar is considered to remove the sins of innumerable lifetimes." (www.khandro.net) The 64mi/100km *kora* takes three to five days.There are a number of monasteries around the lake to visit, among them Trugo, Gotsuck, Chiu, Langbona, Seralung, and Yerngo. At Chiu Gompa is a cave that Padmasambhava is said to have lived in during the last seven days of his life.

**Namtso (Namtso Chukmo)** ("Sky Lake," "Heavenly Lake") (Damxung) (4718m/15,479 ft, 1920 sq km, max. depth 35m, slightly saline)—highest salt lake in the world, and second largest salt lake in Tibet, after Kokonor. Located 112 km/70 mi northwest of Lhasa. There are a number of gompas to visit around the lake; a circumambulation usually takes around 18 days. On a small peninsula on the southeastern side of the lake is a

*Lake Namtso, Tibet, 2007 (also shows the Nyenchen Tanglha mountain range)*

hermitage cave, Tashidor, said to be associated with Padmasambhava and his consort, Yeshe Tsogyel.

**Phuma Yumtso** ("lake of flying turquoise") (Nakartse) (5009m/16,433 ft, 284 sq km)—located just south of Yamdrok Yumtso. According to legend, the lake flew to Tibet from the sea at the end of the universe, and it was designated by Padmasambhava as an important pilgrimage site.

**Yamdrok (Yamdrak) Yumtso (Yutso, Youtso)** ("Turquoise Lake;" sometimes referred to as "Scorpion Lake" because of its shape) (Nakartse)

*Lake Yamdrok Yumtso, Tibet, 2005 (Mt. Jangsang Lhamo, 6324m, in background)*

(4441m/14,570 ft, 754 sq km, max. depth 59m)—considered to be the soul lake of Tibet, where the soul of Tibet is thought to reside. Located 100 km/62 mi southwest of Lhasa. Should its water dry up, it is said, Tibet will no longer be habitable. There are nine islands in the lake. On one, there is a monastery, Yönpodo, and a stone footprint of Padmasambhava. The circumambulation around the Yamdrok lake/peninsula takes about seven days.

## MOUNTAINS

**Mount Amnye Machen (Machen Kongri, Machen Gangri)** (Amnye: "ancestors of the people of the region;" Machen: "the greatest source of the Yellow River"; Kangri: "snowy mountain") (Golok) (6282m/20,610 ft) —located in northeastern Tibet, the abode of Machen Pomra, sacred to both Bön and Buddhist, a very powerful protector god and one of the most important deities in Amdo (birth province of the 14th Dalai Lama). Circumambulation is done clockwise for both. Full circuit around the mountain is about 193 km/120 mi and takes about nine days. It is said by some that this kora is equal in merit to that of Mt. Kailash in western Tibet. The Yangtse (Drichu), Yellow (Machu), and Mekong (Dzachu) rivers derive their waters from the snows of this range.

**Mount Bönri** (Kongpo/eastern Tibet) (4540m/14,895 ft)—meaning "Bön Mountain," this location is highly revered as a pilgrimage location for Bönpo practitioners. There are many places around the kora relating to Tonpa Shenrab, founder of Bön. (Since this is a Bön religious site, circumambulation is usually done counter-clockwise.)

**Mount Bönri** (Ngari/western Tibet) (5995m/19,668 ft)—located southeast of Mt. Kailash and northeast of Lake Manasarovar. A contest was held long ago between Tibetan poet/saint Milarepa and Bönpo master Naro Bon-chung for possession of Mt. Kailash. The Bönpo came in second, and as a result, nearby Mount Bönri was accorded to the Bön. (Since this is a Bön religious site, circumambulation is usually done counter-clockwise.)

**Mount Dakpa (Takpa) Shelri** ("pure crystal mountain") (Tsari) (5735m/ 18,815 ft)—located in southeastern Tibet near the border with India

(Arunachal Pradesh). Highly revered pilgrimage location, particularly for the Drukpa and Drugung Kagyu lineages. Said to be a power place of the meditational deity Cakrasamvara. Having first been circumambulated in the year of the monkey, it is considered most auspicious to do a pilgrimage in the year of the monkey (which occurs every twelve years in the Tibetan calendar—2016, 2028, 2040).

**Jomolungma** (Chomolungma, "mother goddess of the world," Mt. Everest) (8848m/29,028 ft)—the highest mountain in the world, first scaled in 1953, is on the Tibet-Nepal border. While an important site, Everest does not have a kora—that is, you cannot circumambulate it. "It is, however, seen by Tibetans as the abode of one of the Five Long Life Sisters, sworn to Buddhism by Guru Rinpoche (Padmasambhava). The name of the goddess is often given as Jomolungma, . . . but that is only a contraction; her full name is Miyo-Lang-Sangma, meaning *Immovable Goddess-Protector of Bulls*. Each one of the female deities that dwell on the 5 impressive peaks overlooking Tibet's southern border has the power to confer a special boon. Miyo can bestow plentiful food, Tashi Tseringma's gift is long life, Tekar Dosangma grants luck, Chopen Dinsangma grants wealth, and Thingri Shelsangma can bestow psychic powers." (www.khandro.net) The nearest monastery on the Tibetan side is Rongbuk Monastery (clos-

*Jomolungma (Mount Everest) seen from west of Tingri, Tibet, 2005, with a Tibetan boarding school in the foreground*

est to the Tibetan town of Tingri), said to be the highest monastery in the world (5000m/16,404 ft).

**Mount Kailash** (Kailash, Kelas) (Kang Rinpoche, "precious snow mountain"; "silver mountain"; Ngari [western Tibetan dialect], Gangkar Tesi) (Ngari) (6714m/22,027 ft)—one of the holiest sites in the world to Bönpo, Buddhists, Hindus, and Jains. According to Bön adherents, their founder, Tonpa Shenrab, descended from the heavens and came down on Mt. Kailash. Buddhists see Mt. Kailash as a representation of Mt. Meru (Sumeru), the sacred mountain at the center of the universe in Tibetan cosmology. According to Hindus, Mt. Kailash is the abode of Lord Shiva, and a view of his abode will give them release from ignorance and delusion. Jains have named the mountain Astapada, and believe it to be where Rishaba, first of 24 "crossing-makers," attained liberation. Among the monasteries and gompas around Mt. Kailash are Gyandruk, Selung, Chukku, Drirapuk, and Zutrulpuk. The 32mi/54km kora takes between one and three days to complete, depending on your physical condition, and what you are carrying (a tent and other supplies can slow you down). Bön adherents circumambulate counter-clockwise; all others clockwise. It is said that "In Tibetan Buddhist tradition, circumambulation of Kailash and Lake Manasarovar in the Year of the Horse, especially during Sagadawa, brings far greater merit than at any other time. . . . [The Year of the Horse occurs in 2014, 2026, and 2038]." (www.khandro.net) Mt. Kailash is not a mountain that one climbs—it is considered too sacred. Milarepa, 11th-century Tibetan poet and saint and Bön master Naro Bon-chung fought each other for Mount Kailash. Milarepa's defeat of the shaman displaced Bön as the primary religion of Tibet, firmly establishing Buddhism in its place. (www.sacredsites.com)

**Mount Kawa Karpo** (Dechen) (6740m/22,112 ft)—highest in a line of five glacial peaks, all above 5400m/17700 ft. One of 25 meditation sites in eastern Tibet associated with Padmasambhava, this one symbolizing the body aspect of speech of the Buddha. The sheep year in the Tibetan calendar, occurring every twelve years (2015, 2027, 2039), is considered an auspicious time for pilgrimage to the Kawa Karpo region.

**Lapchi Gang** (Tingri) (7367m/24,169 ft)—one of the holiest pilgrimage sites associated with revered saint Milarepa, who lived here and established a number of meditation caves. Demchok (the wrathful manifestation of Buddha Shakyamuni) is supposed to have subdued local gods and created a Buddhist sanctuary in the region. Peaks in this range are the abodes of meditational deities Avalokiteshvara, Cakrasamvara, Manjushri, and Vajrapani.

**Mount Nyenchen Tanglha** (Damzhung) (7162m/23,497 ft)—mountain, and mountain range, located northwest of Lhasa, on the south side of Lake Namtso. Nyenchen Tanglha was originally a Bönpo deity; he is one of the most important protector guardians of the Buddhadharma. It is said that he is also the protector of Marpo Ri, the hill in Lhasa on which the Potala is built. (Pictured at Lake Namtso, page 153)

**Mount Nyenpo Yurtse** (Golok) (5933m/19,465 ft)—revered as the birthplace of the Golok tribes. Nyenpo Yurtse is the highest peak of the Bayankala Mountain Range; on top of it there are 3 snow-capped peaks, which look like petals of a flower. Marshland and glacial lakes surround the mountain. The 6-day pilgrimage circuit is about 130 km/80 mi.

**Mount Yarlha (Yala) Shampo** (Yarlung) (6636m/21,771 ft)—abode of protector Yarlha Shampo, one of the four chief mountain gods in Tibet. Subdued by Padmasambhava with a mudra as the god projected himself as a white yak; he was then bound to protect the Dharma.

**Mount Zhara Lhatse** (Minyak) (5820m/19,094 ft)—another of the 25 revered Padmasambhava sites in eastern Tibet, this representing the body aspect of the Buddha mind. Many medicinal hot springs are located on the southwest side of the mountain. According to Bön tradition, this mountain is regarded as an offspring of Nyenchen Tanglha.

# 11 Language and Literature

## Language

**Pali** Pali belongs to the Indic group of the Indo-Iranian subfamily of the Indo-European family of languages. It is the language that was used in the time that the Tipitaka (Buddhist scriptures or canon) were committed to writing (c. 25 BCE), and became the main written language of Buddhists at that time. Up until that time, the teachings of the Buddha were an oral tradition only. With the introduction of Hinduism in India, the use of Pali declined. Pali is still used as a liturgical language by Buddhists in Sri Lanka, Myanmar (Burma), and Thailand.

**Sanskrit** Sanskrit is based on a similar root family as Pali, coming from the Indo-Aryan subgroup of the Indo-European family of languages. Sanskrit is the language from which Hindu is based. Buddhism and Hinduism have much in common, so there is much Sanskrit used in Buddhism. Many of the deities, the rituals, and terms of Tibetan Buddhism have their root in Hinduism/Sanskrit.

**Tibetan** Tibetan is a member of the Tibeto-Burman subfamily of the Sino-Tibetan family. The written Tibetan language was devised in the seventh century CE, and was created for the purpose of translating the Sanskrit Buddhist scriptures in India into a form that the monastic community developing in Tibet could use. King Songtsen Gampo sent one of his ministers, Thonmi Sambhota, to India (or some say Kashmir) in 632 CE, to study Sanskrit and Buddhist literature, and to gather materials for constructing an alphabet for the Tibetan language. When he returned, he is said to have worked at a number of locations around Lhasa as he developed the written language. There is a stone at Pabongka Monastery, north of Lhasa, which still exists and upon which, it is said, is inscribed the first writing in the Tibetan language of *Om Mani Padme Hum*.

**Wylie** In 1959, Turrell Wylie published "A Standard System of Tibetan Transcription" in the *Harvard Journal of Asiatic Studies*. This format of transliteration has been widely used in romanization of Tibetan for non-Tibetan speakers. It is a system for representing Tibetan using the character set of a standard English-language typewriter or computer keyboard.

## LITERATURE

### The Canon

**Can · on** 1. an authoritative list of books accepted as Holy Scripture 2. a sanctioned or accepted group or body of related works (from Merriam-Webster Collegiate Dictionary)

There are three widely recognized collections of Buddhist scriptures in the world today: the Pali Canon, the Chinese Canon, and the Tibetan Canon. Called the Tipitaka (Pali, *ti*, three, *pitaka*, basket; Sans. Tripitaka) ("Three Baskets"), the canon is composed of the Vinaya-pitaka (Basket of Discipline [monastic rules]), the Sutta-pitaka (Basket of Discourses), and the Abhidhamma-pitaka (Basket of Higher Teachings).

Why baskets? A number of different explanations have been given:

> ". . . Scholars imagine that originally the three types of text were each kept in a separate basket and thus their name evolved." (www.suite101.com)
>
> ". . . bunches of these [sewn-together leaves] were then stored in baskets." (uwacadweb.uwyo.edu)
>
> ". . . the name refers to the baskets passed from hand to hand by construction workers, and is thus a metaphor for the passing on of tradition." (www.encyclopedia.com)
>
> "The word 'basket' in the 'three baskets,' denoting the Buddhist canon,

does not derive from baskets as storage receptacles of manuscripts, but as means for transportation." (www.birgitkellner.org)

***The Pali Canon*** is considered to be the most complete collection of the Buddha's words. It is the complete scripture of the Theravadan school, and is the only set of scriptures preserved in the language of its composition. It was first written down during the Fourth Buddhist Council in Sri Lanka, c. 25 BCE (or 83 BCE, depending on the source), and was written in Pali "on strips of dried palm leaves cut into rectangles and etched with a metal stylus and rubbed over with carbon ink. A thread was passed through the pages to keep them in order and elaborately painted wooden covers fixed at the ends." (www.thebuddhistsociety.org/library/Scriptures.html)

***The Chinese Canon***, called "Great Scripture Store," had its first complete printing in 983 CE (or in 1410/11 in Peking, depending on the source), and included 1076 texts in 480 cases. "The Chinese canon preserves the Vinaya texts of as many as seven different schools. . . . The Council of Vesali (the Second Buddhist Council) saw the breakup of [the] original body [of the sangha] and as many as eighteen separate schools were known to exist by about the first century [BCE]." (www.buddhanet.net) "The . . . manuscript provided the basis for the first xylographic or woodblock print of the [Kangyur], the Yongle edition made in Beijing in 1410. At this point the printing technology first invented by the Chinese largely for the purposes of propagating Buddhist literature was enthusiastically adopted by the Tibetans, who were to continue to use it up to the twentieth century." (www.thdl.org)

***The Tibetan Canon*** is composed of two parts, the *Kangyur* (the words of the Buddha) and the *Tengyur* (commentaries on the words of the Buddha). "The Tibetan Buddhist canon developed over time as Buddhist texts from India and other areas were translated into Tibetan. There were two main periods of translation activity in Tibet. The first began in the seventh century and came to an end in 842 CE with the collapse of the Tibetan Empire. The second period began in the late tenth century and [lasted] into the fourteenth century, though this activity had begun to trail off since the twelfth century due to the Muslim invasions of India and the resulting decline of Buddhism there. . . . By the close of the first millennium . . . towards the end of its life in its homeland, Indian Buddhism was a complex amalgam of three strains—Mainstream [Theravedan], Mahayana, and Vajrayana—and it is this multi-layered tradition and its equally complex scriptural heritage which the Tibetans have inherited and passed down to the present day." (www.thdl.org) Over time, the then-Kadampa monastery at Narthang came to be the repository of many different versions of the Kangyur. The emergence of a Narthang edition "was the result of the gathering in of texts from various monastic libraries . . . and at the same time the culmination of several centuries of collecting and cataloging activity at a number of centers. . . . [A]s complete entities the texts of the [Kangyur] are thought to be powerful and transformative, as physical objects when seen or touched or as sounds when uttered or heard, whether or not intellectual understanding takes place. And if one text can be powerful, then the complete set of them, the entire canon, represents a total power source of considerable importance." (www.thdl.org)

***Kangyur***—defined as "translations of the pronouncements [of the Buddha]" and consists of texts that are attributed to the Buddha (or in some cases by his disciples, but with his blessing). (www.thdl.org) The Kangyur is composed of the following, according to the Narthang edition (www.buddhanet.net):

1. Vinaya: 13 volumes (monastic discipline)
2. Prajnaparamita: 21 volumes
3. Avatamsaka: 6 volumes
4. Ratnakuta: 6 volumes (a set of 49 Mahayana Sutras)
5. Sutra: 30 volumes (270 texts, 75% Mahayana, 25% Hinayana)
6. Tantra: 22 volumes (more than 300 texts)

***Tengyur***—defined as "translations of treatises [on the pronouncements of the Buddha] and consists of texts attributed to subsequent learned and realized masters of Buddhism [mostly in India]. . . . The history of the Tengyur has received far less study than that of the Kangyur, though further study may reveal more variations than expected." (www.thdl.org) The Tengyur is composed of the following (www.buddhanet.net; here-and-now.org):

1. Sutras: 1 volume (64 texts)
2. Commentaries on the Tantras: 86 volumes (3055 texts)

3. Commentaries on the Sutras: 137 volumes (567 texts)
    a. Prajnaparamita commentaries: 16 volumes
    b. Madhyamika treatises: 17 volumes
    c. Yogacara treatises: 29 volumes
    d. Abhidharma: 8 volumes
    e. Miscellaneous: 4 volumes
    f. Vinaya commentaries: 16 volumes
    g. Tales and dramas, including Jataka tales (the Buddha's previous lives): 4 volumes
    h. Technical treatises: logic (21 volumes), grammar (1 volume), lexicography and poetics (1 volume), medicine (5 volumes), chemistry and sundry (1 volume), supplement (14 volumes)

## Bardo Thodol

*Bardo Thodol—The Great Book of Natural Liberation Through Understanding in the Between* (alternate title: *Liberation Through Hearing in the Intermediate State*) (or *The Tibetan Book of the Dead* [as it is known in the West])—composed by Padmasambhava in the 8th century; discovered by tertön Karma Lingpa in the 14th century; translated by Francesca Fremantle, Robert A. F. Thurman, Gyurme Dorje, and others in the 20th century.

*Bardo* in Tibetan means "between state." Most often it refers to the time between death and rebirth. However, "the late Chogyam Trungpa Rinpoche explained that . . . the *Bardo Thodol* can be read as a guide to life experiences as well as a guide to the time between death and rebirth." (buddhism.about.com/od/vajrayanabuddhism/a/bardothodol.htm?p = 1)

"The so-called *Tibetan Book of the Dead* has been renowned for centuries as a classic of Buddhist wisdom and religious thought. Composed in the eighth century, it is intended to prepare the soul for the trials and transformations of the afterworld. Its profound message is that the art of dying is as important as the art of living. Drawing on Tibetan spiritual traditions, it shows us the workings of the mind in its various manifestations—terrifying and comforting, wrathful and beautiful—which appear more clearly after death in the consciousness of the deceased. By recognizing these manifestations, we can attain a state of enlightenment, both in this existence and the existence to come." (cover copy, *The Tibetan Book of the Dead*, 1998)

“The *Bardo Thodol* traditionally is read to a dying or dead person, so that he or she may be liberated from the cycle of samsara through hearing. The dead or dying person is guided through encounters in the bardo with wrathful and peaceful deities, . . . which are to be understood as projections of the mind.” (www.buddhism.about.com/od/vajrayanabuddhism/a/bardothodol.htm?p = 1)

“Since its first English translation in 1927, the Tibetan guide to spiritual and mental liberation called the *Bardo Thodol* had been known in the West as *The Tibetan Book of the Dead*. . . . W. Y. Evans-Wentz coined the English title for the 1927 edition on the basis of analogies he perceived with the Egyptian funerary text *The Book of Coming Forth By Day*, known in the West as *The Egyptian Book of the Dead*. Both the Tibetan and Egyptian books discuss death and its aftermath. Yet their views of death are sufficiently different from the Judeo-Christian tradition that the English titles are quite misleading.” (www.deathreference.com/Sy-Vi/Tibetan-Book-of-the-Dead.html)

## *Gesar of Ling* Epic

The *Gesar of Ling* epic is to Tibet what *The Odyssey* and *The Iliad* are to Greece and the Arthurian legend is to England.

King Gesar (Tib. “Lotus Temple”) is the name of a mythical hero who inspired the greatest epic of Tibetan Buddhism. This epic was spread in the form of folk tales as far as Mongolia and was transmitted by professional singers or bards. The eastern Tibetan kingdom of Ling is given as the homeland of Gesar. The Gesar legends arose in the 11th century, at a time when Buddhism began to prevail in the belief of the people over the indigenous Bön religion, and the main theme of the epic seems to be the battle of Gesar against evil (i.e. Bön). In these conflicts on behalf of the qualities of Buddhism, Gesar is regarded as the embodiment of Avalokiteshvara and of Padmasambhava [Guru Rinpoche] and his heros as incarnations of the mahasiddhas. Today Gesar is venerated as a warrior god and a god of wealth, and his consort as a dakini. (www.buddhistlinks.org/Gesar.htm)

There is no definitive version. The Gesar stories are still being told throughout the Himalayan region (Ladakh, Mongolia, eastern, western, and central

Tibet), and there are differing versions according to the particular culture or region. The epic existed as an oral tradition for generations before being written down. It is said to be twenty-five times longer than *The Iliad*, and has about a million lines (or a million verses, according to another source). There are about 180 episodes, of which 30 are termed "long episodes." Each long episode takes about three months to recite. (www.timsheppard.co.uk; www.Tibettravel.info)

## The Jataka Tales

The Jataka Tales ("Birth Stories") tell stories of the Buddha's previous lifetimes, as told by the Buddha himself. Jataka, which means "birth-related," are contained in the Buddhist canon, the Tipitaka. There are reported to be 547 tales, which do not represent all of the Buddha's previous millions of lives.

All the Jataka tales illustrate one of the 10 Perfections, or "Paramitas," those traits that lead one to Buddhahood. "The stories illustrate Buddhist virtues through stories of these incarnations, both human and animal—particularly the virtues of charity, compassion, and self-sacrifice." (orias.berkeley.edu/2009/Jataka.htm) The primary perfection is generosity (Sans. *dana*), and many of the Jataka tales illustrate this perfection. (See page 194 for a list of the 10 Paramitas.)

# 12 Tibetan Names and Their Meanings

When a Tibetan is born, it is common for his or her parents to confer with a local monk or lama to choose a name for the child. This is the person's birth name.

When one takes Refuge, a refuge name, or Dharma name, is often bestowed upon one by a teacher. It is sometimes given by a teacher who does not know you well, and hence it then tends to reflect the lineage or tradition from which the teacher comes. If the name is given by someone who knows you or knows something about you, it is often derived with your personal qualities in mind.

If one takes a Bodhisattva Vow, another name is often given.

If one has been accepted into a monastic order, a person will receive one or more ordination names.

During certain empowerments, a Tantric ritual name (*samaya*) is given. This name, unlike the other names, is kept secret. It is explained at the time it is given, and is thought to be the name of one's fully realized being (a Buddha's name).

The following list (from www.khandro.net) lists the most common Tibetan names, a pronunciation guide, and the meaning of the name.

| Name | Pronunciation | Meaning |
|---|---|---|
| Chodak | CHO-dahk | Dharma Spreader |
| Choden | CHO-den | One who is devout, religious |
| Choegyal | CHO-gyel | Dharma king |
| Choejor | CHO-jar | Spiritual wealth |

| Name | Pronunciation | Meaning |
|---|---|---|
| Chophel | CHO-pel | The flourishing of the Dharma |
| Dawa | DAH-wah | Moon, Monday |
| Dhargey | DAR-gyeh | Progress, development, spreading |
| Dolma | DOL-ma | Tara (goddess) |
| Dorje | DOR-jeh | Vajra, indestructible; diamond/ thunderbolt |
| Gephel | Ge-PEL | Increase of merit |
| Gyaltsen | GYEL-tsen | Victory Banner |
| Jampa | JAHM-pa | Loving-kindness (Tib. for Maitreya) |
| Jamyang | JAHM-yahng | Gentle voice (Tib. for Manjushri) |
| Jinpa | JIN-pa | Generosity |
| Jungney | JOONG-nay | Source, origin |
| Kalsang | KEL-sahng | Good fortune |
| Karma | KAR-mah | Action, deed |
| Kunchen | KUN-chen | All-knowing |
| Lhamo | LHA-mo | Goddess |
| Lhundup | HLUN-d(r)oop | Spontaneously accomplished |
| Lobsang | LO-sahng | Noble-minded |
| Ngawang | NGAH-wahng | Powerful speech |
| Ngodup | NGO-d(r)oop | Attainment, accomplishment |
| Norbu | NOR-boo | Jewel |
| Palden | PEL-den | Glorious |
| Pema | PEH-mah | Lotus |
| Phuntsok | PUN-tsok | Excellence |
| Rabten | RAHB-ten | Steadfast |
| Rigzin | RIG-zin | Wisdom holder |
| Rinchen | RIN-chen | Precious, gem (great value) |
| Samdup | SAHM-d(r)oop | Fulfillment (of one's wishes) |
| Sangye | SAHN-gyeh | Buddha |
| Sonam | SO-nahm | Merit |
| Tashi | TAH-shee | Auspicious, fortunate |
| Tenzin | TEN-zin | Holder of the teachings |
| Thekchen | TEK-chen | Mahayana |
| Thokmay | TOK-meh | Unobstructed, unhindered |
| Thubten | TOOB-ten | The Buddha's teaching |
| Tinley | T(R)IN-leh | Enlightened activity |

| Name | Pronunciation | Meaning |
|---|---|---|
| Tsering | TSEH-ring | Long life |
| Tseten | TSEH-ten | Stable life |
| Tsewang | TSEH-wahng | Life empowerment |
| Wangchuk | WAHNG-chook | Lord, mighty |
| Wangdak | WAHNG-dahk | Lordly, protector |
| Wangdue | WAHNG-doo | Subduer |
| Wangmo | WAHNG-mo | Power |
| Yonten | YON-ten | Good qualities |

## NAMES IN THE TIBETAN BUDDHIST CULTURE

*By Ven. Tenzin Gephel*, a resident monk at Namgyal Monastery Institute of Buddhist Studies, Ithaca, NY. This article is used with the kind permission of Ven. Tenzin Gephel.

In Buddhism it is said that everything is imputed by name and thought and nothing exists inherently. Names in Tibetan Buddhist culture are given intentionally. Some examples of sources of names given to children are the Dalai Lama's name, common types of names, and the names of the four major Tibetan Buddhist sects.

In Tibet there are two main sources for personal names. People get their names from either their parents or from great lamas. A lama is a great teacher or holy person. It is very common for people to request names for their children from lamas. Many people nowadays request names for their children from His Holiness the 14th Dalai Lama. Some parents request names while the child is still in the mother's womb. When people go to the Dalai Lama to request a name for their child, he gives a name which is then written on a piece of blessed thread. These blessed items serve as protection from physical and mental negative factors such as negative thoughts or bad dreams. Blessed pills are made from different herbal substances. In brief, the giving of these blessed items is done in order to give the child an auspicious beginning to life and with prayers for the child to develop a healthy body and mind. We Tibetans feel that these blessings are created through the combination of religious power and the compassionate mind of the holy person.

My name is Tenzin Gephel. I was named after Tenzin Gyatso, who is the Fourteenth Dalai Lama. My first name, "Tenzin," means "holder of Buddhist doctrine," and my second name, "Gephel," means "increase of merit." Tenzin is a very popular name among Tibetans because it is the first name of the Dalai Lama. When I was born, I was named Nyima Dhamdul by my parents. Later my parents asked the Dalai Lama to name me. Then Tenzin Gephel became my name. I was very small and not a monk at that time. Although people call me by the first name Tenzin or by both names Tenzin Gephel, I prefer Gephel because it is less common among Tibetans.

I should mention that Tibetans usually do not have or use family names. For instance, in the West, the Smith family would all have the last name of Smith. The family might consist of Bob Smith, Mary Smith, Joe Smith, and Susan Smith. In a Tibetan family, all of the first and last names of all members might be different. The family might consist of Tenzin Wangdu, Dicky Dolma, Dawa Paljor, and Karma Dorje.

In Tibet we do not usually refer to the Dalai Lama by that term. "Dalai" is a Mongolian word and was a title given by the Mongolian King Altan Khan to Sonam Gyatso, who later was named the Third Dalai Lama. Sonam Gyatso was a highly respected Buddhist teacher and friend of the Mongolian king. There was a popular saying about the king and the Third Dalai Lama: "In the sky: sun and moon. On earth: two great symbols of generosity." In appreciation to Sonam Gyatso for his Buddhist teachings, the king, out of respect, bestowed on him the title "Dalai Lama." "Dalai" in Mongolian means "Ocean of Wisdom." A very close spiritual relationship developed between Tibet and Mongolia. Since then the name "Dalai Lama" has been used for all succeeding Dalai Lamas and was also applied to two predecessors of Sonam Gyatso.

The current Dalai Lama is the fourteenth. His Holiness the Fourteenth Dalai Lama's personal name is Tenzin Gyatso and was given to him by his religious tutor. "Gyatso" in Tibetan means "Ocean of Enlightened Qualities." Tibetans refer to His Holiness the Dalai Lama by other names such as "Yeshi Norbu," which means "Wish-fulfilling Gem," and "Kundun," which simply means "The Presence." The Dalai Lama is the religious and political leader of Tibet. The Dalai Lama is currently leading his people [from exile] in their efforts for a free Tibet using methods of nonviolence based on great love and compassion according to the Buddhist teachings. He was awarded the Nobel Peace Prize in 1989.

Names are given to all people and things in order to differentiate who or what they are. Naturally nobody wants to have a bad name or reputation. We all want to be referred to by something nice. In Tibet, a person who gives a name to a child, in accordance with Buddhist tradition, always choses a name with an auspicious meaning in order to create positive predisposition for the future of the child. Many people in Tibet have names related to male or female Buddhas or enlightened beings. Some names, such as "Tenzin" or "Dawa," can be both male or female, although females often take the name of a female Buddha or deity such as "Dolma" (Tara in Sanskrit), which means the "one who liberates others from suffering." There are also female names such as "Dicky Dolma" which means "one who is healthy, happy and liberates other by leading them to Nirvana." Some names such as "Dawa" have several different meanings. "Dawa" means both "moon" and "Monday." "Dawa" can be given to a child who is born on a Monday or it can convey the symbolic meaning of one who "gives light and removes darkness" as moonlight does. People are also named after simple Buddhist terms such as "sherap," which is a word meaning wisdom, or "sopa," which means patience. Tibetan names can come from important religious symbols such as the "Dorje," which symbolizes indestructibility, compassion, and skillful means.

In Tibetan culture, people sometimes change their names. For example, when someone becomes a monk or nun, they are given a new monastic name. Then there are occasions such as when someone becomes sick and medical treatments do not cure the person over a long period of time. At that time, according to a lama's advice, the sick person may have a name change in order to keep away obstacles and harm. When I was in school, I got some kind of mysterious pain in my upper back and chest. I had to go home to live with my parents for special care. It was a very painful sickness. My parents tried their best to treat it. I tried modern treatment and ancient Tibetan herbal medicine for many days, months, and a year. The doctors didn't discover what kind of sickness it was. So the treatment seemed not so helpful. At the same time during those long periods of sickness my parents often asked others to perform many ritual prayers according to Buddhist traditions. Meanwhile my parents brought me to consult with Dhamo Loche Rinpoche, who still lives in Dharamsala. He is one of the greatest lamas among several who escaped from Tibet in 1959. Dhamo Loche Rinpoche advised me to change my name. I was named after him, Losang Tenzin, which means good-hearted dharma holder. But I prefer to use Tenzin Gephel for the rest of my life. It is very auspicious for my present and future life to have this name. After I recovered from that sickness, I reused my name Tenzin Gephel. When I received the monastic vows from the Dalai Lama, H.H. did not change my name Tenzin Gephel into another name because he gave this name to me when I was very small and I became a monk. Another solution is that the sick or troubled person may take a name intentionally unpleasant such as Shilog. It means "one who seems likely to have died but come back to life."

Since the 7th century, Buddhism has served as the basis of Tibetan culture, ethics, and almost every other aspect of Tibetan life. Within Tibetan Buddhism there are four great traditions: Nyingma, Kagyu, Sakya, and Geluk. "Nyingma" means old or early and is one part of Tantric Buddhism that came to Tibet from India first during the seventh century. It is called "Nyingma" because it is the oldest form of Tibetan Buddhism. Subsequently Buddhism was suppressed for a period of seventy years until religion reemerged in the year 978. The great Buddhist traditions founded after this time are referred to as the "New Tantric Buddhist traditions." The second tradition to appear, and the first of the new systems, is the Kagyu tradition. This name means "stream of oral teaching." The Kagyu tradition was passed through a long line of teachers from Vajradhara to the great Tilopa, to Naropa, to Marpa and so forth in an oral manner. The third tradition is the Sakya. "Sakya" means "place of white earth." The founder of this tradition was the master Konchok Gyalpo. In looking to establish his monastery, he examined many places but finally he decided on a place on the side of a mountain called Ponpori that was covered with a whitish earth and built his monastery there. After that the tradition he founded was called "Sakya" for the white earth. The fourth and newest tradition is the Geluk tradition. "Geluk" means meritorious or virtuous tradition. "Ge" means virtue and "luk" means system or tradition. Originally this tradition had the name "Ganden" because that is the name of the monastery founded by the great Lama Tsongkhapa who also founded this tradition. This great teacher lived five hundred years ago.

Names are very important in Tibetan Buddhist culture. In order to begin to understand Buddhist principles of names one could examine areas ranging from children's names or common names to the Dalai Lama's names and names of different sects of Tibetan Buddhism.

# 13 Quotations/ Tibetan Sayings

## Sayings Attributed to The Buddha

Believe nothing merely because you have been told it. Do not believe what your teacher tells you merely out of respect for the teacher. But whatsoever, after due examination and analysis, you find to be kind, conducive to the good, the benefit, the welfare of all beings—that doctrine believe and cling to, and take it as your guide.

Do not believe in anything simply because you have heard it. Do not believe in anything simply because it is spoken and rumored by many. Do not believe in anything simply because it is found written in your religious books. Do not believe in anything merely on the authority of your teachers and elders. Do not believe in traditions because they have been handed down for many generations. But after observation and analysis, when you find that anything agrees with reason and is conducive to the good and benefit of one and all, then accept it and live up to it.

Believe nothing, no matter where you read it, or who said it—even if I have said it—unless it agrees with your own reason and your own common sense.

The gift of Truth excels all other gifts.

If you find truth in any religion, accept that truth!

One who sees my teachings sees me.

In this world hatred can never be appeased by hatred. Hatred can be appeased by love. This is the eternal law.

You will not be punished for your anger, you will be punished by your anger.

Do not dwell in the past. Do not dream of the future. Concentrate the mind on the present moment.

All conditioned things are impermanent. When one sees this in Wisdom, then one becomes dispassionate towards the painful.

Fools wait for a lucky day, but every day is a lucky day for an industrious man.

All things appear and disappear because of the concurrence of causes and conditions. Nothing ever exists entirely alone; everything is in relation to everything else.

The secret of happiness lies in mind's release from worldly ties.

Tolerance, patience, and understanding are the highest virtues every man should develop.

Blessed are they who earn their living without hurting others.

Vast learning, perfect handicraft, a highly trained discipline, and pleasant speech—this is a blessing.

Do not associate with fools, Associate with the wise, Honor those who are worthy of honor—this is a blessing.

He who harms the innocent must bear the fruit of his act, like dust flung against the wind.

The man who is a debauchee, a drunkard, a gambler, and who squanders whatsoever he possess—is the cause of his own downfall.

Health is the greatest wealth; contentment is the greatest happiness.

Let a man apply himself to what is proper before he preaches others. Though one should conquer a million men in battlefield, yet indeed, he is the noblest victor who has conquered himself.

Even as a solid rock is unshaken by the wind, so are the wise unshaken by praise or blame.

As rain penetrates an ill-thatched house, so lust penetrates an undeveloped mind.

Do not depend on others; develop your self-confidence.

Do not forget your spiritual development while serving others.

Wheresoever fear arises, it arises in the mind of the fool, not in that of the wise man.

One should not accept anything with mere faith; but one should use one's common sense and intelligence before accepting anything.

What you are is what you have been, and what you will be is what you do now.

Practice the Middle Path without going to extremes; practice it in every aspect of your life.

Radiate your loving-kindness to every living being without any discrimination.

He who leads a righteous way of life, will find that noble virtue itself to protect and guide him.

He who never thinks of anything as 'mine,' who does not feel the lack of anything, he is never worried by a sense of loss.

According to the seed that's sown, So is the fruit you reap there from.

The doer of good will gather good, The doer of evil, evil reaps.

We are the results of what we were and we will be the results of what we are.

Everything is changeable, everything appears and disappears; there is not blissful peace until one passes beyond the agony of life and death.

Your misdeeds were not committed by your parents, nor by your brothers and sisters, nor by your friends nor kinsfolk, nor by recluses and priests. It is you who are responsible.

Holding anger is like grasping a hot coal with the intent of throwing it at someone else; you are the one who gets burned.

Do not disregard the accumulation of goodness, saying, "This will come to nothing." By the gradual falling of raindrops, a jar is filled.

However many holy words you read, how many you speak, what good will they do you if you do not act upon them?

Acquire wisdom, practice devotion, morality, and charity.

We are shaped by our thoughts; we become what we think.
When the mind is pure, joy follows like a shadow that never leaves.

The accomplishment of persistent effort, the accomplishment of watchfulness, good friendship, and balanced livelihood leads to happiness.

Whatever action you intend to perform by body, speech, or mind, first think: "Will this action be harmful to myself or to others or to both? Will this action produce suffering?" If it is harmful, avoid doing it.

He who is controlled in hand, controlled in foot, controlled in speech, and possessing the highest control (of mind), delighted within, composed, solitary and contented, him they call a bhikkhu.

Nothing is so fragile as action without prayer.

If a man's mind becomes pure, his surroundings will also become pure.

How can one ever know anything if they are too busy thinking.

Be lamps to yourselves. And hold fast to the Truth.

Just as a picture is drawn by an artist, surroundings are created by the activities of the mind.

Your worst enemy cannot harm you as much as your own unguarded thoughts.

See the truth, and you will see me.

There are two mistakes one can make along the road to truth . . . not going all the way, and not starting.

You are all the Buddha. (last words of the Buddha)

## SAYINGS ATTRIBUTED TO HIS HOLINESS THE 14TH DALAI LAMA

Spend some time alone every day.

Remember that not getting what you want is sometimes a wonderful stroke of luck.

The purpose of our lives is to be happy.

This is my simple religion. There is no need for temples; no need for complicated philosophy. Our own brain, our own heart is our temple; the philosophy is kindness.

Our prime purpose in this life is to help others. And if you can't help them, at least don't hurt them.

We can never obtain peace in the world if we neglect the inner world and don't make peace with ourselves. World peace must develop of inner peace.

Follow the three Rs: Respect for self, Respect for others, and Responsibility for all your actions.

When you lose, don't lose the lesson.

Details of various practices can differ to suit the western mentality; and not only to suit the western mentality in general but also to suit the individual practitioner's disposition.

Without a teacher, it is best to limit oneself to small and simple meditations.

I look on religion as medicine. For different complaints, doctors will prescribe different remedies. Therefore, because not everyone's spiritual "illness" is the same, different spiritual medicines are required.

Media people should have long noses like an elephant to smell out politicians, mayors, prime ministers, and businessmen. We need to know the reality, the good and the bad, not just the appearance.

Religion is like going out to dinner with friends. Everyone may order something different, but everyone can still sit at the same table.

Through violence you may "solve" one problem, but you sow the seeds for another.

It seems whenever I travel somewhere, it always creates some inconvenience. So, I am very sorry. But hopefully, it is not my mistake.

It is under the greatest adversity that there exists the greatest potential for doing good, both for oneself and others.

Anything that contradicts experience and logic should be abandoned.

The time has come to educate people, to cease all quarrels in the name of religion, culture, countries, different political or economic systems. Fighting is useless. Suicide.

The ultimate authority must always rest with the individual's own reason and critical analysis.

## SAYINGS OF OTHERS

If you want to know your past life, look into your present condition;
If you want to know your future life, look at your present condition.
—Padmasambhava

When you have an itch, you scratch. But not to itch at all is better than any amount of scratching.—Nagarjuna

Because there are no phenomena which are not dependent arisings, there are no phenomena which are not void.—Nagarjuna

My religion is to live and die without regret.—Milarepa

Know emptiness, Be compassionate.—Milarepa

To cherish oneself brings only downfall.—Guru Puja

To talk to one who cannot understand and reply easily is like one simpleton babbling to another.—Samding Dorje Phagmo

Things are not what they appear to be: nor are they otherwise.
—Surangama Sutra

. . . the more attached we are to our possessions and relationships in the world, the more important and necessary we find them, the more pain we encounter when they change or cease—as they always do.
—H.E. Chagdud Tulku Rinpoche (in Johnson, *The Book of Tibetan Elders*)

Anything that is created must sooner or later die. Enlightenment is permanent because we have not produced it; we have merely discovered it.—Chogyam Trungpa

The recognition of impermanence is the key to freedom from fear of remaining forever stuck in a situation, habit, or pattern.—Dzongsar Jamyang Khyentse Rinpoche

All happiness comes from the desire for others to be happy. All misery comes from the desire for oneself to be happy.—Shantideva

When it is impossible for anger to arise within you, you find no outside enemies anywhere. An outside enemy exists only if there is anger inside.—Lama Zopa Rinpoche

A sick body with a good heart is more beneficial to future lives than a fit, healthy body that is used for self-cherishing.—Lama Zopa Rinpoche

When you check your own mind properly, you stop blaming others for your problems.—Lama Thubten Yeshe

One action produces a reaction; that is karma.—Lama Thubten Yeshe

Buddhist meditation doesn't necessarily mean sitting cross-legged with your eyes closed. Simple observing how your mind is responding to the sense world as you go about your business—walking, talking, shopping, whatever—can be a really perfect meditation and bring a perfect result.—Lama Thubten Yeshe

The narrow mind rejects; wisdom accepts.—Lama Thubten Yeshe

There has always been the pure nature of mind and there has always been fundamental ignorance in the mind.—Kalu Rinpoche

For as long as space endures, And for as long as sentient beings remain, Until then may I too abide, To Dispel the misery of the world.
—Shantideva

## **TIBETAN PROVERBS** (unattributed)

You, yourself, must make the effort. The Buddhas are only teachers.

Goodness speaks in a whisper, evil shouts.

Excellent people are honored wherever they go.

Build a dam before the flood.

Better than the young man's knowledge is the old man's experience.

Sow good and you will reap good; sow bad and you will reap bad.
You don't have to cut down a tree to get its fruit.

If the inner mind is not deluded, the outer deeds will not be wrong.

The life of every being is like a bubble in water.

The wise pursue understanding; fools follow the reports of others.

Honor a king in his own land; honor a wise man everywhere.

Nothing is ever difficult once you get use to it.

One cannot succeed with two minds; one cannot sew with two needles.

The goal will not be reached if the right distance has not been traveled.

Everyone dies, but no one is dead.

Drops of water make the ocean.

Habits of one's birth follow one to the grave.

He gets peace who is silent.

Good in the beginning, good in the middle, good in the end.

Words are neither sharp nor cutting, but they can cut the heart of a human being.

The deliciousness of the sweets is due to the kindness of the butter.

Of two witnesses, take the one that is most important.

It is better to live one year in the life of a tiger than 100 years in the life of a sheep.

If a problem can be solved, then what's the point in worrying?
If a problem can't be solved, then worrying will do no good.

Beat the monastery dog and you will incur the resentment of the priest.

He who curses others a hundred times collects a thousand curses for himself.

We come and go and leave no trace, like a crow that has taken off from a rock.

Just as every valley has it unique dialect, so every teacher has his own doctrine.

If you want to know about your past life, look at your present body;
if you want to know your future, look at what you are doing in this moment.

One day in a sacred site is like a thousand days of meditation.

Wherever you find happiness, that is your home.

If a thread breaks nine times, you should connect it nine times.

The anger of one day obliterates the virtue of a hundred years.

Though you may have knowledge, you should take counsel from someone else.

The good are aware of their own faults, but the wicked seek out the faults of others.

When in the body of a donkey, enjoy the taste of grass.

Do not mistake understanding for realization, and do not mistake realization for liberation.

The highest art is the art of living an ordinary life in an extraordinary manner.

Tomorrow or the next life—which comes first, we never know.

Learn wisdom though you should die tomorrow.

The virtuous are meek, so govern themselves and others well, but the wicked, being proud, hurt or trouble themselves and others.

Lose your way and you can return; say the wrong thing and you cannot revoke it.

A tree falling makes more noise than a whole forest growing.

Your enemies are your best teachers—you should be grateful to them.

You cannot wash your hands in the same river twice.

When you live in the present, you repair the past and prepare the future.

It's a tall order to ask for meat without bones, or tea without leaves.

Wonders are many, yet few are they who can understand them.

To be forewarned is to be four-armed; to be four-armed is to be Chenrezig.

When the student is ready, the teacher will show.

As much as you have great desires, you will never know satisfaction.

Love and service are the two keys to heaven.

Engaging in the practice of virtue is as hard as driving a donkey uphill, whereas engaging in destructive activities is as easy as rolling boulders downhill.

After crossing the mountain . . . more mountains.

If you are patient in one moment of anger, you will avoid a hundred days of sorrow.

Even if you have eyes to see other people, you need a mirror to see yourself.

Much talking can be a source of danger.

The greatest happiness consists in having tranquility of mind.

The talkative parrot is shut up in a cage. Other birds, who cannot speak, fly about freely.

To know thoroughly one's own virtues or powers are the characteristics of an excellent man.

When about to perform any great work, endeavor to have a trustworthy associate.

Gloat not, even though death and misfortune overwhelm your enemies.

He who fails to practice worthy precepts after learning them, could be like someone who lights a lamp and then shuts his eyes.

Relinquish an evil custom even if it is of your fathers and ancestors; adopt a good custom even though it is established among your enemies.

Do not speak—unless it improves on silence.

# 14 Buddhism by the Numbers

**2 Accumulations:** merit and wisdom
**2 Buddha Bodies:** Dharmakaya and Rupakaya
**2 Obscurations:** negative emotions and conceptual obscurations
**2 Stages of Tantra:** Generation and Completion
**2 Truths:** Conventional Truth and Ultimate Truth
**2 Types of Meditation:** stabilizing meditation (shamatha/calm abiding) and analytical meditation (vipassana)

**3 Baskets** (Tripitaka): Sutra-Pitaka (Discourses), Vinaya-Pitaka (Monastic Discipline), and Abhidharma-Pitaka (Higher Doctrine)
**3 Buddha Bodies** (Kayas): Dharmakaya, Sambhogakaya, and Nirmanakaya
**3 Capacities:** the Hinayana, Mahayana, and Vajrayana (see 3 Paths)
**3 Dharma Kings:** Songsten Gampo (609-650 CE), Trisong Detsen (742-798 CE), and Tri Ralpachen (806-841 CE)
**3-Fold Morality:** keeping one's vows, collecting virtue, helping sentient beings
**3 Humours:** bile, phlegm, and wind (according to Tibetan medicine)
**3 Jewels/Gems** (Triple Gem) (Tib. *triratna*): Buddha, Dharma, and Sangha
**3 Levels of Liberation:** hearer vehicle, solitary realizer, Mahayana
**3 Long Life Deities:** Amitayus, Namgyalma, and White Tara
**3 Mandalas:** mandalas of body, speech, and mind
**3 Past Buddhas of this Aeon:** Kakusandha, Konagamana, and Kassapa (Kashyapa)
**3 Paths** (Yanas): Hinayana, Mahayana, and Vajrayana (the three paths leading to different levels of enlightenment)
**3 Poisons:** greed, anger, and delusion; greed, hatred, and ignorance
**3 Realms** (of Samsara): desire, form, and formless
**3 Roots:** Guru (lama), Yidam, and Dharmapala (dakini or protector)

**3 Seats (or Pillars) of the Land:** the three great Gelug monasteries in and near Lhasa—Drepung, Ganden, and Sera

**3 Supreme Methods for Any Practice:** the beginning (checking motivation), the main part (practice without materialistic concepts), and the ending (dedicating merit)

**3 Sweet Foods:** sugar, molasses, and honey

**3 Times:** past, present, and future

**3 Types of Actions:** body (physical), speech (verbal), and mind (mental)

**3 Types of Experiences in Meditation:** bliss, clarity, and non-thought

**3 Types of Laziness:** indolence (the wish to procrastinate), inferiority (doubting you capabilities), and attachment to negative actions (putting great effort into non-virtue)

**3 Types of Vows:** Pratimoksha, Bodhisattva, and Tantric

**3 Universal Laws**: all things are impermanent (*anicca*), all life is subject to suffering (*dukkha*), and there is no permanently abiding self (*anatta*)

**3 Vehicles:** Hinayana, Mahayana, and Vajrayana

**3 White Foods:** milk, butter, and curd

**3 Worlds:** worlds of desire, form, and formlessness; also sometimes above the earth, on the earth, and below the earth (three levels)

**4 Activities** (performed by realized beings)**:** pacifying, increasing, controlling, and fierce subduing

**4 Bardos:** the natural bardo of this life; the painful bardo of dying; the luminous bardo of dharmata; and the karmic bardo of becoming

**4 Boundless States:** loving kindness, compassion, sympathetic joy, equanimity

**4 Classes of Tantra—**kriya (action), carya (performance), yoga, and anuttara yoga (highest yoga)

**4 Continents:** land-masses surrounding Mount Meru—East (Lupagpo, Noble-body-land); South (Dzambuling, Jambu-fruit-land [human world]); West (Balangcho, Cattle Enjoyments); North (Draminan, Unpleasant Voice)

**4 Defeats** (leading to the expulsion of a monk or nun)**:** sexual intercourse, theft, murder, and false claim to spiritual achievement

**4 Dharmas of Gampopa:** the mind turns towards Dharma, Dharma becomes the path, the path dispels confusion, confusion arises as wisdom

**4 Dignities:** mythical animals which represent aspects of Bodhicitta:

the Dragon (power); the Tiger (confidence); the Snow Lion (fearlessness); and the Garuda (wisdom)

**4 Elements:** earth (solidity), water (liquidity), fire (heat), and wind or air (movement)

**4 Empowerments:** vase empowerment, secret empowerment, wisdom empowerment, and precious word empowerment

**4 Foundations of Mindfulness:** mindfulness of body, feeling, mind, and phenomena (dharmas)

**4 Great Streams of Suffering:** birth, sickness, old age, and death

**4 Great Vows** (Zen tradition): sentient beings are numberless, I vow to save them; desires are inexhaustible, I vow to put an end to them; the Dharmas are boundless, I vow to master them; the Buddha Way is unsurpassable, I vow to attain it

**4 Groups of People** (1): Those who go from darkness to darkness, those who go from light to darkness, those who go from darkness to light, those who go from light to light.

**4 Groups of People** (2): Those who look after themselves and ignore others, those who look after others and ignore themselves, those who neglect themselves as well as others, those who look after themselves as well as others.

**4 Guardian Kings:** kings of the four directions who can be found on murals at the entrance to most Tibetan Buddhist temples: Dhritarastra (east), Virudhaka (south), Virupaksa (west), and Vaishravana (north)

**4 Hallmarks of Correct View:** all conditioned existence is impermanent; all deluded experiences are suffering; all phenomena are empty and lack self-identity; nirvana/liberation is true peace

**4 Holy Realms:** Sravaka (sound-hearer Arhat), Praetyka-Buddha (those enlightened to conditions), Bodhisattva, Buddha

**4 Immeasurables** (loving kindness, compassion, sympathetic joy, equanimity):

May all beings possess happiness and the cause of happiness
May all beings be parted from suffering and the cause of suffering
May all beings never be parted from the happiness that has no suffering
May all beings abide in equanimity, free of bias, attachment, and anger

**4 Maras:** Devaputra, death, defilements, and contaminated aggregates

**4 Metaphors:** thinking of oneself as someone who is sick, of the spiritual friend as a doctor, of the Dharma as the remedy, and of practicing his instructions as the way to recover

**4 Noble Disciplines:** avoiding to respond to: anger with anger; physical harm with physical harm; criticism with criticism; and verbal argument with verbal argument

**4 Noble Truths:** suffering, the cause of suffering, the cessation of suffering, the path that leads beyond suffering

**4 Obscurations:** negative emotions, karmic obscurations, conceptual obscurations, and obscurations of habitual tendencies

**4 Opponent Powers** (to purify negative karma)**:** strong regret; apply antidote; promise not to engage in negative action again (make strong resolution); power of the object

**4 Purities** (in Tantric practice)**:** place, body, enjoyments, action

**4 Reliances:** rely on the message of the teacher, not on his personality; rely on the meaning, not just the words; rely on the real meaning, not on the provisional one; and rely on your wisdom mind, not on your ordinary, judgmental one

**4 Reminders:** the preciousness of our human rebirth, the truth of impermanence and death, the law of cause and effect (karma), and the shortcomings of samsara

**4 Royal Monasteries (Regency Monasteries [*Ling Shi*])** (in Lhasa): Tengye Ling, Tsomön Ling, Kunde Ling, Drib Tsemchok Ling—Gelug monasteries whose abbots often served as a Regent of Tibet during the search for and the minority of a reincarnated Dalai Lama

**4 Sacred Hills of Central Tibet:** Hepori, Chakpori, Chuwori, and Zadong Gongpori

**4 Seals** (sometimes called the 'Four Keys of the Buddha's teaching')**:** all composite things are impermanent; all emotions are painful; all phenomena are empty; nirvana is peace

**4 Sights** (of Siddhartha Gautama, leading to his search)**:** a sick person, an old person, a corpse, and a world-renouncing ascetic

**4 Tantra Sections:** Kriya, Charya, Yoga, and Anuttarayoga

**4 Ways of Attracting Beings:** being generous, speaking in a pleasant manner, teaching in accordance with individuals' needs, and acting in accordance with what he teaches

**5 Aggregates** (Sans. *skandhas*)**:** form (*rupa*)—earth, water, fire, wind; feeling (*vedana*)—pleasant, unpleasant, neutral; perception (*samjna*); volition (*samskara*); and consciousness (*vijnana*)—visual, auditory, olfactory, gustatory, tactile, mental

**5 Buddha Families** (or 5 Supreme Buddhas)**:** central: white or blue Vairochana (Illuminator); east: white Vajrasattva (Purity) or blue Akshobya (Unshakable); west: red Amitabha (Radiance); north: green Amoghasiddhi; south: yellow Ratnasambhava. These may vary in arrangement according to the lineage or tradition

**5 Chakras:** brow, crown of the head, throat, heart, and four finger widths below the navel

**5 Circumstantial opportunities:** appearing of Buddha; giving teachings; non-existence of Buddhist teachings without degeneration; existence of followers of Buddhist teachings; and having compassion for others

**5 Dhyani Buddhas:** Amitabha, Akshobhya, Ratnasambhava, Vairochana, and Amoghasiddhi

**5 Faults** (to meditation)**:** laziness, forgetting object of meditation, non-application, over-application, mental laxity/agitation

**5 Heinous Crimes:** killing one's father, killing one's mother, killing an Arhat, attempting to wound a Buddha, causing division amongst the Sangha

**5 Hindrances** (or Obstacles)**:** sensuous lust, aversion and ill will, sloth and torpor, restlessness and worry, and sceptical doubt

**5 Paths:** merit, preparation, insight, meditation, attainment

**5 Perfections**: the perfect teacher, teaching, place, disciples, and time

**5 Personal Opportunities:** to be a human being; being born in a central place (existence of a monastic community); free from negative karma; having faith in Buddhist teachings; and good senses

**5 Poisons:** attachment, anger, ignorance, jealousy, and doubt

**5 Precepts:** do not kill (deliberately), do not steal, do not indulge in sexual misconduct, do not make false speech, do not take intoxicants

**5 Sciences:** grammar, logic, medicine, arts and crafts, religious philosophy; or the making of things, the repairing of things (includes medicine), philology, logic, and philosophy

**5 Sisters of Long Life:** female deities dwelling on peaks on Tibet's southern border; they are Miyo-Lang-Sangma, Tashi Tseringma, Tekar Dosangma, Chopen Dinsangma, and Thingri Shelsangma

**5 Skandhas:** see 5 Aggregates

**5 Traditional Sciences**—language, medicine, art, logic, and astrology

**5 Wisdoms:** wisdom of the absolute space, mirror-like wisdom, wisdom of equality, discriminating wisdom, and all-accomplishing wisdom

**6 Bardos** (an interval between two things, or a transition): the bardo between birth and death, the dream bardo, the bardo of the interval of the ultimate nature of consciousness, the bardo of becoming, the bardo of meditative stability, and the bardo of gestation

**6 Chakras:** browpoint (third eye), crown, heart, throat, navel, genitals

**6 Dharmas of Mahamudra** (Six Teachings of Naropa): heat yoga (tummo, the generation of psychic heat), illusory body yoga, dream yoga, bardo realm yoga, light yoga, and transformation yoga

**Great 6:** six great monasteries of the Gelug school: Ganden, Sera, Drepung, Tashilhunpo, Labrang, and Kumbum

**6 Great Seats of the Nyingma:** Orgyen Mindroling and Thubten Dorje Drak (in central Tibet), Dzogchen Orgyen Samten Chöling and Shechen Tennyi Dhargyeling (in eastern Tibet), and Khatok Dorje Den and Palyul Namgyal Jangchubling (in lower eastern Tibet)

**6 Paramitas:** generosity, self-discipline, joyful effort, concentration, patience, and compassion

**6 Perfections** (or Virtues): giving, ethics, patience, effort, concentration, and wisdom

**6 Realms of Rebirth** (or Existence) (*gati*): gods (*devas*), demi-gods (*ashuras*), humans (*manushyas*), animals (*tiryakas*), hungry ghosts (*pretas*), and hell beings (*narakas*)

**6 Root Delusions:** attachment, anger, pride (ego), ignorance, doubt, and wrong view

**6 Senses:** apperception, sight, hearing, touch, taste, and smell

**6-Syllable Mantra:** the mantra of Chenrezig—*Om Mani Padme Hum*

**6 Tantra Sections:** Kriya, Upayoga, Yoga, Mahayoga, Anuyoga, and Atiyoga

**6 Transcendent Perfections:** generosity, discipline, patience, diligence, concentration, and wisdom

**7 Attributes of Royalty**: precious golden wheel, precious wish-fulfilling jewel, precious queen, precious minister, precious elephant, precious horse, and precious general

**7 Branches** (a form of prayer in seven parts): prostration, offering, confession, rejoicing, requesting the teacher to turn the Wheel of Dharma, requesting the teacher not to pass into nirvana, and dedication of merit

**7 Examined Men** (*misedun*): the first seven men ordained as Tibetan Buddhist monks at Samye Monastery c. 779 CE

**7 Generations of Past Buddhas:** Vipashyin, Shikhin, Vishvabhuk, Krakucchanda, Kanakamuni, Kashyapa, and Shakyamuni

**7 Factors of Enlightenment:** mindfulness, investigation, energy, rapture, tranquility, concentration, and equanimity

**7 Noble Riches:** faith, discipline, generosity, learning, conscientiousness, modesty, and wisdom

**7-Point Mandala:** a mandala composed of Mount Meru (Sumeru), the four continents, the sun, and the moon

**7 Points of Mind Training:** the preliminaries, bodhicitta, transform all unfavorable circumstances into path of the Buddha, condensed practice of mind training in five points, measurement of mind training, engagement of mind training, and precepts of mind training

**7 Preliminaries for Practice:** prostration, offering, admitting shortcomings, rejoicing, requesting teachings, beseeching the teacher not to pass away, and dedication

**8 Auspicious Mountains:** eight mountains surrounding Lhasa (also called 8 Treasures), so named by Princess Wencheng, one of the wives of King Songsten Gampo

**8 Auspicious Symbols** (lucky signs)**:** Umbrella (sign of nobility; Buddha's head); Two Fish (transcendent wisdom; Buddha's eyes); Treasure Vase (long life and prosperity; Buddha's neck); Lotus (truth and purity of speech; Buddha's tongue); Right-turning Conch (announces royalty; Buddha's mouth); Endless Knot/Auspicious Seal (links all Dharma and activity; Buddha's heart); Banner of Victory (victory over obstacles; Buddha's torso); Dharma Wheel (teachings of Buddha; Buddha's limbs)

**8 Bodhisattvas:** Manjushri, Vajrapani, Avalokiteshvara, Kshitigarbha, Sarvanivaranaviskambini, Akashagarbha, Maitreya, Samantabhadra

**8 Buddhist Hells:** Hell of Repetition (for murderers); Black Rope Hell (those who have killed during commission of another crime); Crowded Hell/Fire-Jar Hell (certain type of killing or stealing, along with sexual indulgence/having improper attitudes to physical love); Screaming Hell (misuse of intoxicants); Great Screaming Hell (misdeeds via sound or voice); Hell of Burning Heat/Diamond-beak Hornet Hell (those holding false views); Burning Hell of String-like Worms (sexual defilement of religion); Hell of No Interval (those committing the 5 Heinous Crimes)

**8 Cold Hells:** Blister Hell, Bursting Blister Hell, Brrr Hell, Alasss Hell, Chattering Teeth Hell, Utpala Flower Hell, Cracked Like a Lotus Hell, Greatly Cracked Like a Lotus Hell

**8 Consciousnesses:** eye-consciousness (seeing), ear-consciousness (hearing), nose-consciousness (smelling), tongue-consciousness (tasting), body-consciousness (tactile feeling), mind-consciousness (cognition), defiling-mind consciousness, storehouse consciousness

**8 Dharamapalas** (defenders of Buddhism)**:** Begtse, Changpa, Hayagriva, Kubera, Mahakala, Palden Lhamo, Yama, and Yamantaka

**8-Fold Path:** Right view, right aspiration (thought), right speech, right action, right livelihood, right effort, right mindfulness, right concentration

**8 Freedoms:** not being born in the hell regions, not being born as a hungry ghost (*preta*), not being born as an animal, not being born as a barbarian, not being born as a long-life god, not being born as a heretic, not being born where no Buddha has descended, not being born as a fool

**8 Hot Hells:** Reviving Hell, Black Line Hell, Crushing Hell, Wailing Hell, Great Wailing Hell, Hot Hell, Greatly Hot Hell, Unceasing Hell

**8 Manifestations of Guru Rinpoche:** Padmasambhava, appearing as the one born from a lotus, totally pure; Gyakar Panchen, displaying the qualities of a great Indian scholar; Loden Chokse, having an omniscient mind inseparable from Manjushri; Pema Gyalpo, manifesting as a king controlling all realms of existence; Nyima Oser, dispelling the darkness of ignorance; Shakya Senge, appearing as the monk who became the great liberator of all beings; Senge Dradok, destroying extreme wrong views and the demonic forces that arise when Tantric vows are broken; and Dorje Drolo, appearing as the fierce destroyer of enemies and the obstructions to enlightenment

**8 Ordinary Concerns:** gain and loss, pleasure and pain, praise and criticism, fame and infamy

**8 Perverse Acts:** criticizing good, praising evil, interrupting the accumulation of merit of a virtuous person, disturbing the minds of those who have devotion, giving up one's spiritual master, giving up one's deity, giving up one's Vajra brothers and sisters, and desecrating a mandala

**8 Realizations of Great Beings:** the awareness that all dharmas are impermanent and without a separate self; the awareness that more desire brings more suffering; the awareness that living simply, having few desires, leads to peace, joy, and serenity; the awareness that only diligent effort leads to enlightenment; the awareness that ignorance is the cause of the endless round of birth and death; the awareness that poverty creates hatred and anger, which in turn create a vicious cycle of negative thoughts and actions; the awareness that although we dwell in the world to teach and assist others, we should not become caught up in worldly matters; and the awareness that we do not practice for our individual enlightenment alone, but devote our whole being to guiding all others to the gates of enlightenment

**8 Treasures:** the eight mountains surrounding Lhasa (also called 8 Auspicious Mountains)

**8 Unfortunate Conditions** (not able to practice the Dharma)**:** hell-beings; hungry ghosts; animals; barbarians; long-lived gods; those with wrong views; an age without a Buddha; and mutes

**8 Worldly Dharmas** (and their opposites)**:** praise and compliments (criticism and blame), happiness and pleasure (unhappiness and pain), fame and recognition (disgrace), gain (loss)

**9 Stages of Shamata:** placement, continual placement, repeated placement, close placement, taming, pacifying, thoroughly pacifying, one-pointed, equanimity

**10 Bhumis** (stages on the path of a bodhisattva)**:** happiness (*pramudita*), renounce defilement (*vimala*), emitting light (*prabhakari*), blazing wisdom (*arcismati*), difficult conquest (*sudurjaya*), manifestation (*abhimukhi*), travelling far (*duramgama*), not moving (*acala*), wholesome wisdom (*sadhumati*), Dharma Cloud (*dharmamegha*)

**10 Directions:** east, west, north, south, south-east, north-west, north-east, south-west, below, and above

**10 Endowments:** to be a human being; to be born in a central country; to have perfect faculties; to be engaged in right livelihood; to have faith in the holy Dharma which is the basis; the Buddha appears in this world; He teaches the Dharma; the Dharma remains; the Dharma is followed; and one enjoys the kindness and compassion of others

**10 Fetters of Existence:** self delusion, doubt, clinging to ritual, sensuous lust, ill will, greed for fine material existence, greed for immaterial existence, conceit, restlessness, ignorance

**10 Meritorious Deeds:** charity, morality/taking precepts, mental cultivation/meditation, reverence or respect, services in helping others, transference of merits, rejoicing in the merits of others, preaching or teaching Dharma, listening to the Dharma, straightening one's own views

**10 Non-Virtues:** 3 of body (killing, stealing, sexual misconduct); 4 of speech (lying, slander, abusive speech, gossip); 3 of mind (covetousness, ill-will, wrong view)

**10 Paramitas/10 Perfections:** generosity, morality, renunciation, wisdom, energy, patience, truthfulness, resolution, loving kindness, equanimity

**10 Virtues of a Missionary** (according to the Buddha)**:** virtue of knowing the Dharma, knowing how to teach, fearlessness with the public, debating, tactful preaching, obeying the Dharma, possessing dignity, zealous progress, tirelessness, and power in success

**10 Wholesome Deeds:** abstaining from killing, stealing, sexual misconduct, duplicity, harsh speech, lying, irresponsible speech, greed, anger, foolishness

**11 Virtuous Mental Factors:** faith, shame, embarrassment, non-attachment, non-hatred, non-ignorance, effort, pliancy, conscientiousness, equanimity, and non-harmfulness

**12 Branches of Excellent Speech:** condensed, melodious, prophetic, verse, spoken with a purpose, conversatory, concerning his past lives, marvelous, establishing a truth, biographical, and very detailed

**12 Great Deeds of the Buddha:** existence in Tushita heaven; decent from Tushita; entering the womb of his mother; birth as a prince; proficiency in the worldly arts; life in the palace; departure from home; practice of austerities; defeat of Mara; enlightenment; turning the Wheel of Doctrine; final nirvana

**12 Links of Causation (Interdependence):** ignorance, misperception due to disposition, cognition, names and forms, sensory experience, contact, emotion, craving, attachment, becoming, birth, and sorrow/sickness/old age/death

**13 Possessions of an Ordained Monk:** staff, water pot, water sieve, alms bowl, blanket, three outer robes, two underrobes, a sitting mat, and sandals (2)

**14 Root Downfalls:** contradicting one's lama; contradicting or refuting the teachings of the Buddha or the personal teachings that we receive from our guru; creating disharmony within the sangha; breaking one's bodhisattva vow; impairing the white and red bindu; denigrating or abusing any spiritual system, regardless of whether it is Buddhist or non-Buddhist; revealing secret teachings to those unfit to receive them; regarding our physical bodies, or the skandhas, as impure and base; having doubts or hesitations about one's involvement in tantric practice; for an advanced tantric practitioner, not bringing a halt to a being doing terrible harm; falling into the extreme view of either eternalism or nihilism; refusing to teach a sincere student; during the ganachakra, abstaining from the ritual use of alcohol or meat because it is impure or against our beliefs; and disparaging women, either by a mental attitude of considering women to be lower than men, or by verbalizing these opinions

**14 Unwholesome Mental States:** delusion, shamelessness, unscrupulousness/fearlessness, restlessness, greed, mistaken belief, ill-will (rooted in greed), ill-will (rooted in ill-will), envy, avarice, worry, sloth, torpor, and doubt

**18 Root Bodhisattva Downfalls:** praising ourselves and belittling others; not sharing Dharma teachings or wealth; not listening to others' apologies; discarding the Mahayana teachings and propounding made-up ones; taking offerings intended for the Triple Gem; forsaking the holy Dharma; disrobing monastics or committing such acts as stealing their robes; committing any of the five heinous crimes; holding a distorted, antagonistic outlook; destroying places such as towns; teaching voidness to those whose minds are untrained; turning others away from full enlightenment; turning others away from their pratimoksha vows; belittling the shravaka vehicle; proclaiming a false realization of voidness; accepting what has been stolen from the Triple Gem; establishing unfair policies; giving up bodhicitta

**20 Secondary Delusions:** spite, deceit, jealousy, lethargy, laziness, non-shame, non-faith, resentment, excitement, concealment, miserliness, haughtiness, harmfulness, distraction, belligerence, dissimulation, forgetfulness, non-embarrassment, non-introspection, non-conscientiousness

**25 Disciples**—primary disciples of Padmasambhava, all of whom attained enlightenment; many of the great masters of Tibetan Buddhism are emanations of these disciples. One source (www.rangjung.com/gl/25_disciples.htm) lists them as: Denma Tsémang; Dorje Dudjom of Nanam; Drokben Khyechung Lotsawa; Gyalwa Changchub of Lasum; Gyalwa Choyang; Gyalwe Lodro of Dré; Jnanakumara of Nyak; Kawa Paltsek; Khandro Yeshe Tsogyal, the princess of Karchen; King Trisong Detsen; Konchog Jungné of Langdro; Lhapal the Sokpo; Namkhai Nyingpo; Nanam Zhang Yeshe De; Palgyi Dorje of Lhalung; Palgyi Senge; Palgyi Wangchuk; Palgyi Wangchuk of Odren; Palgyi Yeshe; Rinchen Chok of Ma; Sangye Yeshe; Shubu Palgyi Senge; Vairotsana, the great translator; Yeshe Yang; Yudra Nyingpo of Gyalmo

**32 major marks (of excellence) of a Buddha** (Sans. *dvatrimsadvara-laksana*): he places his foot evenly on the floor; the soles of his feet and the palms of his hands are imprinted with wheels; he has projecting heels; he has long fingers and toes; he has soft and tender hands and feet; he has webbed hands and feet; he has arched feet; he has legs like an antelope; when he stands upright his hands reach down to his knees; his male organ is covered with a sheath; his complexion has a golden sheen; his skin is so smooth that no dust clings to it; each hair on his skin grows from a single pore; the hair on his skin is blue-black, curly, and turns at the end to the right; his limbs are straight like those of a god; there are seven convex surfaces on his body: four behind his limbs, two behind his shoulders, and one behind his trunk; his torso is like that of a lion; the furrow between his shoulders is absent; his body is perfectly proportioned: the span of his arms is the same as his height; his neck and shoulders are evenly proportioned; his taste is exceptionally sensitive; his jaws are like those of a lion's; he has forty teeth; his teeth are even; there are no gaps in his teeth; his teeth are white and shining; he has a long tongue; he has a divine voice; he has deep blue eyes; he has eyelashes like those of an ox; he has soft white hair growing between his eyebrows; his head is shaped like a turban

**80 minor marks (notable characteristics) of a Buddha** (Sans. *anuvyañjana*)**:** characteristics that are more subtle and harder to detect than the 32 major marks: his nails have a red color resembling copper, possess a shiny hue and their centers are raised, being neither concave nor flat; his fingers are rounded, broad and well-tapered; his veins are not visible, and are free from knots; his ankle-bones do not protrude, his feet are even and do not differ in length, and he walks with steps of even length; outshining humans, he walks with the lion's gait; outshining nagas, he walks with the elephant's gait; he walks with the manner of the swan moving through the air; leading the retinue to the desired destination, he walks with the bull's gait; he walks naturally to the right side; he walks elegantly and attractively; and he walks evenly and straight (these were the seven manners of walking); his head is rounded and broad, like a parasol, his hairline is well-defined, and his forehead is broad and well-formed; his hair is shiny black like a bee, attractive, smooth, not tangled or matted, not strutting or unruly, and has a sweet scent; his eyes are long and wide, like the petals of the utpala flower; their black and white parts are well-defined and beautiful, like the petals of a lotus; his two eyes are pure, being free from defects of discoloration; his eyes are perfect, being free from the defilement of blurring when beholding an object; and his eyelashes are thick and attractive (these were the five minor marks of his eyes); above his eyes, the eyebrows are long, have smooth hair, a shiny color, and have hairs of even length; his two ears are of equal size, and his faculty of hearing is totally unimpaired; his nose is prominent and totally clean, being free of mucus or the like; his face is even in size, not too long; and his lips are red, like the bimba fruit, and so bright they can reflect an image; his tongue, like the lotus, is supple, slender and red; his four incisors are round; they have sharp tips; his teeth are white in color, equal in length and are well-tapered; his voice is majestic like thunder, and being free from the harshness of scurrying sounds, is soft and gentle; his hands are long and broad, and are soft like cotton wool; the lines on his palms are distinct and clear, the lines are set deep, and they are long and without interruptions; slender and shapely, his body is well-formed; free from irregular length and thickness, his body is well-proportioned; the details of the major marks are all distinct and complete; with the frame being wide and magnificent, he has a broad physical bearing; his body is extremely youthful; free from bumpiness, his body is smooth; free from the defect of an overlong body, his bearing is not sunken; his flesh is full; his body is firm and not sagging; his fingers and limbs are extremely well-proportioned through their well-defined thickness (these ten are the general qualities of his body); his body is free from moles and discoloration; free from unattractive defects, his body is perfect; it is spotless, being free from the impurities of eye-excretion, plaque on the teeth, and so forth; and being naturally clean, even without bathing, his body looks as if it were polished (these were the four qualities of his immaculate body); his waist is rounded as indicated by 'well-rounded side'; the waist being regular, his belly is perfectly moderate; his belly is not drooping by being too long; and his belly is even since the abdomen, meaning the stomach, does not bulge (these were the four qualities of his lower torso); his navel is deep, and the designs of his navel coils to the right; the conduct of his three doors is pure, and his behavior is lovely to behold; his minor marks captivate people's mind by their mere sight, and the palms and the soles of his feet are marked with auspicious designs, which are counted as one (these three were the general qualities). (rywiki.tsadra.org/index.php/The_Buddha's_80_Minor_Marks)

**100 Syllable Mantra:** the mantra of Vajrasattva

**108:** number of beads in a mala
**108:** volumes of the Kangyur

**253:** number of vows of a fully ordained Tibetan Buddhist monk

**363:** number of vows of a fully ordained Tibetan Buddhist nun

**84,000:** number of teachings given by the Buddha

**500,000 Preliminaries:** five traditional preliminary practices: 100,000 times each of refuge, Bodhicitta, vajrasattva, mandala, and guru yoga

# 15 Tibetan Holidays, Festivals, & Calendar

## TIBETAN HOLIDAYS AND FESTIVALS

There are many major and minor holidays celebrated in Tibetan Buddhism. Most are centered on religious themes, people, and deities; most personal birthdays and anniversaries are seldom celebrated or considered important.

In Tibetan Buddhism, certain days are observed on a monthly basis (some twice a month), while others are annual occurrences. Some traditions celebrate on different days, and some have more observances than others. For example, the Karma Kagyu tradition would celebrate the birthday of the Karmapa, whereas the Gelug tradition would be more likely to honor the Dalai Lama. The listing below contains primarily the observances of the Tibetan Vajrayana and Mahayana traditions as practiced in Tibet and in exile.

The Tibetan calendar is lunar based, which complicates translation. Most of the western holidays fall on the same date each year, but the Tibetan holidays, based on the lunar calendar, change each year. Just as the Gregorian calendar adds an extra day once every four years (leap year), the Tibetan calendar adds and subtracts days and months to make the year come out properly.

The Tibetan calendar also has what are called "multiplier days," which means that whatever positive or negative actions done on that day are multiplied by whatever factor is applied. These also tend to vary by tradition, school, and lineage.

### Four Major Buddha Days

*Düchen* is Tibetan for "festival"; the effects of positive or negative actions on these occasions are said to be multiplied 100 million times

**Chotrul Düchen**—celebrated during the first two weeks of the lunar New Year. It is thought that the Buddha performed a miracle each day to increase the merit and devotion of future disciples

**Saga Dawa Düchen**—the birth, enlightenment, and death (parinirvana) of the Buddha are celebrated on the 15th day of the 4th lunar month. Also called Vesak (for the name of the month in the Indian calendar)

**Chökhor Düchen**—on the 4th day of the 6th lunar month, the first turning of the Wheel of Dharma is celebrated. This is when the Buddha gave his first teachings on the Four Noble Truths at Sarnath

**Lha Bab Düchen**—celebrated on the 22nd day of the 9th lunar month, this is when Buddha descended from Tushita heaven after spending three months giving teachings in the Tushita realm

## Monthly observances

**Medicine Buddha Day/Tara Day**—celebrated on the 8th day of each lunar month

**Guru Rinpoche Day**—celebrated on the 10th day of each lunar month

**Tsog Offering**—the 10th and 25th days of each lunar month are appropriate to perform *tsog* offerings

**Sojong Day**—observed on the 15th and 30th days of each lunar month; a time to practice confession; day of the Buddha

**Dakini's Day**—observed on the 25th day of each lunar month; female energy is said to be at its peak on this day

**Dharmapala's Day**—celebrated on the 29th day of each lunar month to honor the Dharma protectors

## Annual observances

**Losar** (Tib. *Lo* [new], *Sar* [year])—the Tibetan New Year, usually held sometime in February (1st day of 1st lunar month); also celebrates

*Monlan Chenmo*, the Great Prayer Festival. Usually, the first *puja* of the New Year, in the Gelug tradition, is to Palden Lhamo, protective deity of Tibet. Celebration usually lasted 2 weeks in Tibet; now usually 3 days in the diaspora

**Anniversary of Milarepa** (Tibetan poet/saint and early follower of the Kagyu school)—celebrated on the 14th day of the 1st lunar month

**Butter Lamp Festival** (Tib. *Chunga Choepa*)—15th day of the 1st lunar month

**Anniversary of Virupa** (founder of the Sakya school)—celebrated on the 23rd day of the 4th lunar month

**Buddha Unfolding Festival**—14th to 16th days of 5th lunar month; held at Tashilhunpo Monastery near Shigatse, Tibet, where gigantic *thangkas* (40m/131 feet high) are displayed on the monastery's nine-story-high thangka wall

**Universal Prayer Festival** (Tib. *Zamling Chisang*)—15th day of the 5th lunar month, to commemorate Padmasambhava (Guru Rinpoche) (who brought Buddhism to Tibet in the 8th century) and his subjugation and taming of the evil spirits (many of whom became Dharma protectors)

**14th Dalai Lama**—celebration of the birth of the 14th Dalai Lama is held on the 6th day of the 5th lunar month, corresponding to July 6 in the year of his birth, 1935

**Birth of Guru Rinpoche** (founder of the Nyingma school)—celebrated on the 10th day of the 6th lunar month

**Harvest Festival** (Tib. *Ongkor*)—celebrated when the summer crops ripen, usually in August, and usually only in farming communities

**Shoton Festival** (Yogurt Festival)—30th day of the 6th lunar month. The main festival is held at Drepung Monastery in Lhasa and is associated with the Opera Festival, traditionally held at the Norbulingka in Lhasa

**Bathing Festival**—27th day of the 7th lunar month. It is believed when the sacred planet Venus appears in the sky, the water in the river becomes purest and can cure diseases. During its appearance for the first week all go to rivers and springs for bathing

**Tsongkhapa Butter Lamp Festival**—25th day of the 10th lunar month; butter lamps are lit and displayed on rooftops to commemorate Tsongkhapa, who founded the Gelug tradition in the 15th century

**Ill Omen Day**—6th or 7th day of the 11th lunar month; it is advised not to do anything important at this time

**House Cleaning Day** (Tib. *Gütor*)—on the 30th day of the 12th lunar month, prior to Losar, the day for cleaning and for purging all negativity accumulated during the year

**Solar Eclipses** (partial or total)—positive and negative actions during these times are multiplied by 10,000 times (or 100 million, depending on the source)

**Lunar Eclipses** (partial or total)—positive and negative actions during these occurrences are multiplied by 7 million times (depending on the source); since the Tibetan calendar is based on a lunar calendar, lunar eclipses are considered more auspicious than are solar eclipses

## Tibetan weddings

Tibetan weddings are not considered religious events. Marriages are regarded as civil, or secular, in nature. However, as in many other aspects of Tibetan life, monks and lamas are consulted. When a prospective bride and groom (or their parents) are considering a match, the astrological compatibility of the couple is charted, usually by a monk who is trained in astrology. If the match is deemed good, then another chart is done to predict the most auspicious day for the wedding. And while the marriage itself is not a religious ceremony, there are many rituals and ceremonies that take place. The usual custom in traditional Tibet is for the bride to move in with the groom and his family. Many celebrations are held in the houses of both families over many days, which includes a white horse, *chang* (Tibetan beer), and the exchange of dowries, among other rituals.

## Tibetan death and funerals

Death is very important in the tradition of Tibetan Buddhism. Primary tenets are:

- life is impermanent
- death is certain
- the time of death is uncertain
- the only thing that can help us at the time of death is what we have accomplished in this lifetime in terms of our spiritual development

"Tibetan Buddhists say the dying process begins when the five senses start to shut down. This signals that the five elements, which make up the physical body and keep it alive (earth, water, fire, wind, and space [air]), along with the five psychological components (form, feeling, projection, intellect, and consciousness) are beginning to disband. The body is placed in the most auspicious position for the dissolution of these elements and a lama or other available spiritual guide begins to offer prayers. These are designed to: encourage an ideal transformation, to invite enlightened beings to offer their assistance and protection, and to focus on the possibility that 'all the elements of ordinary existence' will 'transform into agents of liberation.' In order to guide the transference of consciousness, the *Bardo Thodol* is read to them. "Near the end of the fourth day, when the separation [of the consciousness] is sure to be complete, a funeral is performed to return the body to the elements. . . . The lama returns once a week for up to forty-nine days to recite passages from the *Bardo Thodol*. . . . Since most people are karmically destined to continue on to the next phase of the journey, it is important for the lama to continue reciting the *Bardo Thodol* after the funeral. This is the point where the deceased officially enters the *bardo* and begins to encounter the Peaceful and Wrathful Deities." (www.mythicarts.com)

". . . the day of death is thought of as highly important. It is believed that as soon as the death of the body has taken place, the personality goes into a state of trance for four days. During this time the person does not know he or she is dead. This period is called the First Bardo and during it lamas (monks) saying special verses can reach the person. It is believed that towards the end of this time the dead person will see a brilliant light. If the radiance of the Clear Light does not terrify them, and they welcome it (which comes as a result of the spiritual teachings during their lifetime), then the person will not be reborn (and they will escape samsara). But most flee from the Light, which then fades. The person then becomes conscious that death has occurred. At this point the Second Bardo begins. The person sees all that they have ever done or thought passing in front of them. While they watch they feel they have a body but when they realize this is not so, they long to possess one again. Then comes the Third Bardo, which is the state of seeking another birth. All previous thoughts and actions direct the person to choose new parents, who will give them their next body." (www.buddhanet.net) The circumstances of their next rebirth will be determined by the karmic imprints left in their mindstream from previous lives. If their karma is good, they will receive a good rebirth. If their karma is not so good, their rebirth circumstances will not be so good. (also see Powa on page 51 and Sky Burial on page 66)

## Tibetan Calendar

The Tibetan calendar is based on the Wheel of Time Tantra (*Sri Kalachakra Tantra*), which was translated into Tibetan from Sanskrit in 1027 CE—therefore, the Tibetan calendar also came into use in 1027 CE. The Tibetan calendar operates on a 60-year cycle, using five elements and twelve animals in combination. A single cycle of 60 years is called a *Rab-byung*. The calendar is lunar based, rather than solar based as is the calendar used in the West (the Gregorian calendar). This means that each month starts on a different day each year. There are also days added at times to make up for the lost days, since each Tibetan month is 30 days long. Also, an additional month is added at times (every 30 months or so) to make up for days. Some days are repeated in some months for the same reason, and some days skipped.

## Table of Years, 1927-2106

| Year | | 16 | 17 | 18 |
|---|---|---|---|---|
| | | **Rab-byungs 16-18** | | |
| 1 | Fire-Rabbit | 1927 | 1987 | 2047 |
| 2 | Earth-Dragon | 1928 | 1988 | 2048 |
| 3 | Earth-Snake | 1929 | 1989 | 2049 |
| 4 | Iron-Horse | 1930 | 1990 | 2050 |
| 5 | Iron-Sheep | 1931 | 1991 | 2051 |
| 6 | Water-Monkey | 1932 | 1992 | 2052 |
| 7 | Water-Bird | 1933 | 1993 | 2053 |
| 8 | Wood-Dog | 1934 | 1994 | 2054 |
| 9 | Wood-Pig | 1935 | 1995 | 2055 |
| 10 | Fire-Mouse | 1936 | 1996 | 2056 |
| 11 | Fire-Ox | 1937 | 1997 | 2057 |
| 12 | Earth-Tiger | 1938 | 1998 | 2058 |
| 13 | Earth-Rabbit | 1939 | 1999 | 2059 |
| 14 | Iron-Dragon | 1940 | 2000 | 2060 |
| 15 | Iron-Snake | 1941 | 2001 | 2061 |
| 16 | Water-Horse | 1942 | 2002 | 2062 |
| 17 | Water-Sheep | 1943 | 2003 | 2063 |
| 18 | Wood-Monkey | 1944 | 2004 | 2064 |
| 19 | Wood-Bird | 1945 | 2005 | 2065 |
| 20 | Fire-Dog | 1946 | 2006 | 2066 |
| 21 | Fire-Pig | 1947 | 2007 | 2067 |
| 22 | Earth-Mouse | 1948 | 2008 | 2068 |
| 23 | Earth-Ox | 1949 | 2009 | 2069 |
| 24 | Iron-Tiger | 1950 | 2010 | 2070 |
| 25 | Iron-Rabbit | 1951 | 2011 | 2071 |
| 26 | Water-Dragon | 1952 | 2012 | 2072 |
| 27 | Water-Snake | 1953 | 2013 | 2073 |
| 28 | Wood-Horse | 1954 | 2014 | 2074 |

| Year | | 16 | 17 | 18 |
|---|---|---|---|---|
| 29 | Wood-Sheep | 1955 | 2015 | 2075 |
| 30 | Fire-Monkey | 1956 | 2016 | 2076 |
| 31 | Fire-Bird | 1957 | 2017 | 2077 |
| 32 | Earth-Dog | 1958 | 2018 | 2078 |
| 33 | Earth-Pig | 1959 | 2019 | 2079 |
| 34 | Iron-Mouse | 1960 | 2020 | 2080 |
| 35 | Iron-Ox | 1961 | 2021 | 2081 |
| 36 | Water-Tiger | 1962 | 2022 | 2082 |
| 37 | Water-Rabbit | 1963 | 2023 | 2083 |
| 38 | Wood-Dragon | 1964 | 2024 | 2084 |
| 39 | Wood-Snake | 1965 | 2025 | 2085 |
| 40 | Fire-Horse | 1966 | 2026 | 2086 |
| 41 | Fire-Sheep | 1967 | 2027 | 2087 |
| 42 | Earth-Monkey | 1968 | 2028 | 2088 |
| 43 | Earth-Bird | 1969 | 2029 | 2089 |
| 44 | Iron-Dog | 1970 | 2030 | 2090 |
| 45 | Iron-Pig | 1971 | 2031 | 2091 |
| 46 | Water-Mouse | 1972 | 2032 | 2092 |
| 47 | Water-Ox | 1973 | 2033 | 2093 |
| 48 | Wood-Tiger | 1974 | 2034 | 2094 |
| 49 | Wood-Rabbit | 1975 | 2035 | 2095 |
| 50 | Fire-Dragon | 1976 | 2036 | 2096 |
| 51 | Fire-Snake | 1977 | 2037 | 2097 |
| 52 | Earth-Horse | 1978 | 2038 | 2098 |
| 53 | Earth-Sheep | 1979 | 2039 | 2099 |
| 54 | Iron-Monkey | 1980 | 2040 | 2100 |
| 55 | Iron-Bird | 1981 | 2041 | 2101 |
| 56 | Water-Dog | 1982 | 2042 | 2102 |
| 57 | Water-Pig | 1983 | 2043 | 2103 |
| 58 | Wood-Mouse | 1984 | 2044 | 2104 |
| 59 | Wood-Ox | 1985 | 2045 | 2105 |
| 60 | Fire-Tiger | 1986 | 2046 | 2106 |

## Elements*

**Fire** (Tib. *me*)—strong, instant, hot, warmth

**Earth** (Tib. *sa*)—stable, strength, ground

**Iron** (Tib. *chak*)—strong, cutting, direct, weapon, changing (similar to earth)

**Water** (Tib. *chu*)—soft, fluid, clear-seeing, flowing, smooth; often connected to the blood and emotional concerns

**Wood** (Tib. *shing*) (wind, air)—long life, beauty, good

## Animals*

**Rabbit/Hare** (Tib. *yö*)—"I am just for myself." The rabbit is independent and does not need or ask others for their help. "I can survive. There is much opportunity in the world to be enjoyed. I am satisfied with that." He tends to be indirect, devious, and possibly dishonest but always skillful. He is stingy but smiles and is generous on the surface. Possible diseases include those of the stomach and gall bladder.

**Dragon** (Tib. *druk*)—The dragon is neither brave nor active but is good. He never does bad. "I am not very powerful, but nobody harms me." He does not make much effort but also does not procrastinate or put things off. When the time comes, he does his duty. He has a short temper but is good minded. He is talkative. He listens to others talk. He has trouble containing himself. He has less disease than some of the other signs, but if he gets sick, it can be serious.

**Snake** (Tib. *trü*)—The snake has a bad temper and is always burning his own mind-stream. However, he has a good heart and is very optimistic or forward-minded. Even if others are jealous of him, no one has the power to put him down. He can, however, destroy himself. He may have a somewhat rough character and can be mean. Once his mind is made up, he won't change it. He tends to diseases of the stomach and liver.

**Horse** (Tib. *ta*)—The horse is said to have miraculous power and is capable of great effort. Even though a thousand enemies chase him, he cannot be defeated. His older life will be better than his youth. He listens to others. He likes horses. He is a fast walker and enjoys play. He has a self-sacrificing character and always helps others. He needs little sleep. His life has a lot of ups and downs.

**Sheep** (Tib. *luk*)—The sheep does not talk much and tends to be not too bright. He can be a rough character. He likes to eat. He causes others no harm but does not sacrifice himself for them either. He is generally good tempered and good hearted. Always relaxed, he does not rush. He is not lazy but can't get things done on time. He does not show either like or dislike. He is a good provider.

**Monkey** (Tib. *tre*)—The monkey is very smart, not very talkative, and tends to have a bad temper. He has a lightweight, weak body. He is not always open minded and is said to have "small" mind power. Not noted for his sense of responsibility, he likes to play and enjoy himself. His words are not to be trusted and he talks, gossips, and lies too much. He is surface oriented. He looks clean but tends to eat dirty things. Very ambitious, he always has great plans. He likes to praise himself.

**Bird** (Tib. *ja*)—It is easy for the bird to loose his possessions, legacy, inheritance, what-have-you. He is always advising others, but seldom takes his own advice. Possessing a very strong sexual desire, he always needs company. He likes to be neat and clean and doesn't require much sleep. He is prone to blindness. He loves style, dressing up, and tends to smile a lot. He enjoys walking and stylish movement. Good with friends.

**Dog** (Tib. *kyi*)—The dog is proud, mean, and somewhat wrathful. He can't seem to get kindness from others no matter how hard he tries. He is self-interested, does only for himself and never for others. His mind is always filled with lots of thoughts. He tries to do things right, but they tend to turn out bad or wrong. He likes meat. He is a fast walker. Very sexual. A traveler. He is high- or good-minded, and elegant people tend to like him.

**Pig** (Tib. *pak*)—The pig is not bright. He likes to eat but is not concerned with what type of food. He eats everything. He likes yoga. He has good self-discipline. Can be greedy and often takes advantage of others. He does not benefit himself. He lies. He has a big stomach. He is good with good people and bad with bad people. He seldom smiles and is often mean. He can be a rough character.

**Mouse/Rat** (Tib. *tsi*)—The mouse is quiet. He is not friendly or outgoing and tends to be stable. He is not rough. Even though he does good to others, others don't seem to respond. On the outside, he is open and relaxed in appearance, but inside he is very strong and critical. Very open-mouthed, he says what he thinks. He is kind but not generous. He misses the big opportunities and takes the small ones. He is always searching.

**Ox/Cow** (Tib. *lang*)—The ox is a difficult person. He is hard to get to work and is not obedient. He likes to sleep. He often exhibits bad behavior. While it is hard to change him, he is most often an agreeable person. However, his slogan is "Don't mess with me!" He is very slow and doesn't care much if things are satisfactory or not. He postpones everything. He is good-tempered. He likes to eat and sleep like a bull.

**Tiger** (Tib. *tak*)—The tiger is brave, active, and bright. Always proud and loyal to close relatives, he tends to have rough behavior and speech. He does a lot of thinking. He likes gambling and makes a good businessman.

* "Elements" and "Animals" used with permission from Michael Erlewine/StarTypes.com

## Hanging prayer flags

The hanging of prayer flags (*lung ta*) or banners should be done in accordance with the Tibetan calendar. These dates refer only to the days when you first put up prayer flags; once they have been hung, they stay up. When they are completely worn out, they should be reverently taken down and taken to a monastery, where they can be disposed of in the proper manner.

Usually a Monday is a good day and a Friday is a very good day to hang prayer flags. The following days are *inauspicious* days for putting up new prayer flags:

1st, 5th, and 9th lunar months—10th and 22nd days
2nd, 6th and 10th lunar months—7th and 19th days
3rd, 7th and 11th lunar months—4th and 16th days
4th, 8th and 12th lunar months—1st and 13th days

According to one source, if prayer flags are hung on an inauspicious day, "You will continuously receive obstacles." (Lama Zopa Rinpoche)

## TIbetan Day

The Tibetan day is broken down into twelve two-hour periods, each with its corresponding animal.

| Time period | Approx. time | Animal sign | Tibetan Name |
|---|---|---|---|
| Daybreak | 5 AM – 7 AM | Rabbit | Namlang |
| Sunrise | 7 AM – 9 AM | Dragon | Nyishar |
| Morning | 9 AM – 11 AM | Snake | Nyidron |
| Noon | 11 AM – 1 PM | Horse | Nyiche |
| Afternoon | 1 PM – 3 PM | Sheep | Cheyöl |
| Evening | 3 PM – 5 PM | Monkey | Nyinyur |
| Sunset | 5 PM – 7 PM | Bird | Nyinub |
| Dusk | 7 PM – 9 PM | Dog | Sasö |
| Start of night | 9 PM – 11 PM | Pig | Sökhor |
| Midnight | 11 PM – 1 AM | Mouse | Namche |
| End of night | 1 AM – 3 AM | Ox | Cheyöl |
| Dawn | 3 AM – 5 AM | Tiger | Thörang |

# 16 References and Sources Drawn Upon for this Book

## BOOKS—NON-FICTION

### About Tibet


Allwright, Gavin, and Atsushi Kanamaru, eds. *Mapping the Tibetan World*. Tokyo: Kotan Publishing. 2000, 2004

Barnett, Robert. *Lhasa: Streets with Memories*. New York: Columbia University Press, 2006

Bass, Catriona. *Inside the Treasure House*. London: Gollancz, 1990

Bernbaum, Edwin. *Sacred Mountains of the World*. Berkeley: University of California Press, 1999

Booz, Elizabeth. *Tibet, Roof of the World*. Chicago: Passport Books, 1994

Chan, Victor. *Tibet Handbook: A Pilgrimage Guide*. Chico, CA: Moon Publications, 1994

Dalai Lama, 5th, Ngawang Lobsang Gyatso. *A History of Tibet*. Translated by Zahiruddin Ahmad. Bloomington, IN: Indiana University Research Institute for Inner Asian Studies, 1995

Dorje, Gyurme. *Footprint Tibet*. 4th ed. Bath, UK: Footprint Handbooks, 2009

Dowman, Keith. The *Power-Places of Central Tibet: The Pilgrim's Guide*. New York: Routledge & Kegan Paul, 1988

——. *The Sacred Life of Tibet*. London: Thorsons, 1997

Dreyfus, Georges, B.J. *The Sound of Two Hands Clapping: The Education of a Tibetan Buddhist Monk*. Berkeley: University of California Press, 2003

Duncan, Marion Herbert. *Customs and Superstitions of Tibetans*. London: The Mitre Press, 1964

French, Patrick. *Tibet, Tibet: A Personal History of a Lost Land*. New York: Alfred A. Knopf, 2003

Gergan, J. *A Thousand Tibetan Proverbs and Wise Sayings*. Kathmandu: Tiwari's Pilgrims Book House, 1991

Goldstein, Melvyn. *A History of Modern Tibet, 1913-1951: The Demise of the Lamaist State*. Berkeley: University of California Press, 1989

——. *A History of Modern TIbet, Vol. 2: The Calm Before the Storm: 1951-1955*. Berkeley: University of California Press, 2007

Huber, Toni, ed. *Sacred Spaces and Powerful Places in Tibetan Culture*. Dharamsala: LTWA, 1999

Johnson, Sandy. *The Book of Tibetan Elders: The Life Stories and Wisdom of the Great Spiritual Masters of Tibet*. New York: Riverhead Books, 1996

Kapstein, Matthew T. *The Tibetans*. Malden, MA: Blackwell Publishing, 2006

Laird, Thomas. *The Story of Tibet: Conversations with the Dalai Lama*. New York: Grove Press, 2006

McKay, Alex, ed. *The History of Tibet*. 3 vols. London and New York: RoutledgeCurzon, 2003

Mariani, Fosco. *Secret Tibet*. London: The Harvill Press, 2000

Mayhew, Bradley, John Vincent Bellezza, Tony Wheeler, Chris Taylor. *Tibet, 7th ed*. Melbourne: Lonely Planet Publications, 2008

Nebesky-Wojkowitz, Rene de. *Oracles and Demons of Tibet*. London: Oxford University Press, 1956

Norbu, Thubten Jigme, Colin M. Turnbull. *Tibet, Its History, Religion, and People*. London: Chatto & Windus Ltd., 1968

O'Reilly, James and Larry Habegger, eds. *Travelers' Tales Tibet*. San Francisco: Travelers' Tales, 2003

Pemba, Lhamo. *Tibetan Proverbs*. Dharamsala: LTWA, 1996

Rajesh, M.N. *Gompas in Traditional Tibetan Society*. New Delhi: Decent Books, 2002

Richardson, Hugh E. *A Short History of Tibet*. New York: E.P. Dutton & Co., Inc., 1962

Shakabpa, W.D. *Tibet: A Political History*. New Haven: Yale University Press, 1967; New York, Potala, 1984

Shakya, Tsering. *The Dragon in the Land of Snows: A History of Modern Tibet Since 1947*. New York: Columbia University Press, 1999

Snellgrove, David, and Hugh Richardson. *A Cultural History of Tibet*. Boston: Shambhala, 1995

Sorenson, Per K. *The Mirror Illuminating the Royal Genealogies—An Annotated Translation of the XIVth Century Tibetan Chronicle*. Wiesbaden: Harrasowitz Verlag, 1994

Stein, R.A. *Tibetan Civilization*. Stanford, CA: Stanford University Press, 1972

Thurman, Robert, and Tad Wise. *Circling the Sacred Mountain: A Spiritual Adventure Through the Himalayas*. New York: Bantam Books, 1999

*Tibet at a Glance*. Dharamsala, HP, India: The Tibet Museum, Department of Information and International Relations, 2005

## Buddhism

Burlingame, Eugene Watson. *Buddhist Parables*. Delhi: Pilgrims Book, 1999

Maguire, Jack. *Essential Buddhism: A Complete Guide to Beliefs and Practices*. New York: Pocket Books, 2001

Naht Hahn, Thich. *Old Path White Clouds: Walking in the Footsteps of the Buddha*. Berkeley, CA: Parallax Press, 1991

Powers, John. *A Concise Encyclopedia of Buddhism*. Oxford: Oneworld Publication, 2000

## Dalai Lamas

Avedon, John F. *In Exile from the Land of Snows*. New York: HarperPerennial, 1994

Barry, Catherine, ed. *Reflections from the Journey of Life: Collected Sayings of the Dalai Lama*. Berekely, California: North Atlantic Books, 2002

Bell, Sir Charles. *Portrait of a Dalai Lama: The Life and Times of the Great Thirteenth*. London: Wisdom Publications, 1946, 1987

Chhaya, Mayank. *Dalai Lama: Man, Monk, Mystic, An Authorized Biography*. New York: Doubleday, 2007

Craig, Mary. *Kundun: A Biography of the Family of the Dalai Lama*. Washington, DC: Counterpoint, 1997

Dalai Lama, 14th, Tenzin Gyatso. *Freedom in Exile: The Autobiography of the Dalai Lama*. New York: HarperCollins, 1990

Mullin, Glenn H. *The Fourteen Dalai Lamas*. Santa Fe, NM: Clear Light Publishers, 2001

Norman, Alexander. *Secret Lives of the Dalai Lama*. New York: Doubleday, 2010

Strober, Deborah Hart and Gerald S. Strober. *His Holiniess the Dalai Lama: The Oral Biography*. Hoboken, NJ: John WIley & Sons, 2005

Tsering, Diki, and Khendroob Thondup. *Dalai Lama, My Son: A Mother's Story.* New York: Viking, 2000

## Meditation

Dalai Lama, 14th, Tenzin Gyatso. *Path to Bliss, A Practical Guide to Stages of Meditation.* Translated by Geshe Thubten Jinpa, edited by Christine Cox. Ithaca, NY: Snow Lion Publications, 1991

Dalai Lama, 14th, Tenzin Gyatso. *Stages of Meditation.* Ithaca, NY: Snow Lion Publications, 2001

Lamrimpa, Gen. *Calming the Mind: Tibetan Buddhist Teachings on Cultivating Meditative Quiescence.* Translated by B. Alan Wallace, edited by Hart Sprager. Ithaca, NY: Snow Lion Publications, 1992

McDonald, Kathleen. *How to Meditate: A Practical Guide.* Boston: Wisdom Publications, 1984, 2005

## Tibetan Buddhism

Bell, Sir Charles. *Religion of Tibet.* Oxford: Oxford University Press, 1931

Berzin, Alexander. *Relating to a Spiritual Teacher.* Ithaca, NY: Snow Lion Publications, 2000

Dalai Lama, 14th, Tenzin Gyatso. *Kindness, Clarity, and Insight.* Translated and edited by Jeffrey Hopkins. Ithaca, NY: Snow Lion Publications, 1984, 2006

Dzongsar Jamyang Khyentse Rinpoche. *What Makes You* Not *a Buddhist.* Boston: Shambhala, 2007

Jamgön Kongtrul the Great. *The Teacher-Student Relationship.* Translated by Ron Garry. Ithaca, NY: Snow Lion Publications, 1999

Ladner, Lorne. *Wheel of Great Compassion: The Practice of the Prayer Wheel in Tibetan Buddhism.* Boston: Wisdom Publications, 2000

Landaw, Johnathan, and Andy Weber. *Images of Enlightenment: Tibetan Art in Practice.* Ithaca, NY: Snow Lion Publications, 1993

Lopez, Don S., Jr., ed. *Religions of Tibet in Practice.* Princeton, NJ: Princeton University Press, 1997

Pabongka Rinpoche. *Liberation in the Palm of Your Hand: A Concise Discourse on the Path to Enlightenment.* Edited by Trijang Rinpoche. Translated by Michael Richards. Boston: Wisdom Publications, 1991

Patrul Rinpoche. *The Words of My Perfect Teacher.* Translated by the Padma-kara Translation Group. San Francisco: HarperCollins Publishers, 1994

Powers, John. *Introduction to Tibetan Buddhism*. Ithaca, NY: Snow Lion Publications, 1995, rev. 2007

Ray, Reginald A. *Indestructible Truth: The Living Spirituality of Tibetan Buddhism*. Boston: Shambhala, 2000

Samuel, Geoffrey. *Civilized Shamans: Buddhism in Tibetan Societies*. Washington, D.C.: Smithsonian Institution Press, 1993

*The Tibetan Book of the Dead (Bardo Thodol)*. Composed by Padmasambhava. Discovered by Karma Lingpa. Translated by Robert A. F. Thurman. New York: Bantam Books, 1994

Too, Lillian. *Mantras & Mudras: Meditations for the Hands and Voice to Bring Peace and Inner Calm*. London: Element, 2002

Tucci, Giuseppe. *The Religions of Tibet*. Translated by Geoffrey Samuel. Berkeley and Los Angeles: University of California Press, 1980

Tuttle, Gray. *Tibetan Buddhists in the Making of Modern China*. New York: Columbia University Press, 2005

Vessantara. *Meeting the Buddhas: A Guide to Buddhas, Bodhisattvas, and Tantric Deities*. Birmingham, England: Windhorse, 1993

## "People"

Arjia Rinpoche. *Surviving the Dragon: A Tibetan Lama's Account of 40 Years Under Chinese Rule*. New York: Rodale, 2010

Brauen, Martin, ed. *Peter Aufschnaiter's Eight Years in Tibet*. Bangkok: Orchid Press, 2002

Ford, Robert. *Captured in Tibet*. Oxford: Oxford University Press, 1990

Foster, Barbara, and Michael Foster. *The Secret Lives of Alexandra David-Neel: A Biography of the Explorer of Tibet and Its Forbidden Practices*. Woodstock, NY: Overlook Press, 1998

Gyatso, Palden, and Tsering Shakya. *The Autobiography of a Tibetan Monk*. New York: Grove Press, 1997

Harrer, Heinrich. *Seven Years in Tibet*. New York: Tarcher, 1997; first published in 1953 in Great Britian

Hilton, Isabel. *The Search for the Panchen Lama*. New York: W.W. Norton & Company, 1999

Khétsun, Tubten. *Memories of Life in Lhasa under Chinese Rule*. New York: Columbia University Press, 2008

Kimura, Hisao and Scott Berry. *A Japanese Agent in Tibet: My Ten Years of Travel in Tibet*. London: Serindia, 1990

Martin, Michele. *Music in the Sky: The Life, Art & Teachings of the 17th Karmapa Ogyen Trinley Dorje*. Ithaca, NY: Snow Lion Publications, 2003

McDonald, David. *Twenty Years in Tibet*. London: Seeley Service & Co., 1932

McGovern, William Montgomery. *To Lhasa in Disguise: An Account of a Secret Expedition Through Mysterious Tibet*. London: Kegan Paul, 2004

## Books—Fiction

Adam, Paul. *Oracle Lake*. New York: Thomas Dunne Books/St. Martins, 2007

Alai. *Red Poppies*. Boston: Houghton Mifflin, 2002

Ekvall, Robert Brainerd. *Tents Against the Sky: A Novel of Tibet*. Farrar, Straus & Young, 1955

Falla, Jonathan. *Blue Poppies*. New York: Random House, 2001

Frutkin, Mark. *Invading Tibet*. New York: Soho Press, 1991

Hilton, James. *Lost Horizon*. New York: Macmillan, 1933

Hyde-Chambers, Fredrick. *Lama, A Novel of Tibet*. London: Souvenir Press Ltd., 1984

Jamyang Norbu. *Sherlock Holmes: The Missing Years; The Adventures of the Great Detective in India and Tibet*. New York: Bloomsbury Publishing, 1999

Magee, Bill. *She Still Lives: A Novel of Tibet*. Ithaca, NY: Snow Lion Publications, 2006

Ma Jian. *Stick Out Your Tongue*. New York: Farrar, Straus and Giroux, 2006

Michie, David. *The Magician of Lhasa: A Novice Monk, A Quantum Scientist, An Ancient Secret*. Lyons, CO: Trapdoor Books, 2010

Mitchell, Ken. *Stones of the Dalai Lama*. New York: Soho Press, 1993

Pattison, Eliot. *Beautiful Ghosts*. New York: St. Martin's, 2004

———. *Bone Mountain*. New York: St. Martin's, 2002

———. *The Lord of Death*. New York: Soho Press, 2009

———. *Mandarin Gate*. New York: Minotaur Books, 2012

———. *Prayer of the Dragon*. New York: Soho Press, 2007

———. *Skull Mantra*. New York: St. Martin's, 1999

———. *Water Touching Stone*. New York: St. Martin's, 2001

Peterson, Jeanne M. *Falling to Heaven*. New York: Thomas Dunne Books, 2010

Tshe-rin-dban-rgyal, Mdo-mkhar. *Tale of the Incomparable Prince*. Trans. by Beth Newman. New York: HarperCollins, 1996

Xinran. *Sky Burial, An Epic Love Story of Tibet*. New York: Vintage, 2004

Yongden, Albert. *Mipam: The First Tibetan Novel*. 1938. Berkeley, CA: Snow Lion Graphics, 2000

## Periodicals/Journals

(also see www.dharamsalanet.com/links/articles.htm)

**Harvard Journal of Asiatic Studies**
www.jstor.org/

**Mandala, A Tibetan Buddhist Journal**
www.mandalamagazine.org/

**Sangha Journal**
www.sanghajournal.com/

**Shambhala Sun**
www.shambhalasun.com/

**Tibetan Bulletin**
www.tibet.net/w-p-content/uploads

**Tricycle Magazine**
www.tricycle.com

## Websites

There are hundreds of thousands of websites having something to do with Buddhism, or Tibetan Buddhism, or Tibet. A keyword search on any search engine will give you a list of many sites, which are being added, and added to, each day, from all around the world—commercial sites, non-profit sites, and personal sites. The web addresses listed below are some of those that have been found useful. While nothing is permanent, most of these sites have been on the web for some time, and are likely to remain active. In most cases only the root address for the site is listed. In addition, almost all sites have links to other sites, which can lead to more sites. Be aware that the Web is a double-edged sword—it is an unlimited resource for information, but it is also mostly uncensored, so one must be aware of the source of the information. This list includes primarily nonprofit, or organizational, listings. However, you can often find very useful information from commercial sites. For example, if you do a keyword search for "phurba," you will come up with many sites that will sell you a phurba, but will also sometimes have very useful information on what a phurba is and what it is used for.

www.beliefnet.com/
www.berzinarchives.com
www.buddhanet.net
www.dalailama.com
www.dharmanet.org
www.drepung.org/
www.dzogchen.org/
www.fpmt.org/
www.himalayanart.org/
www.hinduwebsite.com/links/buddhism/organizations.asp
www.kagyu.org
www.kalachakra.org
www.khandro.net/
www.kotan.org/tibet/directory/index.html
www.metaxu.to
www.nalandabodhi.org/
www.palyul.org/
www.sacred-texts.com/bud/tib/
www.sakya.org/
www.samye.org/
www.samyeling.org
www.shambhalamountain.org/
www.tbrc.org/ (Tibetan Buddhist Resource Center)
www.thlib.org (Tibetan & Himalayan Digital Library)
www.tibet.net (site of the Central Tibetan Administration Government-in-Exile)
www.tibetanculture.org/
www.tibetfund.org/
www.tricycle.com

## Publishers of Buddhist Books

Publishers whose books are primarily Buddhist, Tibetan Buddhist, or spiritual in nature, or who have a significant number of Buddhist books or significant titles among their lists.

**Asian Classics Input Project**
www.asianclassics.org

**Clear Light Publishers**
www.clearlightbooks.com

**Columbia University Press**
www.cup.columbia.edu/

**Counterpoint Press**
www.perseusbooksgroup.com

**Dharma Publishing**
www.dharmapublishing.com

**Inner Traditions International**
www.innertraditions.com

**Kotan Publishing**
www.kotan.org

**Lotus Press**
www.lotuspress.com

**North Atlantic Books**
www.northatlanticbooks.com

**Paljor Publications**
www.paljorpublications.com

**Parallax Press**
www.parallax.org

**Princeton University Press**
www.pup.princeton.edu

**Red Wheel/Weiser**
www.redwheelweiser.com

**Shambhala Publications, Inc.**
www.shambhala.com

**Tuttle Publishing**
www.tuttlepublishing.com

**The University of California Press**
www.ucpress.edu
**The University of Chicago Press**
www.press.uchicago.edu
**The University of Hawai'i Press**
www.uhpress.hawaii.edu
**Windhorse Publications**
www.windhorsepublications.com
**Wisdom Publications**
www.wisdompubs.org

## Finding a Dharma Center

The most comprehensive, and up-to-date, listings of Dharma centers of all types can be found online. The links below will lead to a wealth of information. Be mindful of the fact that all websites are not updated as often as others, and that some go out of existence while new ones are started, as is also the case for Dharma centers (impermanence, you know). Some list all schools while some only list the centers of that particular school or lineage.

www.fpmt.org/centers
www.kagyuoffice.org/dharmacenters.html
www.dharmanet.org/listings/centres/country/United_States
www.buddhist-directory.org
www.shambhalasun.com/
www.pluralism.org/directory/search
www.gosit.org

## Educational Opportunities

**Columbia University**
www.columbia.edu
**Cornell University**
www.cornell.edu

**Drepung Loseling Institute Center for Tibetan Buddhist Studies**
(affiliated with Emory University)
www.drepung.org

**Harvard University**
www.harvard.edu

**Indiana University**
www.indiana.edu

**Namgyal Monastery Institute of Buddhist Studies**
www.namgyal.org

**Naropa University**
www.naropa.edu

**Princeton University**
www.princeton.edu

**Rice University**
www.rice.edu

**Tibetan and Himalayan Digital Library (Education section)**
www.iris.lib.virginia.edu/tibet/education

**University of California at Santa Barbara**
www.ucsb.edu

**University of Chicago**
www.uchicago.edu

**University of Michigan**
www.umich.edu

**University of Virginia**
www.virginia.edu/religiousstudies

**University of Washington**
www.washington.edu

**University of Wisconsin**
www.wisc.edu

In addition, many other universities and colleges have courses in various aspects of Buddhism, Asian Studies, language, and literature. Check them online.

## Films on Tibet, Buddhism, the Dalai Lama, and Other Topics of Interest

Many of the films listed here are commercially available; some are feature movies, others are documentaries. Other sources of films include: meridian-trust.org, www.hartleyfoundation.org, and www.tibetnetwork.org/films-about-Tibet. More in-depth information on many of these films can be found at the Internet Movie Database (www.imdb.com), or by searching the internet for the title of the film.

***Angry Monk—Reflections on Tibet*** (2005/Switzerland/Tibetan & English/documentary/97 minutes)—story of Gendun Choepel, a Tibetan monk who lived during the first half of the twentieth century (1903-1951). After rejecting monastic life, he traveled in Tibet and India, learning more about the history of his country. He eventually came to criticize aspects of Tibet's religion and government, and was imprisoned in 1946 for three years by the Tibetan government as a political subversive.

***Buddha*** (est. 2013/India/English/c. 120 miniutes)—the planned release in 2013 of a movie on the life of the Buddha is based on the book *Old Path White Clouds* by Vietnamese monk Thich Nhat Hanh. The "Dalai Lama reportedly gave his blessing to this project and took on an advisory role with the development of the script." (www.imdb.com)

***Compassion in Exile: The Story of the 14th Dalai Lama*** (1993/US/English/documentary/60 minutes)—portrait of the Dalai Lama, as he describes how he was raised and the key moments in his life.

***The Cup*** (1999/Bhutan/Hindi & Tibetan with English subtitles/93 minutes)—young Tibetan monks at a monastery in exile try to talk the abbot into letting them rent a television and a satellite dish to watch the World Cup soccer finals. Based on a true story. Made by Khyentse Norbu Rinpoche.

***Dalai Lama: The Soul of Tibet*** (1994/US/English/A&E Biography TV/documentary/50 minutes)—the story of the 14th Dalai Lama, from childhood to exile, including footage of his life and interviews. Includes his acceptance of the 1989 Nobel Peace Prize and interviews with Chinese scholars.

***Daughters of Wisdom*** (2007/US/Tibetan/documentary/68 minutes)—"an intimate portrait of the nuns of Kala Rongo, . . . a Buddhist Monastery exclusively for women situated in Nangchen, in remote and rural northeastern Tibet." (www.imdb.com)

***Dreaming Lhasa*** (2005/India/English & Tibetan/90 minutes)—the story of a 30-year-old Tibetan woman raised in New York, who travels to Dharamsala, India, to make a film about the exile community. Joining with a local Tibetan youth and an ex-monk, they end up on a quest to find a CIA-trained resistance fighter who has been missing for 15 years.

***Dreams of Tibet*** (1997/US/English/documentary/55 minutes)—the history of Tibet, and the desire of its people for independence, is examined through interviews with politicians, actors, directors, and others.

***Heart of Tibet: An Intimate Portrait of the 14th Dalai Lama*** (1992/US/English/documentary/60 minutes)—portrait of the 14th Dalai Lama, made in 1989 while in Los Angeles for a Tibetan Buddhist initiation ritual. He talks about human rights, nonattachment, compassion, and peace.

***Himalaya*** (1999/UK/Tibetan & German/English subtitles/108 minutes)—different generations and rivals compete in this tale of travels on hostile terrain in Tibet to trade salt for grain. Beautiful cinematography.

***Himalaya*** (2004/UK/English/documentary/360 minutes)—in this documentary series, writer/host/actor Michael Palin travels the Himalaya from Pakistan to Myanmar (Burma), including Tibet, and in the process meets many different people, from Royals and Ministers to ordinary shepherds, and even the Dalai Lama. On his journey through visually stunning landscape, he shows those whose livelihoods depend on the mountains of the Himalaya.

***The Knowledge of Healing*** (1996/Switzerland/German & Tibetan/documentary/93 minutes)—the first feature documentary dealing extensively with Tibetan medicine. Taught for hundreds of years, this is a thorough and objective look at a highly developed medical system.

***Kundun*** (1997/US/English/128 minutes)—directed by Martin Scorsese, this is the story of the discovery of the 14th Dalai Lama up until the time he flees Tibet in 1959 after nine years of Chinese occupation. One of the first of the major Hollywood films with Tibet or Buddhism as a theme. Filmed in Morocco. ***In Search of Kundun with Martin Scorsese*** (1998/US/English/documentary/85 minutes)—"a mini documentary of the filming of the movie ***Kundun***, along with interviews with Martin Scorsese and the cast." (www.imdb.com)

***Little Buddha*** (1993/UK/English/123 minutes)—film within a film, the first being the story of a young American boy who is thought to be the reincarnation of a Tibetan Buddhist Rinpoche; interspersed is the story of the historical Buddha (played by Keanu Reeves), who lived in Nepal and India in the 5th century BCE. Directed by Bernardo Bertolucci.

***Lost Horizon*** (1937/US/English/132 minutes)—a plane crashes in the remote Himalayan mountains, and the survivors are rescued by the inhabitants of a strange, mystical valley, protected by the mountains from the world outside—Shangri-la. Hollywood's idea at the time of what Tibet was like, based on James Hilton's book of the same name.

***Milarepa*** (2006/India & Bhutan/Tibetan/96 minutes)—story of the first half of the life of Tibet's great poet/saint, who lived 1040-1123. Milarepa's life started out by his becoming a sorcerer to avenge the death of his father and the treatment of his family by his uncle, but who later renounces his earlier ways and devotes his life to Buddhist practice. Filmed on location in the Spiti Valley on the Indian-Tibetan border with non-professional actors, including some who had appeared in *The Cup* by Khyentse Norbu Rinpoche. The date of release of the second half of the film is still to come.

***Oracles & Demons of Ladakh*** (2003/US/English/documentary/71 minutes)—located in the Himalayas in the northwest province of India, Ladakh is in the western region of the Tibetan plateau, and has been spared the encroachment of the Chinese. This region maintains the ways of Tibetan Buddhism (of all four schools) that have become minimalized in Tibet. The practitioners are believed to have direct contact with spirits, with whom they communicate through the Oracles. As they did in historic Tibet, and in the exile community, the Oracles are called upon to divine the future, ward off harmful deities, and cure bodily illnesses. Made by Khyentse Norbu Rinpoche.

***Robert A. F. Thurman on Buddhism*** (2002/US/English/documentary/220 minutes)—Tibetan scholar and former Buddhist monk Robert Thurman shares his unique insight into Tibetan Buddhism in college lecture format, and explores: the Three Jewels; Boddhicitta; Merit; Wisdom; the Four Noble Truths; the Three Wheels of Dharma; the Three Vehicles of Dharma; Buddhahood; and many others.

***Robert A. F. Thurman on Tibet*** (2002/US/English/documentary/240 minutes)—in lecture format, former Tibetan Buddhist monk and currently professor at Columbia University Robert Thurman gives the history of Tibet, from the pre-Buddhist Bön shamanistic folk religion, to the warrior-like early dynastic kings conquering their neighbors, to the introduction and peaceful nature of Buddhism from India, to the institution of the Dalai Lamas.

***The Saltmen of Tibet*** (1997/Germany & Switzerland/German & Tibetan with English subtitles/documentary/108 minutes)—four men from a nomadic Tibetan tribe undertake their annual pilgrimage to a sacred salt lake, Lake Tsento. Salt gathered in the traditional fashion will be sold to provide the economic livelihood of the tribe for the coming year. The journey incorporates a number of rituals necessary for their culture to survive in the modern world.

***Seven Years in Tibet*** (1997/US/English/139 minutes)—story of Austrian mountain climber Heinrich Harrer (and Peter Aufschnaiter, a fellow Austrian) who escape a prisoner-of-war camp in northern India during the Second World War and make their way across the Himalayas and Tibet to Lhasa. He was eventually to become a teacher and confidant to the young 14th Dalai Lama, before they both fled in 1959 as a result of an onslaught by the Chinese. Major Hollywood production, starring Brad Pitt as Harrer.

***The Spirit of Tibet: The Life and World of Dilgo Khyentse Rinpoche*** (aka ***Journey to Enlightenment***) (1995/US/English/documentary/47 minutes)—born in 1910, Dilgo Khyentse Rinpoche was one of Tibet's most revered teachers of the 20th century, including among his students the 14th Dalai Lama. Shows rarely photographed regions of Tibet and Bhutan, and includes interviews with the Dalai Lama. Directed by Matthieu Riccard, a Buddhist monk, who traveled with Rinpoche for more than 14 years before his death in 1991.

***The Sun Behind the Clouds: Tibet's Struggle for Freedom*** (2010/Austria, France, India, Netherlands, China, US, UK, & Germany/English, Mandarin, and Tibetan/documentary/79 minutes)—"a uniquely Tibetan perspective on the trials and tribulations of the Dalai Lama and his people as they continue their struggle for freedom in the face of determined suppression by one of the world's biggest and most powerful nations." (thesunbehindtheclouds.com)

***10 Questions for the Dalai Lama*** (2006/US/English/documentary/85 minutes)—filmmaker Rick Ray combines interviews with His Holiness the Dalai Lama, asking 10 fundamental questions, along with historical footage and filming done under cover in Tibet, to create a film that is "part biography, part philosophy, part adventure, and part politics." (www.10questionsforthedalailama.com)

***Tibet: A Buddhist Trilogy*** (1979; reissued in 2005/UK/Tibetan with English commentary and subtitles/documentary/134 minutes)—a trilogy of insights into the Tibetan Buddhist community: Part I is filmed in Dharamsala, India, home to the exiled Dalai Lama, and at Sera Monastery, rebuilt in southern India; Part II looks at monastic life in Nepal, with lamas from the Phulwary Sakya Monastery; and Part III is set in Ladakh, in northwestern India, following farmers and monks during a day, ending with monastic rituals as a result of a death in the community.

***Tibet: Cry of the Snow Lion*** (2003/US/English/documentary/104 minutes)—filmed over the course of ten years worth of travel in Tibet, this movie examines the history of devastation in Tibet, the significance of the Tibetan issue today, and the spiritual beliefs, both inside Tibet and in the diaspora, that continue to inspire hope for the future. The documentary gives a concise, though passionate, overview of the history of Tibet, focusing on the suffering of the people over the past five decades at the hands of the People's Republic of China. The story of the invasion is told through translated interviews, film footage, and still photographs. Narrated by Martin Sheen.

***Tibet in Song*** (2009/US/Tibetan with English subtitles, English/documentary/86 minutes)—a "tale of cultural exploitation and resistance, which includes Ngawangs' [the director] own eventual imprisonment for recording the very songs at the center of the film. . . . provides raw and uncensored look at Tibet as it stands today, a country plagued by Chinese brutality, yet willing to fight for the existence of its unique cultural heritage." (www.tibetinsong.com)

***Travellers and Magicians*** (2003/Bhutan/Dzongkha with English subtitles/108 minutes)—directed by Khyentse Norbu Rinpoche, this is a mystical tale of lust, jealousy, and murder, involving two men in the Buddhist kingdom of Bhutan who seek to escape their mundane lives, yearning for a better and different life from the one they have been living. The scenery, along with the songs of traditional Buddhist chanting, make the film seem blurred between fantasy and reality, which, coincidentally, is what the film is all about. (www.travellersandmagicians.com)

***Unmistaken Child*** (2008/Israel/English, Tibetan, Hindi, and Nepali/102 minutes)—"follows the four-year search for the reincarnation of Lama Konchog, a Tibetan master who passed away in 2001 at age 84. The Dalai Lama charges the deceased monk's disciple, Tenzin Zopa (who had been in his service since the age of seven), to search for his master's reincarnation." (www.unmistakenchild.com)

***We're No Monks*** (2004/India/Tibetan/129 minutes)—the story of four youths living in exile in Dharamsala, India, home to the Tibetan government-in-exile. They are torn between trying to do something for the Tibetan diaspora and the country many have never seen and their need to find their way into the modern world of work, money, and a dream of emigrating to the United States. Written and directed by Pema Dhondup, the film portrays both the aspirations and frustrations of Tibetan youth.

***What Remains of Us*** (2004/Canada/Tibetan & English/documentary/77 minutes)—this Canadian documentary won the Best Documentary Prize at the 2004 Hollywood Film Festival. It shows how Kalsang Dolma, an Indian-born Tibetan women who moved to Montreal, carried a portable video player into Tibet that contained a message the 14th Dalai Lama had recorded especially for the Tibetan people. The film covers the intense emotional reactions of Tibetans who have not heard from or about him for more than fifty years due to Chinese censorship.

***Wheel of Time*** (2003/German/English & German/documentary/80 minutes)—a thoughtful and highly personal look at what Buddhism means, written and directed by Werner Herzog. The film focuses on the Kalachakra Initiation ceremony, this one held in 2002 in Bodh Gaya, India, where the historical Buddha Shakyamuni gained enlightenment, and on the creation of the intricate sand mandala that is at the heart of the ceremony.

***When the Dragon Swallowed the Sun*** (2010/US/English & Tibetan/documentary/115 minutes)—"The Tibetan people's ongoing struggle for freedom is examined by director Dirk Simon in this documentary about the history of China's occupation of Tibet, and the protests, both violent and peaceful, that have resulted around the world. Tibetan exiles from all walks of life are interviewed, including the 14th Dalai Lama, as well as supporters such as Richard Gere and Archbishop Desmond Tutu." (movies.netflix.com)

***Windhorse*** (1998/US/English/97 minutes)—this powerful movie, shot on location in various parts of Tibet and in Kathmandu, Nepal, is about the treatment of the Tibetan people by the Chinese, who have occupied Tibet since 1950. It focuses on three Tibetans, a brother and sister (one of whom does nothing but drink and whine, the other sings songs for the Chinese about the glory of China), and their cousin, a Tibetan nun. While the scenery is stunning, much of the action was shot surreptitiously due to the oppressive nature of Chinese surveillance in Lhasa.

***Words of My Perfect Teacher*** (2003/Canada/English/documentary/103 minutes)—Dzongsar Khyentse Norbu Rinpoche is a renown, charismatic Buddhist teacher, with his primary monastery in Bhutan. He crosses many different bridges, being a teacher and a filmmaker, a high lama and a rabid soccer fan, a Rinpoche with duties to his monastery and a world-traveling, cell-phone-toting director scouting out locations. The story focuses on three of his students (one of whom is the director, Lesley Ann Patten) as they follow him for teachings, and deal with disappointments. "The film's point of view is inspired by Buddhist philosophy—which says that we can't really change human behavior until we learn to deal with our mind. . . . And to study the mind, you need a teacher." (www.wordsofmyperfectteacher.com)

**Yatra Trilogy** (UK/English/documentary)—"'Yatra' is a Sanscrit word for a sacred journey or pilgrimage. In this ancient tradition, revered in every major faith, pilgrims travel to religious sites to share in the unique presence of the place. This trio of movies is a cycle of meditative journeys created to give viewers a profound experience of sacred space." (www.directpictures.com)

***Dharma River: Journey of a Thousand Buddhas* (Laos, Thailand, Burma)** (2004/81 minutes)—"travels on legendary rivers to mystical sites of Laos, Thailand and Burma."

***Prajna Earth: Journey into Sacred Nature* (Bali, Cambodia, Java)** (2004/85 minutes)—"This second film of the Yatra Trilogy is a cinematic journey to the legendary temples of Angkor in Cambodia, the spiritual sites of Bali and finally, the marvel of Buddhist Borobudur in Java."

***Vajra Sky: Journey into Luminous Faith* (Tibet)** (2005/87 minutes)—"Discovering the temples, festivals, and monasteries of Tibet, one is continually greeted by luminous faces of faith. Through mountains, rivers, and sky, the journey leads to the revered sites of Shigatse and Gyantse. It echoes within the bustling Jokhang Temple and the empty Potala Palace, home of His Holiness the Dalai Lama."

# 17 Glossary

Much of this glossary is oriented towards Tibetan Buddhism; there are, however, terms included here from other traditions.
Chin.—Chinese; Jap.—Japanese; Pali—Pali; Sans.—Sanskrit; Tib.—Tibetan

**Abbess** (Tib. *khenpa*)—the head official of a nunnery
**Abbot** (Tib. *khenpo*)—the head official of a monastery
**Abhidharma** (Sans.)—scholastic system derived from the discourses of the Buddha which summarize key points and classifies teachings
**Abhidharma-pitaka** (Sans.)—a philosophical systematization of the Buddha's teaching, including a detailed analysis of Buddhist psychology
**Acharya** (Tib.)—teacher; equivalent of a spiritual master
**Adept**—a person who is highly skilled, proficient, or knowledgable at something; a highly realized master
**Aggregates**—see Skandhas
**Alms**—the offering of food to monks or nuns on their daily rounds and the donation of goods and money to monasteries
**Amida Butsu** (Jap.)—Japanese version of Amitabha Buddha. See Amitabha
**Amitabha** (Sans.)—one of the Five Transcendant Buddhas, the Buddha of the western direction and also of the western paradise, or Pure Land. Associated with the Buddha Amitayus (Infinite Life) and considered the spiritual father of the bodhisattva Avalokiteshvara
**Anapanasati** (Pali)—mindfulness of in-and-out breathing used in many forms of meditation
**Ananda**—friend, cousin, and favorite disciple of the Buddha, and monk who remembered the Sutras
**Ani** (Tib.)—nun
**Ani gompa** (Tib.)—nunnery
**Annitya** (anicca) (Sans.)—impermanence

**Arahant** (Pali; Sans. *Arhat*)—Worthy One, a name for the Buddha; a person who has destroyed the mental defilements and become detached from the phenomena of cyclic existence, a kind of nirvana, but not quite yet Buddhahood; a Buddhist monk who is free from all illusions and who has achieved personal enlightenment (primarily Theravadan)

**Ascetic**—one whose life or practice is characterized by abstinence from all worldly pleasures, and who perceives these actions as virtuous, helping to purify the body to further the chance for enlightenment

**Asuras** (Sans.)—"demi-gods," beings of one of the six realms of existence, sometimes considered to be the chief of the evil spirits

**Atisha**—great Indian scholar who arrived in Tibet in 1042 at the invitation of rulers of western Tibet. He worked to reform and revive Buddhist teachings and practices and first formulated the Lam Rim teachings

**Atman** (Sans.)—Hindu concept of a soul: the individual consciousness that is continually reborn

**Attachment**—inability to separate from a person or thing, although it will ultimately lead to suffering; usually exaggerates the good qualities of the object; one of the primary delusions which prevents the achievement of enlightenment

**Auspicious**—marked by lucky signs or good omens, and by the promise of success or happiness; can be a date or a symbol or a number or a name

**Avalokiteshvara** (Sans.) (Tib. *Chenrezig*)—Bodhisattva of Compassion; see Chenrezig

**Avidya** (Sans.)—ignorance, delusion

**Bardo** (Tib.)—an intermediate state; most often referring to the time between death and rebirth

***Bardo Thodol*** (Tib.)—Tibetan name for *The Tibetan Book of the Dead*, which describes the process of dying and how one can improve one's chances of a good rebirth

**Barkhang** (Tib.)—middle or second floor

**Barkhor** (Tib.)—intermediate circumambulatory passage; kora around the Jokhang Temple in Lhasa, which also contains many shops selling Tibetan goods

**Beyül** (Tib.)—"Hidden valley" in which people can take refuge during times of upheaval and where Buddhism can be safely practiced

**Bhagavan** (Sans.)—the Blessed One, a name for the Buddha

**Bhikkshu** (Sans.; Pali, *Bhikku*)—monk

**Bhikkshuni** (Sans.; Pali, *Bhikkuni*)—nun
**Bod** (Tib.)—Tibet
**Bodh Gaya**—town in Indian state of Bihar where the historical Buddha is said to have attained enlightenment sitting beneath the Bodhi Tree
**Bo Tree**—see Bodhi Tree
**Bodhi** (Pali)—term meaning "awakening," sometimes translated as enlightenment
**Bodhi Tree**—the tree beneath which Siddhartha Gautama sat meditating while he attained enlightenment
**Bodhicitta** (Sans.)—the "mind of enlightenment;" the altruistic intention to become enlightened in order to benefit all sentient beings
**Bodhidharma**—monk who brought Buddhism to China in the 6th century
**Bodhisattva** (Sans.)—an enlightened being; one who has generated bodhicitta and seeks enlightenment for the benefit of all sentient beings
**Bön** (Tib.)—pre- and non-Buddhist religion of Tibet
**Bön-po (Bönpo)**—practitioners of the Bön tradition of Tibet
**Brahma** (Sans.)—the supreme Hindu deity, who convinced Buddha to teach after he became enlightened
**Brahman** (Sans.)—a member of the priestly caste of Hinduism
**Buddha** (Tib. *sangye*)—the historical Shakyamuni Buddha, born as Siddhartha Gautama, who is credited with establishing Buddhist doctrine in the present era; a term meaning enlightened one or one who has awakened
**Buddha-nature**—the nature innate in every sentient being; the potential for attaining Buddhahood; the inherent potential in each being to become a Buddha, one who is awake
**Bumpa** (Tib.)—a ritual vase used during initiation, healing, and purification rites
**Butsu-dan** (Jap.)—Japanese Buddhist household altar

**Calm abiding**—term for samatha, the meditation that one does to calm or make the mind more tranquil
**Cat** (Tib. *shimi*)—a small, usually furry, carnivorous mammal
**Chaitya** (Tib.)—assembly hall for monks
**Cham** (Tib.)—monastic ritual dance
**Ch'an** (Chin.)—form of Mahayana Buddhism practiced in China; Japanese tradition is called Zen
**Chakra** (Sans.)—one of a series of focal points of the system of circulation of prana throughout the body

**Chakstal** (Tib.)—prostration

**Chandaka**—squire to Siddhartha Gautama, who aided him in leaving his princely life

**Chenrezig** (Tib.) (Sans. Avalokiteshvara)—the Buddha of Compassion; patron deity of Tibet; the Dalai Lamas are emanations of Chenrezig

**Chikhor** (Tib.)—outer circumambulatory passage

**Chöd** (Tib.)—meditational practice involving visualizing one's body being cut up and offered to deities and other beings; a key practice for many Tibetan lay tantric practitioners

**Chokhang** (Tib.)—offering hall

**Chömay** (Tib.)—butter lamp

**Chöra** (Tib.)—debating courtyard

**Chorten** (Tib.)—see Stupa

**Chu** (Tib.)—river or stream

**Circumambulation** (Tib. *kora*)—walking a circular route around a holy place (clockwise in Buddhist and counter-clockwise in the Bön tradition); one of the most frequent of merit-making activities in the Buddhist world

**Citta** (Sans.)—basic mind or consciousness

**Citta-matra** (Sans.)—mind only; idealism

**Compassion** (Sans. *karuna*)—sympathy and love for all beings; one of the two principle Buddhist virtues (the other being wisdom); leads to the wish to free all sentient being from dukkha (suffering)

**Daka** (Sans.)—male equivalent of Dakini

**Dakini** (Sans.)—female tantric Buddha and women who are the keepers of the secret lore of Tantra, which they pass on to adepts

**Dalai Lama** ("Dalai" is Mongolian for "Ocean of wisdom")—term bestowed on Tibetan lama Sonam Gyatso by Mongolian ruler Altan Khan in the 15th century; the spiritual and temporal leader of Tibet and the emanation of Chenrezig; the current Dalai Lama, the 14th, Tenzin Gyatso, lives in Dharamsala, India, with the Tibetan government-in-exile. Also known as Kundun ("The Presence") and Yeshi Norbu ("Wish-fulfilling Jewel")

**Damaru** (Tib.)—two-sided hand drum, usually round, having two "strikers" attached, which hit the heads of the drum when the drum is quickly rotated side to side

**Damchen** (Tib.)—a deity protector of the Dharma, and one who has been bound under oath by Padmasambhava

**Darchen** (Tib.)—flagpole used for prayer flags

**Deer Park**—located in Sarnath, near Benares, India, where the Buddha gave his first sermon, also called the first turning of the Wheel of Dharma; a sacred place to Buddhists

**Defilements** (Tib. *dripb pa*, "veil")—that which would prevent us from gaining knowledge or insight; the root defilements are ignorance, desire, hostility, self-centeredness, and skeptical doubt

**Deity**—symbolic form of a pure being, manifested from Buddha's wisdom

**Delusion**—"that which afflicts from within;" the main delusion is ignorance, out of which grow attachment, hatred, and jealousy

**Demigod** (Sans. *asura*)—one of the six classes (realms) of beings, whose predominant emotion is jealousy

**Dependent origination**—doctrine that refers to cause and effect; one of the key realizations attained by Buddha during his awakening

**Devadatta**—"evil cousin" of Buddha, blamed for causing a schism within the monastic order; he is thought to have tried to have Buddha assassinated three times

**Devas** (Pali)—beings that inhabit the god realm, the highest of the six levels within cyclic existence

**Dhamma** (Pali)—Dharma

**Dharma** (Sans.; Tib. *chö*)—Buddhist doctrine, teachings, and practice; one of the Three Jewels (along with the Buddha and the Sangha); other definitions include: the basic building blocks of reality; a law of rule to be followed; good qualities; and truth

**Dharmapala** (Tib.)—see Dharma protector

**Dharma protector** (Tib. *dharmapala*)—those entities that protect the teachings of Dharma—Buddha's words—from being diluted or distorted. They are sometimes emanations of Buddhas or bodhisattvas; other times they might be spirits or demons that have been subdued by a master (such as Padmasambhava) and made to protect the teachings

**Dharmakaya** (Sans.)—truth body of a Buddha; the pure, omniscient mind of a Buddha, the result of the transformation of the ordinary mind

**Dhyana** (Sans.)—meditation, or internal contemplation; the practice of mind control by which we seek to realize the truth

**Disrobe**—when a monk or nun leaves monastic life, giving back his or her vows, it is called disrobing

**Dog** (Tib. *kyi*)—it is said that many of the dogs that congregate around monasteries are the reincarnations of naughty monks

**Dogen**—monk who brought Soto Zen to Japan

**Dorje** (Tib.; Sans. *vajra*)—in tantric Buddhism, a five-pronged scepter, the two ends of which are said to represent wisdom and compassion. As a whole, it represents the unbreakable union of wisdom and compassion; in ceremonies, a dorje is usually used in conjunction with a bell (*drilbu*)

**Drilbu** (Tib.)—hand bell that is used in Tibetan Buddhist ceremonies, almost always in conjunction with a Dorje

**Drubkhang** (Tib.)—meditation hermitage

**Duchen** (Tib.)—large assembly hall in a monastery

**Dukhang** (Tib.)—assembly hall in a monastery

**Dukkha** (Pali)—suffering, the First Noble Truth; a primary goal of Buddhism is overcoming dukkha

**Dungchen** (Tib.)—long horns that are played during ceremonies, creating very deep bass tones; due to the lengths (up to 15 feet long), the horns are made to telescope for easy transport and storage

**Dungkhor** (Tib.)—large prayer wheel, usually permanently attached to a wall, to be spun by pilgrims

**Dzogchen** (Tib.) ("Great Perfection," "Great Completeness")—meditation practice associated with the Nyingma school based on the concept that all appearances are creations of the mind

**Dzong** (Tib.)—fort or fortress

**Ecumenical**—teachings that do not identify with only one particular school or lineage, but include all schools and paths in its Dharma; Rimé is an example of such a school

**Eightfold Path** (Sans. *magga*)—the path, described by Buddha, that leads to the cessation of suffering: right view, aspiration, speech, action, livelihood, effort, mindfulness, and concentration

**Emanation**—a thing which comes from a source, i.e., the Dalai Lama is an emanation of Chenrezig

**Empowerment**—ceremony which introduces the practitioner to the powerfield of a certain Buddha aspect. It may be given as a blessing or at the start of a practice. Examples of prominent empowerments would be Tara and Kalachakra. Sometimes also termed an initiation, which empowers one to practice the teachings of a particular deity

**Emptiness** (Sans. *sunyata*)—the doctrine that all concepts and phenomena lack inherent existence, that lack independent self-existence, and that everything is dependent on something outside of itself in order for it to exist

**Enlightenment** (Sans. *bodhi*)—highest level of development, having forever

eliminated all defilements and karmic imprints, and having developed all good qualities and wisdom to their fullest extent; full awakening; Buddhahood
**Equanimity**—being unbiased; the state of mind in which one does not distinguish or discriminate between, for example, good/indifferent/bad or friend/stranger/enemy
**Excellent Words**—the words of the Buddha

**Five sadhus**—the five ascetics who practiced self-mortification with Siddhartha Gautama (one of the early paths the Buddha experienced in his search)
**Four Noble Truths** (Sans. *Arya-Satya*)—the Doctrine as taught by the Buddha: 1. the truth of suffering (*dukkha*); 2. the truth of the arising (causes) of suffering (*trishna*); 3. the truth of the cessation of suffering (*nirodha*); and 4. the truth of the path that leads beyond suffering (the Eightfold Path) (*magga*)

**Ganachakra** (Tib.)—vajra feast
**Gassho** (Jap.)—hand gesture, placing the fingertips and palms together in a prayerlike position. Used to show reverence to the Buddha or teachers
**Gati** (Sans.)—realm; used for the six realms (gods, demi-gods, humans, animals, hungry ghosts, and hell-beings)
**Gautama** (Gotama)—family name of the historical Buddha of this age
**Gelug** (Geluk) (Tib.)—largest order of Tibetan Buddhism, founded by Tsongkhapa in the 15th century; sometimes called Yellow Hats. Main emphasis is on ethics and sound scholarship prior to serious meditation. It claims to be a more authentic version of Indian Buddhism than other schools. Dalai Lama is of this school, although traditionally the Dalai Lama would study all schools and many traditions
**Gen** (Tib.) (Gen-la)—respected teacher (title)
**Geshe** (Tib.)—degree/title awarded to monks (and nuns as of April 2011), similar to Doctor of Theology, although it may take 15 to 20 years to attain. Includes such areas of study as monastic discipline, logic, debate, epistemology, cosmology, and traditional medicine. Levels of the degree are: Lharampa (highest, meaning "divine scholarly spiritual friend"), Tsokrampa, Lingse, and Dorampa
**Gompa** (Tib.)—monastery, a place of meditation; spiritual community
**Göngkhang** (Tib.)—chapel in a monastery where protective deities are worshipped

**Götshang** (Tib.)—mountain hermitage

**Guardian deity**—the deity with which a practitioner has a special relationship, based on specific criteria with which the deity reveals to the individual; also known as protector deity or tutelary deity. For example, Palden Lhamo is the guardian deity of the Dalai Lama

**Guru** (Sans.)—spiritual teacher

**Guru Rinpoche**—see Padmasambhava

**Guru-yoga** (Sans.)—form of meditation through which one realizes that one's own mind is inseparable from the mind of the teacher and from the ultimate reality—enlightenment; practice of connecting one's mind with the mind of the teacher

**Gyaling** (Tib.)—musical reed instrument, similar to an oboe, played during ceremonies

**Gyaltsen** (Tib.)—victory banner mounted on the roof of a monastery

**Gyalwa** (Tib.)—usually translated as "the Victorious One." In a more general context, "Gyalwa" refers to a Buddha (Martin, *Music in the Sky*)

**Habitual tendencies**—thoughts, speech, or actions that are exhibited through what one has done in past lives

**Heart disciple**—a person receiving and knowing and acting upon all of his or her teacher's teachings and the teachings and actions of the teacher's lineage. A teacher can have more than one "common" heart disciple, but only one "uncommon" heart disciple. Not all teachers will have a heart disciple

**Hell Being** (Tib. *dmyalba*; Sans. *naraka*)—a resident of the lowest of the six realms of existence

**Hinayana** (Sans.)—Buddhist path leading to individual (rather than collective) liberation from samsara; sometimes called lesser vehicle (Mahayana being called the greater vehicle)

**HE**—His Eminence (e.g., HE Tai Situ Rinpoche)

**HH**—His Holiness (e.g., HH the 14th Dalai Lama)

**Ignorance** (Sans. *avidya*)—unawareness, lack of enlightenment; not knowing the principles of karma; not seeing that which exists, or the way in which things exist; one of the three poisons (along with attachment and anger)

**Inherent existence**—that which exists in its own right and is not dependent on anything else to exist

**Initiation**—similar to Empowerment

**Kadam** (Tib.)—Tibetan Buddhist tradition founded by Indian teacher Atisha, who came to Tibet in 1042; it emphasizes monastic discipline and the cultivation of Bodhicitta; many of its teachings were taken up by other schools, particularly Tsongkhapa in founding the Gelug school

**Kagyü** (Tib.)—group of Tibetan Buddhist schools founded by Tilopa, Naropa, and Marpa, and continuing with the disciples of the 11th century saint, poet, and lama Milarepa and his student Gampopa; emphasizes practice of tantric yoga

**Kalachakra** (Sans.)—"wheel of time;" a Tantra containing a complex cosmology, including apocalyptic theory of history involving a great war at the end of history, and triumph in Shambhala

**Kalpa** (Sans.)—lifetime of a universe; millions of years; an eternity

**Kamma** (Pali)—Karma

**Kangling** (Tib.)—ritual musical instrument—a trumpet/horn—traditionally made from a human thighbone

**Kangyur** (Kanjur) (Tib.)—collection of all Sutras and Tantras spoken by Shakyamuni Buddha translated from Sanskrit into Tibetan; reportedly stored in 1334 in Shalu Monastery, it comprised 108 volumes, and became the basis for all later editions. Tengyur is the collection of commentaries on the Sutras and Tantras. Also see Tengyur

**Karma** (Sans.; Tib. *lay*)—universal law of cause and effect which governs rebirth and the world of samsara; the concept that binds beings to an endless cycle of birth, death, and rebirth and, according to one's deeds in life, determines the condition of one's rebirth

**Karmapa** (Tib.)—"the one who carries out Buddha-activity;" suborder of the Kagyu school of Tibetan Buddhism, also known as the Black Hats; title of the reincarnate lama who heads the order, currently the 17th Karmapa, Orgyen Trinley Dorje

**Karuna** (Pali)—compassion or mercy, the special kindness shown to those who suffer; an attitude of active concern for the suffering of sentient beings

**Kaya** (Sans.)—"body;" in Mahayana, the three aspects of the body of a Buddha: the body of dharma, the body of bliss, and the body of transformation

**Khang** (Tib.)—house; house within a college within a monastery

**Khangtsen** (Tib.)—house in a monastic college; residential quarters of monks

**Khata** (Kata, Katag) (Tib.)—scarf, usually white (but can be ivory, blue, or yellow), of fine cotton or silk, used for ceremonial purposes, as a ritual offering or a gift

**Khenpa** (Tib.)—abbess of a nunnery
**Khenpo** (Tib.)—abbot of a monastery
**Khorla** (Tib.)—Dharma wheel, often seen above the entry to a monastery
**Koan** (Jap.)—a riddle, tale, or short statement used in Zen to bring practitioners to sudden insight (such as "What is the sound of one hand clapping?")
**Kora** (Tib.)—ritual circuit; path along which one circumambulates (clockwise for Tibetan Buddhists, counterclockwise for practitioners of Bön)
**Kudung khang** (Tib.)—reliquary room, where sacred relics are kept
**Kumbum** (Tib.)—large, multi-leveled, multi-chapel stupa, such as those found at Kumbum Jampaling Monastery in Amdo in northeast Tibet, and in Gyantse, southwest of Lhasa
**Kundun** (Tib.)—name for the Dalai Lama, meaning "The Presence"; title of a book (1997) and a movie (1997) about the Dalai Lama and his family from the time of his discovery as a reincarnation at the age of two until the time he went into exile from Tibet to India in 1959
**Kushinagara** (Pali)—town in northern India where Shakyamuni Buddha attained parinirvana. One of the major Buddhist pilgrimage sites
**Kuten (Kuden)** (Tib.)—"the physical basis;" term used for the person through which a deity is able to communicate with the human realm from the spirit realm
**Kwannon** (Jap.)—name for Avalokiteshvara
**Kwan Yin** (Chin.)—name for Avalokiteshvara
**Kyabje** (Tib.)—honorific title bestowed on revered teachers, meaning "glorious refuge"

**La** (Tib.)—pass (as in a high mountain pass); honorific, placed at the end of someone's name, such as Jamyang-la; "soul" or "spirit"
**Labrang** (Tib.)—residence of an abbot
**Lama** (Tib.)—literally translated as "none higher" or "superior one." It indicates a person who has been recognized as a spiritual guide; a teacher, capable of giving initiations and guiding students along the Vajrayana path. It can mean a personal religious teacher, or the head or leading figure within a spiritual community, or a properly qualified performer of Tantric ritual. A lama plays a crucial role in Tibetan Buddhism particularly in the transmission of teachings and rituals to students. Different orders and sects have different qualifications for this title. The role of a monk and a lama are different—most monks are not lamas, and all lamas are not necessarily monks. Corresponds to Sanskrit *guru*, but has a wider range of meanings in Tibetan

**Lamaism**—term used in the late 19th and 20th centuries by some western scholars to describe their concept of Tibetan Buddhism
**Lha gyal lo** (Tib.)—"victory to the gods;" traditional Tibetan phrase of celebration or rejoicing
**Lha** (Tib.)—general term for deities, including local gods as well as Tantric deities
**Lhakhang** (Tib.)—"deity house;" chapel or temple
**Lhasa** ("Abode of the Gods")—capital city of Tibet, and center of Tibetan culture
**Liberation**—state of being after defilements and karma (which cause samsara) have been removed; freedom from samsara
**Lineage**—the succession of Buddhist teachers who transmit a particular tradition from teacher to student in a continuous line; the chronological listing of teachers belonging to a specific line of tantric practice
**Lingkhor** (Tib.)—external (from a monastery) circumambulatory circuit
**Lokapala** (Tib.)—"worldly protector;" any of the protector deities that have not reached complete enlightenment
**Losar** (Tib.)—Tibetan New Year's festival, taking place in the first week of the first lunar month of the Tibetan calendar (often February)
**Lower Realms**—of the six realms of existence, the three lower regions: hells, hungry ghosts, and animals
**Lu** (Tib.; Sans. *naga*)—water-dwelling, serpent-like spirits
**Lumbini Grove**—located in Nepal, near the border with India; where Siddhartha Gautama, the future Buddha, was born in 563 BCE. An important Buddhist pilgrimage site
**Lungta** (Tib.)—"wind horse;" prayer flag

**Madhyamaka** (Sans.)—Middle Way school, whose doctrines are based on the notion that all phenomena are empty of inherent existence
**Magga** (Pali)—path leading to the cessation of suffering, the Eightfold Path—the fourth of the Four Noble Truths
**Mahakala** (Sans.)—wrathful aspect of Avalokiteshvara. Considered by Mongolians to be that country's patron Buddha and by Tibetans as a Dharma protector
**Mahamaya** (Mayadevi, Maya)—Siddhartha Gautama's mother, who died seven days after giving birth to him
**Mahamudra** (Sans.)—"great seal;" meditation system found in all schools of Tibetan Buddhism, based on a direct, personal realization of truth

**Mahaprajapati**—stepmother and aunt of the Buddha, and founder of the order of Buddhist nuns

**Mahayana** (Sans.)—Buddhist path which leads to Buddhahood for the benefit of all sentient beings; sometimes called the greater vehicle (see Hinayana)

**Maitreya**—the Buddha of the future; the next (fifth) Buddha of this era, following Buddha Shakyamuni

**Mala** (Sans.; Tib. *treng ah*)—sometimes called prayer beads, they are used to count the repetitions of one's mantras, or of other spiritual practices. Buddhists traditionally use a 108-bead mala. The beads, strung together in a circle on a string, can be made of any type of material, most commonly seeds, wood, glass, bone, or gemstones

**Mandala** (Sans.)—circular diagram used in meditation as an aid to visualization, which represents the residence and perfected attributes of a Buddha; symbolic representation of the universe; can occur as either a two- or three-dimensional form

**Mani stone** (Tib.)—stone inscribed with a Buddhist prayer, usually *Om Mani Padme Hum*

**Mani wall** (Tib.)—wall made up of mani stones; pilgrims would traditionally visit a shrine or holy place and add a mani stone to the mani wall, thus acquiring merit

**Manjushri** (Sans.)—Mahayana and Vajrayana deity of transcendent insight (prajna), patron of scholarship and wisdom; often depicted holding a flaming sword of wisdom (that cuts through false views) in one hand and a Perfection of Wisdom text in the other

**Mantra** (Sans.; Tib. *ngag*)—a series of syllables designed as a tool to focus the mind through repetition, and often used during meditation; commonly invokes the power of a particular Buddha. A widely used mantra is *Om Mani Padme Hum* ("Hail the Jewel in the Lotus"), the mantra of Chenrezig

**Mara** (Sans.)—demon associated with death and hindrances to enlightenment. It was Mara who tempted Buddha beneath the Bodhi Tree. According to Buddhist mythology, there are many maras, whose goal is to tempt people into ignorance, delusion, hatred, and desire

**Marga** (Sans.)—the path; general term for Buddhist practice that leads to liberation from cyclic existence; specifically, the Eightfold Path, that leads beyond suffering

**Marpa**—main disciple of Naropa

**Maya**—mother of Shakyamuni Buddha

**Meditation** (Tib. *gom*)—general term that encompasses a wide range of mental practices. Some aim at pacifying the mind and quieting the mental confusion that afflicts people (shamatha), while others are concerned with developing clear understanding and insight of Buddhist practices (vipassana).

**Meditational deity**—a deity that one visualizes during meditation to represent a particular aspect of the full enlightenment of Buddhahood

**Mendicant**—a beggar; a member of a religious order (monks) who because of a vow of poverty, must be supported by alms

**Merit** (Sans. *punya*)—good actions in one of a person's successive states of existence which help to determine his or her fate in the next or future states; positive imprints left on the mind; spiritual credit held to be earned by performance of righteous acts and to ensure beneficial future rebirths

**Merit field**—a technique used in some tantric practices where one visualizes a field (sometimes in the form of a tree) with your lama, lineage masters and teachers, Buddhas, and Bodhisattvas in front of you; see Refuge Tree

**Middle Way**—the path taught by the historical Buddha, Shakyamuni, that leads to enlightenment by avoiding the extremes of self-indulgence on one end or self-mortification on the other, but rather takes the middle path, or the Middle Way

**Milarepa**—great poet/saint in Tibetan Buddhism (1040-1123) particularly revered as an ordinary person who attained enlightenment in one lifetime

**Mindstream**—"that which is clear and knowing;" continuity of the mind from one lifetime to another

**Monlam Chenmo** (Tib.)—great prayer festival/ceremony initiated by Tsongkhapa in 1409. Celebrated annually, beginning at Tibetan New Year (Losar), involving both lay and monastics, and includes prayer, chanting, prostrations, and public lectures

**Mount Meru (Mount Sumeru)**—huge mountain in the center of the universe, as conceived by Tibetan Buddhist cosmology. Underneath Mount Meru are the hungry ghosts and hell-beings; at the base of Mount Meru is the animal realm; above that is the human realm, and higher up the slopes are the demi-gods and the gods, making up the six realms of existence within samsara. Mount Kailash in western Tibet is considered by many to be Mount Meru

**Mudra** (Sans.)—hand gestures, often seen in Buddhist iconography (such as statues and thangkas), which have various meanings, such as meditation, reassurance, earth-touching, and teaching

**Mundane attachment**—the feelings one has for all worldly things, or that which is mundane

**Nagarjuna**—Indian sage of the 1st-2nd century CE, renowned for his writing on the Middle Path

**Nagas** (Sans.; Tib. *lu*)—beings with serpent-like bodies and human heads said to inhabit rivers, lakes, or oceans. According to legend, Buddha gave "Perfection of Wisdom" texts to the nagas to keep until someone who was able to interpret them came along, which happened in the early second century CE, when Nagarjuna retrieved the books

**Namu Amida Butsu** (Jap.)—mantra used in the Pure Land traditions of Buddhism, "Praise to Amitabha Buddha"

**Nangkhor** (Tib.)—inner circumambulatory passage

**Naraka** (Sans.)—hell beings, the lowest realm of rebirth

**Naropa**—student of Tilopa

**Nekhor** (Tib.)—pilgrimage circuit (kora) around a holy site

**Nibbana** (Pali)—Nirvana

**Nichiren** (Jap.)—Japanese school of Buddhism, emphasizing chanting

**Nirodha** (Sans.)—cessation of suffering (the Third Noble Truth)

**Nirvana** (Sans.)—liberation, enlightenment, liberation from the cycle of rebirth and suffering (samsara); a goal of spiritual practice in Buddhism

**Non-duality**—the absence of an ultimate distinction between the self and divine reality

**Nyingma**—oldest Tibetan Buddhist tradition, founded in the 8th century with the teachings of Padmasambhava; emphasizes Tantric tradition and Dzogchen practice

**Obscurations**—those things that have been put in front of us that do not allow us to see reality

**Obstructions**—those things which make it difficult to progress (towards enlightenment)

**Om Mani Padme Hum**—mantra of Chenrezig

**Padmasambhava**—also known as Guru Rinpoche, this great Indian tantric master came to Tibet around 760 CE and, after dispelling evil forces, introduced Buddhist teachings

**Pali**—language similar to Sanscrit, but a different dialect from a particular area of northwestern India

**Pali canon**—body of Buddhist texts written in Pali and regarded as the canon by Theravadan schools; the Tibetan equivalent is the Kangyur

**Pancha shila** (Sans.)—the five moral precepts: avoid killing or harming any living being; avoid stealing; avoid sexual misconduct or irresponsibility; avoid lying or any hurtful speech; and avoid alcohol and drugs which diminish clarity of consciousness

**Panchen Lama** (Tib., "Great Scholar")—title of successive incarnations of Sakya Pandita, traditionally residing at Tashilhunpo Monastery; the second highest incarnation of Tibet, after the Dalai Lama

**Pandita** (Sans.)—scholar (or great scholar), most often associated with those from India, who are learned in the five traditional sciences (language, medicine, art, logic, and astrology)

**Pañña** (Pali)—Prajña

**Paramita** (Sans.)—see Perfections

**Parinirvana** (Sans.)—final nirvana and passing away of the Buddha

**Pecha** (Tib.)—religious text, usually horizontal pages block-printed on one side only; bound between two "covers" usually made of wood

**Pehar** (Pekar) (Tib.)—important guardian deity who manifests through a spirit medium (kuten, in this case the Nechung Oracle) to advise the Dalai Lama and his government

**Perfections**—qualities (usually six) that, bringing to perfection, define the path of a bodhisattva: generosity, ethical discipline, patience, perseverance, meditative concentration, and discriminative awareness

**Phuk** (Tib.)—cave

**Phurba** (Tib.)—small dagger with a triangular blade, used in Buddhist rituals

**Pitaka** (Sans.)—"basket," referring to the Tripitaka, or Buddhist scriptures

**Prajña** (Sans.)—wisdom, or discriminative awareness; it represents the wisdom obtained during enlightenment, and one of the key insights is emptiness

**Prajña-Paramita Sutra**—collection of Mahayana texts, including the Heart and Diamond Sutras, dealing with Prajna and its attainment

**Prana** (Sans.)—"breath," "wind," "energy;" wind/energy in Tantra which is the vehicle of consciousness

**Prateyaka-buddha** (Sans.)—a solitary Buddhist practitioner who has attained personal enlightenment and Nirvana without the aid of a teacher

**Preta** (Sans.)—hungry ghost; a being obsessed by attachment, living in the preta-realm within the desire realm (one of the six realms of existence), mainly suffering from lack of food, drink, and shelter

**Protective deity**—see Guardian deity

**Puja** (Sans.)—a traditional religious ceremony during which offerings and prayers are made to Buddha or other deities, to request help from them or to ask for their blessings

**Purba**—see Phurba

**Pure Land**—realms where pure beings—such as Buddhas and Bodhisattvas—abide, where samsara does not exist, and where all conditions are conducive for practicing Dharma

**Rahula**—son of the historical Buddha Shakyamuni

**Refuge** (Tib. *skyabs*)—when one has reached the conclusion that he or she wants to commit to a Buddhist practice, refuge vows are taken, when one declares that one has decided to rely on the Three Jewels of Buddhism—the Buddha, the Dharma, and the Sangha

**Refuge Tree**—a visualization, either mental or physical as in the form of a thangka, where your spiritual guru sits, and all about him are the lineage of gurus and teachers that came before. Each school of Tibetan Buddhism has a thangka representing the lineage of that school, called a Refuge Tree; in the Gelug version, for example, Tsongkhapa would have a prominent position as founder of the sect. (see example on page 69)

**Reincarnation**—the belief that the spirit/consciousness/essence/mindstream of a sentient being returns to life through rebirth in a new body, bringing with it positive and negative karmic imprints from previous lives

**Relic** (Sans. *sarira*, Pali *dhatu*)—originally the cremated remains of the Buddha; the bodily remains, usually after cremation, of a holy or revered person

**Reliquary**—a container or shrine in which sacred relics are kept; a chorten would be an example of a reliquary

**Renunciation**—the determination to be free from samsara

**Retreat**—a time (and place) of personal solitude when one engages in reflection, meditation, and spiritual practices. In Tibet, this was often done in caves remotely located for this purpose

**Ri** (Tib.)—mountain

**Rimé** (Tib.)—"unbiased;" movement begun in Tibet towards the end of the 19th century stressing the common grounds of Buddhist lineages and meditation, and minimizing the differences among the schools

**Rinpoche** (Tib.)—"Precious one;" honorific applied to reincarnate lamas and other highly respected individuals
**Root lama**—the individual who comes to be one's personal spiritual guide and from whom one learns about enlightenment and the nature of the mind
**Rupa** (Sans.)—form; the physical body; senses; a Buddhist statue

**Sadhana** (Sans.)—tantric meditational ritual usually focusing on a particular deity or group of deities; normally involves visualization, recitation of verses and mantras, physical gestures, and real or visualized offerings to a particular deity in order to attain enlightenment
**Sadhu** (saddhu) (Sans.)—in Hinduism, an ascetic or practitioner of yoga (yogi) who has given up pursuit of worldly pleasures and is solely dedicated to achieving liberation. The term sadhu has its roots in Hinduism, but is also used for followers of other religions if they live the sadhu lifestyle. Perhaps the most famous non-Hindu following the sadhu lifestyle was Siddhartha Gautama, who became a Buddha
**Sakya** (Tib.)—one of the four major Tibetan Buddhist schools, which stresses scholarship and tantric practice; monastery founded in 1073 by Kon Chögyal Pho in central Tibet
**Samadhi** (Sans.)—one-pointed meditation where the meditation object and the meditator are experienced as inseparable
**Samatha** (Pali)—Shamatha
**Samaya** (Sans.)—commitment, promise; sacred link between a teacher and disciple
**Samsara** (Sans.; Tib. *kor wa*)—the cycle of repeated existence; the world where we must continuously be reborn, die, be reborn, die, due to the accumulated negative karma of previous lifetimes
**Samudaya** (Sans.)—arising of suffering, the Second Noble Truth
**Sangha** (Sans.)—the community of Buddhist practitioners; sometimes used to mean monks and nuns, sometimes meant to include all followers on the path; one of the Three Jewels, along with Buddha and Dharma
**Sanskrit**—early language of northern India, modified and used as a religious language by some Buddhists
**Satori** (Jap.)—Zen term for enlightenment
**Sentient being** (Sans. *sattva*)—a being that has consciousness. The five factors necessary for this are feeling, discrimination, intention, mental activity, and contact
**Shakyamuni** (Sakyamuni)—family name of the historical Buddha, living

in the 6th century BCE. Literally means sage of the Shakya (clan); the Buddha of our time, and the fourth Buddha of this era

**Shamatha** (Samatha, Shamata) (Tib.)—one form of meditation, also called calm abiding, used to pacify and calm the mind

**Shambhala** (Shambala) (Tib.)—mythical Buddhist kingdom said to be in a hidden valley, protected from outsiders, in the north of Tibet; branch of Mahayana Buddhism developed in the early 1980s by Chögyam Trungpa Rinpoche

**Shravaka** (Sans.)—"hearer," one who needs the help of others to become enlightened

**Shunyata** (sunyata) (Sans.)—emptiness; the belief that all things are empty of inherent existence—that they do not exist except in relationship with other things

**Siddha** (Sans.)—one who had acquired supernatural powers

**Siddhartha Gautama**—birth name of the historical Buddha of this time

**Silnyen** (Tib.)—large flat cymbals played during ceremonies

**Six realms of existence** (Tib. *rikdruk*)—gods, demi-gods, humans, animals, hungry ghosts, and hell-beings

**Skandhas** (Sans.)—aggregate, parts of the self: form (body), feeling, recognition, volition, and primary consciousness

**Spiritual companions**—students with whom one has received teachings, or students of the same teacher

**Spiritual friend**—spiritual teacher, but not necessarily one's root lama

**Stupa** (Sans.; Tib. *chörten*)—traditionally, dome-shaped monuments containing relics of the Buddha or his disciples. In Tibetan Buddhism, they are of a particular shape and proportion, representing the Buddha's mind, and may contain relics of a deceased teacher or sacred objects. They also serve to identify important Buddhist sites

**Suchness**—see Emptiness

**Suffering** (Sans. *dukkha*)—the First Noble Truth as defined by Buddha; a condition that results in physical and/or mental pain

**Sumeru**—see Mount Meru

**Sungkhang** (Tib.)—chapel of a protective guardian deity

**Sutra** (Sans.)—an oral teaching directly attributed to the historical Shakyamuni Buddha

**Sutra pitaka** (Sans.)—section of Buddhist canon containing sermons attributed to the historical Buddha

**Sutta** (Pali)—Sutra

**Tantra** (Sans.)—Buddhist texts that outline the practices of vajrayana

**Tara** (Sans.)—popular Buddha in Tibetan cosmology. Female in gender, she has twenty-one main emanations, the most popular being White Tara (Tib. *Drolma*) and Green Tara (Tib. *Drolkar*)

**Tashi Delek** (Tib.)—a phrase of greeting used throughout the Tibetan diaspora. Not exactly meaning hello, it is said to mean "blessings and good luck" or "good fortune" or "may everything be well" or "may all auspicious signs come to this environment." In traditional Tibet, it was used primarily during Losar, as a New Year's greeting

**Tathagata** (Sans.)—"One thus gone"—an epithet of Buddhas signifying the attainment of awakening and a transcendent state that surpasses all mundane attachments. "It is thus taken to signify one who, having thus gone, will not come again, i.e., who will have no rebirths—hence, one who has attained supreme enlightenment." (www.exoticindia.com)

**Tengyur** (Tenjur) (Tib.)—collection of commentaries of Buddha's teachings translated from Sanskrit into Tibetan, comprising 225 volumes including philosophical treatises and commentaries. In 1334 it was stored at Shalu Monastery (southwest of Shigatse), and became the basis for all later editions. See also Kangyur

**Terma** (Tib.)—"hidden treasure;" general term for relics and/or texts hidden by Padmasambhava or his disciples during the eighth century, to be discovered later by the appropriate finder. See Tertön

**Tertön** (Tib.)—"treasure discoverer" or "finder of terma;" some believed to be rebirths of disciples of Padmasambhava, they were preordained to find certain objects or texts when the time was right for their discovery

**Thangka** (tangka) (Tib.)—painting on a cloth, meant to be able to be rolled up for transport or storage, typically of a religious nature, and considered sacred

**Theraveda** (Sans.) ("The Teachings of the Elders")—dominant Buddhist tradition found in Southeast Asia, and following the Hinayana school

**Three fires** (poisons)—the basic causes of suffering: ignorance/delusion (*moha*), attachment/greed (*lobha*), and anger/hatred (*dosa*); the three poisons are subdued by using the antidote—the three jewels: meditation, non-attachment, and compassion and love.

**Three Jewels/Gems**—the Buddha, the Dharma, and the Sangha

**Thusness—**the nature of things; emptiness

**Tibet** (Tib. *Bod*)—Asian country, north of India, and west of China. Historically independent from the 7th century CE until the 1949 invasion and occupation by the People's Republic of China, which claimed that Tibet was, and is, an integral part of China. Prior to the occupation, Tibet was virtually 100 percent Buddhist, and ruled spiritually and temporally by the Dalai Lamas since the 17th century

**Tilden** (Tib.)—altar cloth, usually of brocade

**Tilopa**—Indian Tantric sage (988-1069 CE) who is credited with starting the Kagyu school of Tibetan Buddhism

**Tipitaka** (Pali)—Tripitaka

**Tonglen** (Tib.)—mind training/meditation to overcome selfishness and develop compassion for others; giving up one's own happiness and taking other's suffering (often called give and take); generally undertaken to prepare the mind for attainment of Bodhicitta

**Torma** (Tib.)—offering used during rituals, made of butter and barley flour, shaped and dyed in many sizes and shapes, in homage to Buddhist deities

**Tratsang** (Tib.)—monastic college

**Tripa** (Tib.)—head of the Gelug sect of Tibetan Buddhism; also serves as the abbot of Ganden Monastery

**Tripitaka** (Sans.)—"three baskets;" the three collections of Buddhist scriptures: 1. Vinayana pitaka; 2. Sutra pitaka; and 3. Abhidharma pitaka

**Triple Jewels** (Triple Gems)—the Buddha, the Dharma, and the Sangha

**Trishna** (Sans.)—"desire;" the second of the Four Noble Truths; divided into three types: 1. craving for sensual pleasures; 2. craving for continued existence; and 3. craving for non-existence

**Tsa Tsa** (Tib.)—a small clay Buddha, deity, or stupa, made from a mold; sometimes they will have the ashes from a deceased person combined with the clay they are made from; a merit-making activity

**Tsamkhang** (Tib.)—hermitage; meditation room

**Tsampa** (Tib.)—a staple food in Tibet, made of roasted barley (including the husk) ground into very fine flour, then usually mixed with tea and rolled into small balls and eaten with the fingers; it may be mixed with butter, sugar, or curds to add flavor

**Tshokchen** (Tib.)—great assembly hall

**Tshokhang** (Tib.)—assembly hall

**Tso** (Tib.)—lake

**Tsog** (Tsok) (Tib.)—"gathering;" a ceremony for the Buddhas when one makes offerings of food and drink, along with prayers; one method for purifying negativity, receiving blessings, and accumulating merit

**Tsongkhapa** (1357–1419)—founded Ganden Monastery (1409), which became the basis for the Gelug ("Virtuous Ones") school

**Tsuglag Khang** (Tib.)—Tibetan name for the Jokhang Temple in Lhasa, and also for the Central Temple in Dharamsala, India

**Tubo** (Tib.)—Ancient name for Tibet. Nowadays, many Tibetans living in Tibet prefer to use this name for Tibet rather than the Chinese name "Xizang" since it only includes central Tibet and leaves Amdo (north-east Tibet) and Kham (south-east Tibet) out. After Chinese occupation, Amdo was incorporated into the Chinese provinces of Qinghai and Gansu, and Kham into the provinces of Sichuan and Yunnan

**Tulku** (Tib.)—recognized reincarnation of a lama

**Tumo** (Tummo) (Tib.; "inner fire")—tantric yogic meditation technique whereby the practitioner can raise the temperature of his or her body

**Tushita** (Sans.)—Joyous Land; the Bodhisattva pure realm of the 1000 Buddhas of this aeon

**Tutelary deity**—see Yidam

**Upali**—one of the ten main disciples of Buddha, and the first person ordained by him as a monk; after ordination, he specialized in the study of the Vinaya, or monastic rules

**Urna** (Sans.)—mark on the Buddha's forehead between his eyes, signifying his great intuition

**Ushanisha** (Sans.)—protuberance on top of the Buddha's head, signifying his great wisdom

**Vajra** (Sans.)—see Dorje

**Vajrasattva** (Sans.)—important Buddha in Tibetan tantric Buddhism, specially relating to purification practices; the practice/ceremony of purifying negative actions

**Vajrayana** (Sans.)—Tibetan tantric Buddhist practice

**Ven.**—Venerable (used for a monk or nun who has been ordained)

**VV**—Very Venerable

**Vihara** (Sans.)—cave dwelling for monks; monastery, temple

**Vinaya pitaka** (Sans.)—one of the three major divisions of Buddhist scriptures, governing the rules of discipline for the monastic community (monks and nuns)

**Vipashyana** (Sans.)—seeing beyond, superior or excellent seeing, insight; meditation technique involving the analysis of a meditative object, aiming at direct realization of its final nature (called Vipassana meditation)

**Virtue**—merit, positive potential; positive actions imprinted on the mindstream, leading to future happiness

**Visualization**—to form a mental image of something, often a deity

**Wat** (Thai, from Sans.)—term used in Therevadan countries, such as Cambodia and Thailand, for a Buddhist temple or monastery, such as Angkor Wat, in Cambodia

**Wheel of Dharma** (Tib. *khorla*)—a symbol of the Buddha's teachings (often shown in conjunction with two deer, to symbolize his first teaching at a deer park in Sarnath, India); to turn the Wheel of Dharma means to teach the Dharma; during his lifetime, the Buddha gave three major series of teachings, which are referred to as the first, second, and third turning of the Wheel of Dharma

**Wisdom**—understanding of things that goes beyond intellectual knowing; one of the two Buddhist virtues (the other being compassion)

**Wrathful manifestation/deity**—the manifestation of a deity or bodhisattva whose purpose is to assist one in removing obstructions and negative influences to Dharma practice, to tame destructive forces, and protect Buddhism against its enemies. For example, Mahakala is a wrathful manifestation that destroys mind chatter and brings the mind back into focus. Despite the ferocious appearance of the wrathful and semi-wrathful deities—their symbolic gestures and implements, dramatic colors, fantastic anatomies, and theatrical poses and gestures—these fierce and violent-looking deities are benign agents and protectors

**Yab-Yum** (Tib.) ("father-mother")—in the Buddhist art of India, Nepal, and Tibet, the representation of the male deity in sexual embrace with his female consort; the pose is generally understood to represent the mystical union of the active force, or method (*upaya,* conceived of as masculine), with wisdom (*prajna,* conceived of as feminine)—a fusion necessary to overcome the false duality

**Yama** (Sans.)—god of death and king of the hells in Buddhist mythology

**Yamantaka** (Sans.)—wrathful manifestation of Manjushri, the Buddha of wisdom

**Yana** (Pali; Tib. *thegpa*)—"vehicle;" refers to the path to salvation and enlightenment; often meaning the Hinayana, Mahayana, and Vajrayana

**Yashodhara** (Yasodhara)—wife of the Buddha, whom he left to pursue liberation from suffering for all beings
**Yidam** (Tib.)—term for the Buddhas who are the focus of tantric visualization practices; mental image of a god or other entity used for meditation; also known as tutelary deities
**Yoga** (Sans.)—referring to any physical and/or mental discipline
**Yogi** (Sans.)—practitioner of yoga

**Zazen** (Jap.)—sitting meditation in Zen Buddhist tradition
**Zen** (Jap.)—"meditation Buddhism," the east Asian Buddhist tradition emphasizing the struggle to realize one's original nature; known as Ch'an in China, Son in Korea, and Tien in Vietnam
**Zimkhang** (Tib.)—hermitage
**Zimphuk** (Tib.)—cave retreat

APPENDIX 1

# Chronology

## CHRONOLOGY OF BUDDHISM AND BUDDHIST TIBET

The outline of the major events in Buddhism/Tibetan Buddhism are covered here, mostly in the Gelug lineage. Although events are listed here from around the world, concentration is on the Indian subcontinent and Tibet. Dates are from generally accepted sources.

| | |
|---|---|
| 563-483 BCE | Shakyamuni Buddha/Siddhartha Guatama |
| 563 | Birth at Lumbini |
| 534 | Renunciation |
| 528 | Enlightenment at Bodh Gaya |
| 483 | Death/Parinirvana at Kushinagara |
| 483 | First Buddhist Council, held at Rajagaha soon after the death of the Buddha in order to recite the Buddha's sayings (Sutras) and to codify the monastic rules (the Vinaya) |
| 383 | Second Buddhist Council, at Vaisali |
| 272-236 | Reign of Ashoka in India |
| 240 | Third Buddhist Council, at Pataliputra (or 253 BCE) |
| 200 | Beginnings of Mahayana Buddhism |
| 25-17 | Fourth Buddhist Council (Theravadan tradition), Sri Lanka; Pali Canon committed to writing (or 29 BCE) |
| 100 CE | Fourth Buddhist Council (Sarvastivada/Mahayana tradition), Gandhara/Kashmir |
| 1st Century | Buddhism enters Central Asia and China |
| c. 150-250 | Nagarjuna, Indian Buddhist philosopher |

| | |
|---|---|
| 2nd Century | Founding of Nalanda Monastic University, India |
| 3rd Century | Buddhism spreads to Burma, Cambodia, Indonesia, Laos, Vietnam |
| 372 | Buddhism enters Korea |
| 520 | Bodhidharma arrives in China, spreading Buddhism |
| 552 | Buddhism enters Japan from Korea |
| 617-650 | King Songtsen Gampo (Tibet)<br>Marriages of Songtsen Gampo to Nepalese Princess Bhrikuti (632) and Chinese Princess Wencheng (641), both of whom encouraged Buddhism in Tibet |
| 742-798 | King Trisong Detsen |
| 760 | Buddhism arrives in Tibet with Padmasambhava, who, along with Shantarakshita, starts first major dissemination |
| 775-779 | Samye Monastery founded |
| 792-794 | Great Debate between Indian/Tibetan and Chinese Ch'an Buddhism at Samye Monastery; Indian/Tibetan view won, and became the religion of Tibet |
| 806-841 | King Tri Ralpachan |
| 838-842 | End of first dissemination of Buddhism in Tibet with the reign of Langdarma |
| 978 | Beginning of the second major dissemination of Buddhism in Tibet |
| 982-1054 | Atisha |
| 988-1069 | Tilopa |
| 993-1077 | Drogmi, founder of Sakya order |
| 1012-1096 | Marpa, founder of Kagyu order (Red Hats) |
| 1016-1100 | Naropa |
| 1040-1123 | Milarepa, great Tibetan poet and saint |
| 1057 | Reting Monastery founded (center of Kadam order) |
| 1073 | Sakya Monastery founded (first of the Sakya order) |
| 1158 | Thil Monastery founded (Kagyu) |
| 1175 | Tshal Monastery founded (Kagyu) |
| 1179 | Drigung Monastery founded (Kagyu) |
| 1189 | Tsurphu Monastery founded (Kagyu Karmapa) (Black Hats) |
| 1182-1251 | Sakya Pandita |
| 1197 | Destruction of Nalanda Monastic University in India during an invasion; Buddhism largely disappears in India |

| | |
|---|---|
| 1270 | Kublai Khan (in Mongolia) converts to Tibetan Buddhism |
| 1357-1419 | Tsongkhapa, founder of Gelug tradition (Yellow Hats) |
| 1365-1438 | First Panchen Lama, Kedrup Geleg Pelzang (posthumous) |
| 1391-1474 | First Dalai Lama, Gedun Druba (posthumous) |
| 1409 | Ganden Monastery founded by Tsongkhapa (first of the Gelug order) |
| 1416 | Drepung Monastery founded (Gelug) |
| 1419 | Sera Monastery founded (Gelug) |
| 1437 | Chamdo Monstery founded in Kham (Gelug) |
| 1439-1504 | Second Panchen Lama, Sonam Choglang (posthumous) |
| 1447 | Tashilhunpo Monastery founded in Tsang by first Dalai Lama (future seat of Panchen Lamas) |
| 1475-1542 | Second Dalai Lama, Gedun Gyatso (posthumous) |
| 1505-1566 | Third Panchen Lama, Lobsang Dondrup (posthumous) |
| 1543-1588 | Third Dalai Lama, Sonam Gyatso |
| 1578 | Title of Dalai Lama (Ocean of Wisdom) bestowed on Sonam Gyatso by Mongol ruler Altan Khan |
| 1567-1662 | Fourth Panchen Lama, Lobzang Cholyi Gyaltsen |
| 1589-1617 | Fourth Dalai Lama, Yonden Gyatso |
| 1617-1682 | Fifth Dalai Lama, Ngawang Lozang Gyatso (often referred to as the Great Fifth) |
| 1645 | Construction begins on the Potala in Lhasa by Fifth Dalai Lama; completed in 1694 after his death |
| 1659 | Dorje Drak Monastery founded (Nyingma) |
| 1663-1737 | Fifth Panchen Lama, Jetsun Lobzang Yeshey |
| 1665 | Palyul Monastery founded (Nyingma) |
| 1676 | Mindroling Monastery founded (Nyingma) |
| 1683-1706 | Sixth Dalai Lama, Tsangyang Gyatso |
| 1685 | Dzokchen Monastery founded (Nyingma) |
| 1708-1757 | Seventh Dalai Lama, Kelsang Gyatso |
| 1738-1780 | Sixth Panchen Lama, Panchen Rinpoche |
| 1758-1804 | Eighth Dalai Lama, Jambel Gyatso |
| 1782-1854 | Seventh Panchen Lama, Lobzang Tenpai Nyima |
| 1815-1815 | Ninth Dalai Lama, Lungtok Gyatso |
| 1816-1837 | Tenth Dalai Lama, Tsultrim Gyatso |
| 1838-1855 | Eleventh Dalai Lama, Khedrub Gyatso |
| 1854-1882 | Eighth Panchen Lama, Tenpai Wangchuck |

| | |
|---|---|
| 1856-1875 | Twelfth Dalai Lama, Trinley Gyatso |
| 1868-1871 | Fifth Buddhist Council, Mandalay, Burma |
| 1876-1933 | Thirteenth Dalai Lama, Thupten Gyatso (often referred to as the Great Thirteenth) |
| 1881 | Founding of the Pali Text Society |
| 1883-1937 | Ninth Panchen Lama, Lobzang Chokyi Nyima |
| 1903-1904 | British invade Tibet, under Colonel Francis Younghusband |
| 1909-1910 | Chinese incursion into Tibet, prior to fall of the Qing dynasty |
| 1935- | Fourteenth Dalai Lama, Tenzin Gyatso |
| 1938-1989 | Tenth Panchen Lama, Choekyi Gyaltsen |
| 1949- | Invasion/occupation of Tibet by People's Republic of China |
| 1951 | Seventeen-Point Agreement |
| 1954-1956 | Sixth Buddhist Council, Rangoon, Burma |
| 1956 | Buddha Jayanti Year, celebration of the 2500th anniversay of Buddha's birth |
| 1959 | 14th Dalai Lama goes into exile to India |
| 1966-1976 | Chinese Cultural Revolution |
| 1989 | 14th Dalai Lama awarded Nobel Peace Prize |
| 1989- | Eleventh Panchen Lama, Gedun Choekyi Nyima |
| 2000 | 17th Karmapa escapes from Tsurphu Monastery in Tibet to go to India |

APPENDIX 2

# Schools and Sub-Schools

## Major Buddhist Schools and Sub-Schools

### Mahayana

**Pure Land**

Unified Buddhist Church—founded in France in 1969 by Vietnamese monk Thich Nhat Hanh

Jodo Shinshu—founded by Tendai Japanese monk Shinran Shonin (1173-1263)

Vietnamese Pure Land/Zen—various traditions came to Vietnam from the beginning of the common era through the 15th century; a combination of Pure Land and Zen Buddhism dominates Buddhist life in Vietnam. Zen practice is followed mostly by monks and nuns while Pure Land is preferred by the laity

**Yogacara**—founding traditionally ascribed to two half-brothers, Asanga and Vasubandhu, in fourth-fifth century CE India

**Zen**—a form of Buddhism practiced initially in Japan around 1200 CE, based on the practice of Buddhism from China, then mixed with the practice of Taoism

### Vajrayana (Tibetan Buddhism)

**Nyingma**

Aro gTér—The Aro teachings descend from a lineage of enlightened women—beginning with Yeshé Tsogyel. Aro is a small family lineage within that tradition—founded by the female visionary Lama Aro Lingma in 1909

Chagdud Gonpa—international Nyingma Buddhist organization, founded in 1983 by H.E. Chagdud Tulku Rinpoche (1930-2002)

Dzogchen—"a system of practice leading to enlightenment and involves a view of reality, way of meditating, and way of behaving. It is found earliest in the Nyingma and Bön (pre-Buddhist) traditions." (www.berzinarchives.com)

Palyul—origins go back to the eighth century reign of the Dharma King Trisong Deutsen in Tibet. The main practices are emphasized in the three inner tantras of Maha Yoga, Anu Yoga, and Ati Yoga. (www.palyul.org)

Rigpa—meaning "the innermost nature of the mind," Sogyal Rinpoche (author of *The Tibetan Book of Living and Dying*) gave this as the name for his work and to the vehicle he was developing to serve the Buddha's teaching in the West. Rigpa has more than 130 centers in 41 countries around the world.

**Kagyu**

Shangpa Kagyu—founded by Khyungpo Nyaljor (978-1079)

Dakpo Kagyu—founded by Gampopa (Dagpo Lhaje) (1084-1161)

***Four "Main" Schools****

Baram (Barom) Kagyu—founded by Baram Darma Wangchuk (unk.)

Karma (Kamtsang) Kagyu—founded by Dusum Khyenpa (1110-1193)

Tsalpa Kagyu—founded by Zhang Yudakpa Tsondu Dakpa (1123-1193)

Pagtru (Phaktru) Kagyu—founded by Phagmo Drupa (1100-1170)

***Eight "Branch" Schools****

Drikung Kagyu—founded by Jigten Sumgon (1143-1217)

Drukpa Kagyu—founded by Ling Repa (1128-1189); state religion of Bhutan

Martsang (Martshang) Kagyu—founded by Marpa Rinchen Lodoe (unk.)

Shukseb (Shugseb, Shuksep) Kagyu—founded by Chokyi Sengey (1144-1204)

Taklung Kagyu—founded by Taglung Thangpa Tashe Pel (1142-1210)

Trobu (Trophu) Kagyu—founded by Rinpoche Gyaltsa (unk.)

Yazang (Yasang) Kagyu—founded by Yeshi Senge (?-1207)
Yerpa (Yelpa) Kagyu—founded by Yelpa Yeshe Tseg (unk.)

* "The different Kagyu lineages are not referred to as major and minor in terms of the instructions they contain; they are equal in that respect. The four main lineages are known as main in that they originate with Gampopa himself, whereas the eight branch lineages originate with a later generation of masters." (www.karma-kagyu .org)

**Sakya**

Ngorpa School—founded by Ngorchen Kunga Zangpo (1382-1457)
Tsarpa School—founded by Tsarchen Losal Gyatso (1502-1556)
Dechen—founded in 1988 in UK and Europe by Lama Jampa Thaye
Dzogchen—founded in 1685
Shambhala—founded in the 1970s by Chögyam Trungpa Rinpoche
Shingon—founded in 804 CE in Japan by Kobo Daishi

**Gelug**

Foundation for the Preservation of Mahayana Tradition (FPMT)—founded in 1975 by Lama Thubten Yeshe (1935-84) and Lama Zopa Rinpoche (1946- )
Mongolian

**Newer Schools**

**Friends of the Western Buddhist Order**—founded in 1968 in London by Sangharakshita
**Nichiren**—schools derived from Japanese Buddhist monk Nichiren (1222-1282), which bases the practice on the Lotus Sutra
**Rimé**—Rime means "non-sectarian" and offers teachings from all Tibetan Buddhist traditions, including Mahayana and Tantrayana. The movement was started in Tibet in the 19th century

APPENDIX 3

# Buddhism Around the World

Buddhism is the world's fourth largest organized religion (following Christianity, Islam, and Hinduism). It is estimated that there are more than 376 million Buddhists worldwide, representing approximately 6 percent of the world's population.

There are ten countries where Buddhism is the religion of the majority of the population. They are:

Thailand (95 percent)
Cambodia (90 percent)
Myanmar (Burma) (88 percent)
Bhutan (75 percent)
Sri Lanka (70 percent)
Tibet (65 percent)
Laos (60 percent)
Vietnam (55 percent)
Mongolia (50 percent)
Japan (50 percent)

In addition, Buddhism is practiced widely in China and North Korea, although it has been suppressed by the Communist governments. In Tibet prior to 1959, the country was virtually 100 percent Tibetan Buddhist; it was also estimated that 20 percent of the population was in some way connected with monasteries and nunneries.

The ten countries with the largest Buddhist populations are:

China (102,000,000)
Japan (89,650,000)

Thailand (55,480,000)
Vietnam (49,690,000)
Myanmar (Burma) (41,610,000)
Sri Lanka (12,540,000)
South Korea (10,920,000)
Taiwan (9,150,000)
Cambodia (9,130,000)
India (7,000,000)

In terms of the number of adherents of the major branches of Buddhism worldwide:

Mahayana—56 percent (Nepal, China, Japan, Vietnam, North Korea, South Korea)
Theravada—38 percent (Myanmar, Thailand, Laos, Cambodia, Sri Lanka)
Vajrayana—6 percent (Tibet, Mongolia, Bhutan [state religion])

In the United States, Buddhism is the fourth largest organized religion (following Christianity, Judaism, and Islam), with an estimated number of more than 2.1 million adherents as of 2009, making up approximately 0.7 percent of the population. During the last decade of the 20th century, the Buddhist population in the U.S. increased by 170 percent.

## Tibetan Buddhism in the West

Prior to 1950, Tibetan Buddhism was largely unknown in the West. There were a number of people who had penetrated the almost totally isolated "Rooftop of the World" prior to 1950, including: Frenchwoman Alexandra David-Neel; Italians Giuseppe Tucci and Fosco Maraini; Englishmen Sir Charles Bell, Hugh Richardson, David Snellgrove, L. Austine Waddell, Francis Younghusband (who invaded Tibet), and radio operator Robert Ford; Austrian mountain climbers Heinrich Harrer and Peter Aufschnaiter; and a few missionaries over the centuries.

Not until the flight of Tibetans into exile to India starting in 1959 did the spread of Tibetan Buddhism begin (although there had been adherents of Tibetan Buddhism in Nepal, Bhutan, and parts of India for centuries). When Tibetans settled in India, their monasteries followed, on land that had been generously donated by the Indian government. In some areas, notably in the south, the climate was drastically different from what Tibetans were used to; many perished because of the hard work of rebuilding, the climate, the loss of homeland and loved ones, and diseases that did not exist in Tibet.

The Tibetan government-in-exile was set up in the Indian hill station of Dharamsala, Himachal Pradesh, in northwestern India, where the Dalai Lama took up residence in April 1960. His Holiness did not visit anywhere outside of India until 1967, when he went to Japan and Thailand. His first visits to the West were September through November 1973, when he went to Italy, Switzerland, The Netherlands, Belgium, Ireland, Norway, Sweden, Denmark, UK, West Germany, and Austria. A number of these countries had taken in Tibetan refugees. His first visit to the United States was September and October 1979; he has made more than 30 visits to the U.S. since then.

The first real interest in Buddhism in the West came from the teachings of Zen Buddhists from Japan at the end of the 19th and beginning of the 20th centuries. In 1905-1906, Soyen Shaku and a number of his students (including Nyogen Senzaki, Sokatsu Shaku, and Sokei-an) came to the U.S. and initially worked on the west coast, primarily in the San Francisco and Los Angeles areas. D.T. Suzuki (1870-1966), another student of Soyen Shaku, came to the U.S. in 1897 and returned to Japan in 1907. In 1939 he returned to the U.S., first working in Hawaii and California, then later moving to New York, where he gave seminars at Columbia University from 1951 through 1957. Among his students were Allen Ginsberg and Jack Kerouac. In 1957, he helped establish the Cambridge Buddhist Association (Massachusetts). Suzuki is generally credited with bringing Zen Buddhism to the American scene through his teaching and books. *Essays in Zen Buddhism* (1926), *Manual of Zen Buddhism* (1934), and *An Introduction to Zen Buddhism* (1964) were some of his well-known books. One of the first western teachers of Zen was Alan Watts (1915-1973), who wrote and lectured widely, after choosing Buddhism at the age of 16 over his strict Christian upbringing. One of his best-selling books was *The Way of Zen* (1958).

In 1955, Geshe Ngawang Wangyal, a Gelug teacher of Mongolian descent, founded the first Buddhist monastery in North America. The Lamaist Buddhist Monastery of America, located in Howell, New Jersey, later became the Tibetan Buddhist Learning Center. Both Jeffrey Hopkins and Robert Thurman were early students.

One of the first Tibetan Buddhists to make an impact in the United States was Chögyam Trungpa Rinpoche (1940-1987), a lineage holder in both the Kagyu and Nyingma schools. After leaving Tibet for India in 1959, he attended Oxford University in England (1963-1967), and in 1969, became the first Tibetan British subject, also relinquishing his monastic vows. He arrived in the United States in 1970 and established a meditation center, now known as Karme Chöling, in Vermont. In 1971, he began teaching at the University of Colorado and also established what is now known as the Shambhala Mountain Center. In 1973, Trungpa incorporated Vajradhatu, now known as Shambhala International, an association of Buddhist meditation and study centers. Shambhala now has more than 150 branches in North America and Europe. Trungpa later founded Shambhala Training to promote a secular approach to meditation practice.

APPENDIX 4

# Tibetan Diaspora

## TIBETANS IN THE DIASPORA

**di-as´-pora.** n. a dispersion of a people from their original homeland

According to the latest figures available (2009), more than a hundred thousand Tibetans are currently living outside of Tibet. The figures for India and Nepal might vary widely—Tibetans cross the borders to and from these two countries daily.

| | 1998 Census* | 2009 Census* |
|---|---|---|
| India | 85,000 | 94,203 |
| Nepal | 14,000 | 13,514 |
| US/Canada | 7,000 | 11,112 |
| Bhutan | 1,600 | 1,298 |
| Switzerland | 1,540 | 2,830 |
| Taiwan | 1,100 | 376 |
| Rest of Europe | 640 | 2,700† |
| Australia/NZ | 220 | 545 |
| Scandinavia | 110 | 142‡ |
| Japan | 60 | 176 |
| TOTAL | 111,170 | 126,896 |

* Figures courtesy of the Planning Commission of the Central Tibetan Administration.

† Austria, Belgium, Czech Republic, England, France, Germany, Hungary, Ireland, Italy, Liechtenstein, Luxemborg, Netherlands, and Spain.

‡ Denmark, Finland, Iceland, Norway, and Sweden.

APPENDIX 5

# Unifying Beliefs Among Buddhist Traditions

## COMMON GROUND BETWEEN THERAVADA AND MAHAYANA BUDDHISM (www.buddhanet.net)

1. Sakyamuni Buddha is the original and historial founder of Buddhism
2. The Three Universal Seals, Four Noble Truths, Eight Fold Path, and Twelve Links of Dependent Origination are basic to all schools
3. Three-fold training of Precepts, Meditation, and Wisdom is common
4. Organization of Buddhist teachings (Dharma) into Sutra, Vinaya, and Sastra (Sans.; commentary on the Sutras) is widely practiced
5. Mind as the principal area of taming and control in all schools

## THE BASIC POINTS IN BUDDHISM (www.religionfacts.com)

In the 2,500+ years since the Buddha was enlightened under the Bodhi Tree, Buddhism has spread over many countries, split into numerous sects, and adopted a wide variety of beliefs, practices, rituals, and customs. However, an essential unity centered around the teachings of the Buddha underlies these differences.

In 1966, leading monks from both the Theraveda and Mahayana traditions met in Sri Lanka with the goal of bridging the differences between the two groups and identifying the essential points of agreement. The World Buddhist Sangha Council, unanimously approved the following *Basic Points Unifying the Theravada and Mahayana*:

1. The Buddha is our only Master
2. We take refuge in the Buddha, the Dharma, and the Sangha
3. We do not believe that this world is created and ruled by a God

4. Following the example of the Buddha, who is the embodiment of Great Compassion and Great Wisdom, we consider that the purpose of life is to develop compassion for all living beings without discrimination and to work for their good, happiness, and peace; and to develop wisdom leading to the realization of Ultimate Truth
5. We accept the Four Noble Truths, namely *Dukkha*, the Arising of Dukkha, the Cessation of Dukkha, and the Path leading to the Cessation of Dukkha; and the universal law of cause and effect as taught in Dependent Origination
6. We understand, according to the teaching of the Buddha, that all conditioned things are impermanent and *dukkha*, and that all conditioned things (Dharma) are without self
7. We recognize the thirty-seven qualities conducive to Enlightenment as different aspects of the Path taught by the Buddha leading to Enlightenment
8. There are three ways of attaining Enlightenment, according to the ability and capacity of each individual: as a disciple, as a Pratyeka-Buddha, and as a Samyak-sam-Buddha. We acknowledge that it is most appropriate to opt for the career of a Bodhisattva and to become a Samyak-sam-Buddha in order to safeguard others
9. We admit that in different countries there are differences with regard to the life of Buddhist monks, popular Buddhist beliefs and practices, rites and ceremonies, and customs and habits. These external forms and expressions should not be confused with the essential teachings of the Buddha

# Photography/ Illustration credits

All images, except for the following, were supplied by the author.

Page ii—Eight Auspicious Symbols combined, courtesy Bob Johnson/ Osel Shen Phen Ling, Missoula, MT

Pages 32-33—Eight Auspicious Symbols, courtesy Bob Johnson/Osel Shen Phen Ling, Missoula, MT

Page 38—Lotus, courtesy Bob Johnson/Osel Shen Phen Ling, Missoula, MT

Page 41—3-D Kalachakra Mandala, courtesy Arjia Rinpoche, TMBCC

Page 62—Skull Cup (*kapala*), courtesy Robyn Buntin, Honolulu, HI

Page 105—Panchen Lama, courtesy International Campaign for Tibet

Page 116—17th Karmapa, courtesy KTD, Woodstock, NY

Page 148—Srinmo, courtesy www.american-buddha.com/dalai .avalok.htm

# About the Author

Richard Farkas is a student of Buddhism and Tibet, and a practicing Tibetan Buddhist. He was co-founder (with wife Julie) of the Tibetan Buddhist Community of Lexington (Kentucky).

He has traveled to India, Tibet, Nepal, Bhutan, and has visited Dharamsala, home of the the Dalai Lama and the Tibetan government-in-exile. He has done freelance design and typesetting for Snow Lion Publications, worked with the Tibetan Mongolian Buddhist Cultural Center in Bloomington, Indiana, and served on the board of directors of the Drepung Gomang Institute in Louisville, Kentucky.

He has a degree in journalism/photography and English from the University of Maryland, and has been a freelance photographer (covering the Dalai Lama six times since 2000). Most recently, he worked at the University Press of Kentucky designing and typesetting books.

Semi-retired, he lives in Lexington, Kentucky, with his wife, Julie (author of *Morning Call*), and their two cats, Karma and Kitty.

# Index